Intellectual Property Law

The editors would like to thank Matthew J. Acocella for his considerable editing and research assistance.

Intellectual Property Law

Economic and Social Justice Perspectives

Edited by

Anne Flanagan

Queen Mary, University of London, UK

Maria Lillà Montagnani

Università L. Bocconi, Italy

Edward Elgar

Cheltenham, UK • Northampton, MA, USA

Published by
Edward Elgar Publishing Limited
The Lypiatts
15 Lansdown Road
Cheltenham
Glos GL50 2JA
UK

Edward Elgar Publishing, Inc.
William Pratt House
9 Dewey Court
Northampton
Massachusetts 01060
USA

A catalogue record for this book
is available from the British Library

Library of Congress Control Number: 2009941165

Mixed Sources
Product group from well-managed forests and other controlled sources
www.fsc.org Cert no. SA-COC-1565
© 1996 Forest Stewardship Council

ISBN 978 1 84844 627 4

Printed and bound by MPG Books Group, UK

Contents

Contributors

Rosa Castro Bernieri, Università degli Studi di Bologna, Italy
Rosa Castro Bernieri is a Ph.D. candidate for the European Doctorate in Law and Economics at the University of Bologna and Erasmus Rotterdam University. She holds a law degree from Venezuela and a Master degree in Law and Economics from the University of Bologna and Hamburg University. She has been a visiting fellow at the Erasmus Rotterdam University and Max Plank Institute for Intellectual Property, Competition and Tax Law and has lectured on 'Industrial property' and 'Comparative Law and Economics' courses at the University of Bologna. She is the author of several articles and short pieces about intellectual property and investment and her current research focuses on the law and economics of patent law.

Valeria Falce, LUISS Guido Carli and Università Europea di Roma, Italy
Valeria Falce, Ph.D. in Competititon Law, LL M, London School of Economics, is Assistant Professor in Commercial Law at the Università Europea di Roma, where she teaches Commercial Law, Intellectual Property and Competition Law. Dr. Falce is Senior Research Fellow at the Intellectual Property, Competition and Communications Observatory, LUISS Guido Carli University of Rome. She has been appointed as Independent Expert of the Italian Committee for the Reform of Copyright and has extensively published in competition law, IP and regulation. Her publications include *Profili Pro-concorrenziali Dell'istituto Brevettuale* (Giuffrè ed., 2008).

Anne Flanagan, Queen Mary, University of London, UK
Anne Flanagan, BA, JD, LL M (Lon), is Senior Lecturer of Law at the Centre for Commercial Law Studies at Queen Mary, University of London and a licensed New York attorney. She teaches on various courses of the Queen Mary's LL M and M.Sc. in IP Management including Information Law, Telecommunications Law, Cyberspace Law and Competition Law. She is the Chief Examiner and author of the University of London External LL M course in Telecommunications Law and Deputy Examiner and co-author of *Intellectual Property on the Internet*. Anne has been a Visiting Professor of Law at Università L. Bocconi in Milan, Visiting Scholar at Brooklyn Law School, NY and served as Senior

International Expert to the EU-China Information Society Law Project. Anne has participated in law reform, research and training projects for the European Bank for Reconstruction and Development, UNCTAD and the EU. Her research interests include intellectual property, competition law, privacy and data protection, cybercrime and freedom of information law. Before coming to Queen Mary, she practiced law for 16 years in the US financial services industry.

Maria Mercedes Frabboni, Queen Mary, University of London, UK
Maria Mercedes Frabboni, Ph.D. (London), LL M (Hamburg), is the holder of a post-doctoral research position at the Centre for Commercial Law Studies at Queen Mary, University of London. Her research interests principally relate to competition and copyright legal analysis, with particular attention to the management of rights in the creative industries. She has commented extensively on the legal and economic implications of the European reforms concerning music collecting societies, both at conferences and in legal journals. Dr. Frabboni's current research explores aspects of commercial transactions in the art markets.

Federico Ghezzi, Università L. Bocconi, Italy
Federico Ghezzi is Head of Angelo Sraffa Department of Law at Bocconi University and Professor of Commercial Law. He is a member of CREDI and Baffi research centres. His research focuses mainly on competition law and corporate law, but he has also published in the field of intellectual property law. He is co-director and editor of a Commentary on the 'New Italian Corporate Law' (12 volumes, Giuffré-EGEA, Milano 2005–09).

Gustavo Ghidini, Università degli Studi di Milano, Italy
Gustavo Ghidini is Professor of Intellectual Property, Faculty of Law, Milan University. He is also Professor of IP and Competition Law, Faculty of Law, LUISS Guido Carli University, Rome where he is Director of the Intellectual Property, Competition and Communications Observatory. He has been President (2006–08) of ATRIP, International Association for Teaching and Research in Intellectual Property, and founded the law review 'Concorrenza e Mercato – Orientamenti dell'Autorità Garante' (Giuffré publisher) of which he is currently co-director. His latest publications include *Intellectual Property and Competition Law. The Innovation Nexus* (Edward Elgar, Cheltenham, UK 2006).

Jerzy Koopman, Utrecht University, the Netherlands
Jerzy Koopman, LL M (Utrecht 2000), LL M (NYU 2001) is an associated Ph.D. researcher at the Centre for Intellectual Property Law (CIER), Molengraaff Institute, School of Law, Utrecht University, the Netherlands. Jerzy's work focuses on the patentability of biotechnological

inventions from both a narrow legal-technical perspective and a broad societal perspective, which involves notions of sustainability, ethicality and justice. In 2006, his article 'Patenting biotechnological inventions and morality: law in the line of fire!', published in Dutch in the journal *B.I.E.*, was awarded the AIPPI/VIE prize. Jerzy also works as an independent life science law counsel for a variety of corporate, public and indigenous stakeholders in life science research and development.

Mariateresa Maggiolino, Università L. Bocconi, Italy
Mariateresa Maggiolino is Assistant Professor of Commercial Law at Angelo Sraffa Department of Legal Studies at Bocconi University. She has a LL M in Comparative Law (University of Iowa). Her latest English publication is the book *Intellectual Property and Antitrust: A Comparative Economic Analysis of US and EU Law* (Edward Elgar, Cheltenham, UK, forthcoming 2010). She is also widely published in Italian legal journals.

Maria Lillà Montagnani, Università L, Bocconi, Italy
Maria Lillà Montagnani is Assistant Professor of Commercial Law at Angelo Sraffa Department of Law of Bocconi University and associate faculty member of ASK Research centre. She has a Ph.D. in Competition Law and a LL M in Intellectual Property Law (Queen Mary, University of London). She has extensively published in the field of Intellectual property (in particular in copyright) and competition law. She has been a Visiting Scholar at the Centre for Commercial Law Studies, Queen Mary, University of London, August 2003, and at the Max Planck Institute for Intellectual Property and Competition Law, Winter 2007/2008.

Federico Morando, NEXA Center for Internet & Society, DAUIN, Politecnico di Torino, Italy
Federico Morando is managing director and research fellow at the NEXA Center for Internet & Society of the Politecnico di Torino and adjunct lecturer of Advanced Intellectual Property Law at Bocconi University in Milan. He is an economist (with a Master in Economic Theory and Econometrics from the University of Toulouse) with multidisciplinary research interests. He recently defended his Ph.D. dissertation concerning interoperability issues in software markets within the International Programme in Institutions, Economics and Law (Carlo Alberto, Torino).

Giovanni B. Ramello, Università del Piemonte Orientale, Italy
Giovanni Battista Ramello is Associate Professor of Industrial Economics at the Università del Piemonte Orientale, Italy and chairs the International Programme in Institutions, Economics and Law at Collegio Carlo Alberto (Torino). His research interests include industrial economics, antitrust and regulation, economic analysis of law and institutions, intellectual property,

information goods and knowledge production. He is currently president-elect of the Society for Economic Research on Copyright Issues and has recently published several books and articles on the law and economics of intellectual property rights.

Sharon K. Sandeen, Hamline University, USA
Sharon K. Sandeen is a Professor of Law at Hamline University in St. Paul, Minnesota where she teaches and writes in the area of intellectual property law, with an emphasis on the law of trade secrecy. Prior to becoming a law professor, she practiced intellectual property law in Sacramento, California for over 15 years. Professor Sandeen received her LL M from U.C. Berkeley School of Law (Boalt Hall), her JD from the University of the Pacific, McGeorge School of Law, and her BA from U.C. Berkeley.

Intellectual property law: economic and social justice perspectives: introduction

Anne Flanagan and Maria Lillà Montagnani

Intellectual property (IP) is deemed grounded in economics incentives and societal balancing of rights to fruits of one's own labour, personality and good name with others' interests in knowledge, progress and their by-products. Such foundations have underpinned the granting of patents, trademarks and copyrights (as well as the development of trade secret and industrial design laws) for centuries. Yet the recognition that intellectual property in the form of literature, science, knowledge and its fair dissemination and access to knowledge has a broader role to play in the development of all individuals as well as the fabric of society and democracy is not novel, although some would label it 'neo-liberal'. This is made clear by the declaration on the role of law in this regard and the duty of policymakers to foster it made by John Adams, then future president, during a time when the United States of America could legitimately be called a developing country. Contained in the first Massachusett's state constitution of 1780, entitled 'Encouragement of Literature, etc.' this unique and then radical constitutional provision states:[1]

> Wisdom and knowledge, as well as virtue, diffused generally among the body of the people, being necessary for the preservation of their rights and liberties; and as these depend on spreading the opportunities and advantages of education in the various parts of the country, and among the different orders of the people, it shall be the duty of legislatures and magistrates, in all future periods of this commonwealth, to cherish the interests of literature and the sciences, and all seminaries of them; . . . public schools, and grammar-schools in the towns; to encourage private societies and public institutions, rewards and immunities, for the promotion of agriculture, arts, sciences, commerce, trades, manufactures,

---

[1]   David McCullogh, *John Adams* (Simon & Schuster, 2001), pp. 222–3. (Noting this provision to be 'like no other declaration to be found in any constitution ever written until then, or since'.)

and a natural history of the country; to countenance and inculcate the principles of humanity and general benevolence, public and private charity, industry
and frugality, honesty and punctuality in their dealings; sincerity, and good
humor, and all social affections and generous sentiments, among the people.[2]

Despite the broader potential envisioned thus, in the context of more
recent IP developments it is the incentive and societal trade-off between
exclusivity and accessibility that generally remain the rationales under
which IP scholars seek to explain and to ground the changes occurring in
IP laws at both international and national levels.[3] This also serves to place
the current reinforcement of intellectual property rights (IPRs) in terms of
length, scope and strength[4] within a well-known framework and one that
is deemed to be still capable of supporting the current IP system. Indeed,
even when confronting the much-debated overgrowth of IP protection
– and the consequent disequilibria that the current IP system reveals –
many still advocate the solution to rest merely in restriking somewhat the
balance between the individual private and the public interests.[5]

Not properly questioning the utilitarian approach and its incentives-
to-innovate rationale – but rather taking them for granted – results in
the failure to account adequately for the increasing importance of IP to
situations and persons beyond the customary and historical, and that
IP implications extend far beyond maximizing cultural and scientific
progress. As Madhavi Sunder has astutely noted: '[p]roperty rights today
balance myriad values, from efficiency to personhood, health, dignity, and
distributive justice,'[6] values that are not yet comprised, though, within IP
which is, by contrast, still underpinned on market efficiency and welfare

---

[2] MASS. CONSTIT., ch. vi., sec. II (1780).

[3] Neil W. Netanel, 'Why has copyright expanded? Analysis and critique', in
Fiona Macmillan (ed), 6 *New Directions in Copyright Law* (Edward Elgar, 2008)
(discussing the multiple causes for copyright's expansion). Also available at: http://
papers.ssrn.com/sol3/papers.cfm?abstract_id=1066241.

[4] Among the broad literature of those advocating the overgrowth of IP law see
Lucie M C R Guibault, P Bernt Hugenholtz (eds), *The Future of Public Domain*
(Kluwer, 2006).

[5] For a different interpretation of the balance between the private and public
interest see Abraham Drassinower, 'From distribution to dialogue: remarks on
the concept of balance in copyright law' **34**, *Journal of Corporation Law* (2009)
991 (arguing that copyright should be thought less as a balance between authors
and users and more as a 'dialogue' between them since the concept of balance is
not adequate to overcome the sweat of the brown theory). Also available at: http://
papers.ssrn.com/sol3/papers.cfm?abstract_id=1474374.

[6] Madhavi Sunder, 'IP3', **59**, *Stanford Law Review* (2006) 257, 250 (questioning the economic foundations of IP law).

maximization.[7] At the moment 'there are not "giant-sized" intellectual property theories capable of accommodating the full range of human values implicit in intellectual production'.[8]

This analysis holds true as well when we look at the debate revolving around the 'balance' between intellectual property and public domains. A law and economics approach would justify the public domain and advocate the 'tragedy of the anti-commons' through the lens of efficiency.[9] Information as commons deserves protection against propertization because the public domain is considered a key element of an efficient economic growth: a deposit of raw material for authors and inventors to make use of in order to create and invent.[10] The balance here is customarily considered the key as impoverishing the public domain in favour of stronger IPRs limits innovation and creativity; weakening IPRs in favour of an empowered public domain prevents them from working as efficient incentives. This binary choice between IP and public domain, which has been central over the last few decades, still relies on the economics incentives and the societal trade-off between exclusivity and accessibility. But again, this approach neglects the distributive consequences of the commons.[11] It has been observed that 'leaving a resource in the public domain is not enough to satisfy societal ideals. It matters how that public domain is to be structured'.[12] The failure to focus beyond the original dimension[13] prevents the possible perspective that IP's pervasiveness has grown to the extent of exposing the fragility of its economics foundations[14] and of amplifying its social and cultural impacts, perhaps synergistically given the layering and overlapping of various forms of IPRs and their means of deployment beyond mere protective defenses to encroachments.

---

[7]   While the reality of what IP law has achieved may not reflect this 'myriad' of values.

[8]   Sunder, *supra* note 6 at 260.

[9]   James Boyle, 'The second enclosure movement and the construction of the public domain', **66**, *Law and Contemporary Problems* (2003) 33, 44.

[10]   Jessica Litman, 'The public domain', **30**, *Emory Law Journal* (1990) 965.

[11]   Anupam Chander and Mandhavi Sunder, 'The romance of the public domain', **92**, *California Law Review* (2004) 1331, 1332 (exploring an international intellectual property order that holds the possibility of enabling an equalitarian exploitation of the public domain).

[12]   Chander and Sunder, *supra* note 11 at 1337.

[13]   This does not intend to suggest that there have been no significant efforts in this regard, see, Pamela Samuelson, 'Mapping the digital public domain: threats and opportunities', **66**, *Law & Contemporary Problems* (Winter/Spring 2003) 147 but rather that this is not as comprehensive or pervasive as it needs to be.

[14]   Sunder, *supra* note 6 at 260.

Criticism of the utilitarian foundation for IP also lies in the fact that the law and economics perspective[15] of incentivizing innovation and creativity in order to maximize cultural production – though still central to the IP discourse – overlooks discussion of the true impact of cultural production maximization, on the one hand, and changes that are taking place within society and communities, on the other. A realistic consequence of this is that the utilitarian and law and economics' vision of IPRs will overlook the IP social dimension, situating the choices for IPRs solely in the realm of individual right holders' decision-making and control.[16] Without purposive examination and full consideration of such issues, we might well find ourselves further down a track of greater imbalance between public and private interests almost by autopilot. As was recently observed, 'Until 1990, there was a system of open access to knowledge but "we have moved in a completely opposite direction and there is no answer why we have moved away."'[17]

Therefore, consideration must be given not only to the economic-oriented incentive dimension of IP laws, but also to the regulatory dimension in terms of social goals that can be achieved through their construction. This approach is essential, if not the only one that can be employed to this end as several chapters here consider, if IPRs are truly to be granted for the ultimate goal of welfare maximization. Without regulating distributive justice issues through IPRs themselves that will share resources among creators and users, and among generations, it is questionable whether this ultimate goal will be met.[18] Put it in another more radical way, the current IP system has been condemned for ignoring 'matters of inegalitarian distribution of benefits arising from IP rights between persons within a nation,

---

[15]   See, e.g., William M Landes and Richard A Posner, *The Economic Structure of Intellectual Property Law* (Belknap Press of Harvard University Press, 2003).

[16]   Shuba Ghosh, 'When property is something else: understanding intellectual property through the lens of regulatory justice', in Alex Gosseries, Alain Marciano and Alain Strowel (eds), *Intellectual Property and Theories of Justice* (Palgrave Macmillan, New York 2008) 106, 114 (arguing that IP can better be understood as systems of laws meant to define and regulate creative activity instead of a set of property rights).

[17]   Catherine Saez, 'Panel Sees Tension Between IP and Human Rights' (IP Watch March 20, 2009) (quoting Phillipe Cullet, director International Environmental Law Research Center), available at: http://www.ip-watch.org/weblog/2008/03/20/panel-sees-tension-between-ip-and-human-rights/.

[18]   Shuba Ghosh, 'The fable of the commons: exclusivity and the construction of intellectual property markets', **40**, *U.C. Davis Law Review* (2007) 855, 859 (discussing how notions of distributive justice should inform management of the commons through the construction of intellectual property law).

between various nations, and between different regions and areas of the globe'.[19] Enhancing the regulatory dimension (as well as the normative effects) of IP laws would thus bring right into the policy picture those goals that have been so far kept outside. It would morph IPRs from sources of exclusivity to means for any number of social ends, such as combating disease or providing access to educational content, or to the technology needed to build capacity to address such issues as global warming.[20]

Some of these features of the IP discourse are those that underpin the topics discussed in this book. Without neglecting the importance of the utilitarian approach and the law and economics perspective as a means to shape IPRs as tools of market efficiency, the social dimension of IP is analysed in different areas: from the traditional IPRs, such as patents and copyright to less traditionally IP contexts, such as unfair competition and unfair commercial practices.

Ramello in Chapter 1 posits that, as far as knowledge is concerned, the law and economics theory does not give due weight to the complexity of knowledge production, thereby distorting the meaning of maximizing cultural production. Rather, he considers that a social justice approach can simultaneously produce IP-enhancing distributive effects and realize market efficiency with the precondition being a lower level of IP protection. This outcome is obtained given the nature of knowledge as simultaneously an input, output and productive technology and the specificity of its productive process, which belongs to the collective context and is renewed through the sharing among individuals as an indispensable feature for creative activity. In other words, it is not only a matter, as the utilitarian approach would maintain, of maximizing production regardless of the distributive effects that such maximization generates.

That changes taking place at the level of society and in online and other communities may be best addressed by other than the current balance

---

[19]   Keith Aoki, 'Distributive and syncretic motives in intellectual property law (with special reference to coercion, agency, and development) markets', **40**, *U.C. Davis Law Review* (2007) 717, 735 (examining the distributive effects of American and international property regimes). See also Margaret Chon, 'Intellectual property and the development Divide', **27**, *Cardozo Law Review* (2006) 2813, 2823, 2877 (proposing a normative principle of global intellectual property beyond utilitarian measures of social welfare, to face challenges derived from the encounter between intellectual property and development).

[20]   See, K Mara, 'Informal UN Climate Talks Indicate Continued Divergence On IP Issues' (IP Watch 28 August 2009); William New 'UN Climate Report Envisions Modified TRIPS As Governments Seek Progress (IP Watch 1 September 2009).

between the private and public interest is also tackled here. As illustrated by Morando in Chapter 2, the impact of the Web 2.0 revolution changes the economics and status of authorship, calling into question the effectiveness and efficiency of the current copyright defaults. He shows that alternative copyright regimes premised on Creative Commons licenses could efficiently accord sufficient protections without undermining fairness or distributive social justice.

Sandeen in Chapter 3 questions why the utilitarian approach and its incentives-to-innovate rationale is so ingrained and narrow, given the other motivations to create that have always existed. She suggests that these 'irrational' values beyond efficiency could be promoted by IP policies to promote innovation for the benefit of society.

The increasingly stronger appropriation regime of intellectual property law affects the spread of knowledge to the detriment of not only efficiency, but also societal justice, which can be defined in various ways as shown herein. Definitions adopted include not only the fair societal-level distributive access to knowledge and products of knowledge, such as drugs or biomedical procedures,[21] or the more restrictive concept of the means by which a society distributes burdens and benefits,[22] but also the ability of a society to redress situational inequities in the balance of IPR exercised to the detriment of others, or flying in the face of the policy justifications underlying the grant of the IPR.[23] The book addresses such phenomena in relation to patent and copyright law, which though indeed tools to incentivize innovation and creativity – and to reward inventors and creators for such activities – might now be addressed to other social ends.

Koopman in Chapter 4 considers how changes to disclosure requirements in patent could redress some inequities in the exploitation of traditional knowledge and bio-chemical materials and at the same time enable examiners to more readily ascertain the novelty and innovation so as to avoid undue propertization, which could undermine distributive justice and as well help to conserve traditional knowledge and biodiversity.

These authors have focused on how societal and distributive justice considerations can be addressed primarily in the context of existing or tweaked IP legal frameworks. Other authors, however, focus on how the current balance of interests under IP law can be changed by considerations of fairness or justice via the operation of legal frameworks external to IP

---

[21] See Castro Bernieri, infra at Chapter 5.
[22] See Koopman, infra at Chapter 4, note 5 and accompanying text.
[23] See Flanagan, et al. infra at Chapter 6, Section 2.1.

law itself, such as antitrust/competition law and equity.[24] Castro Bernieri in Chapter 5 explores how the recent intervention of the US Supreme Court in the test for whether a defendant may be enjoined from practicing a patent while the outcome of a patent case is determined has reset a balance in the principles of equitable relief, that is, injunction, which may serve to redress a growing offensive use of patents to preclude innovation and competition. She considers the impact that this rebalancing will have in the context of biomedicine, where offensive use of patents as a strategy can preclude whole lines of research and thereby create a biomedical 'anti-commons'. While the significance in this important area of innovation may be therefore singular, the use of this equitable remedy, although recognized under the Patent Act (and thus technically an internal tool), was prevalent in most patent case appeals under the Federal Circuit's exclusive jurisdiction due to its limitations on its availability. With this Supreme Court decision, injunctions will continue as a potential interim remedy to patent cases only where the traditional tests developed by courts at equity are met and the balance of the equities lie in its favour. Thus, substantive justice may ultimately be possible on the ultimate issues in many more cases since competitors will not be forced out of business if they are able to continue to practice their innovations where monetary damages will suffice to make the complainant whole.

The principles of equity, whether premised on historical notions of fairness, redressing balances or restoring situational justice according to the values of a society as determined to have been set in the original IP bargain, are also considered by Flanagan, Ghezzi and Montagnani in Chapter 6. They explore IP misuse doctrines in the US premised alternatively on equity and antitrust law in evaluating whether parallels may be found in the EU, under competition law or possibly its abuse of rights doctrine. Although US IP misuse can be considered an internal tool of IP, since after its untethering from equity it looks to the policy underpinning the grant of the IP right in question, it retains features of equity, including the great discretion of the courts in when to apply it. Abuse of rights in the EU, while very similar in its application, has other doctrinal limitations. As these are likely to address only the occasional IP over-appropriation in specific cases, the normative effect of these legal frameworks in their interaction with IP is to be questioned. In contrast, while the relationship between competition law and IP remains much debated, the former serves

---

[24]   Morando's proposals involving Creative Commons licenses clearly encompasses not only copyright frameworks but contract law that would enforce these licenses.

as a broader external tool to compensate for the latter's disequilibria and supports a balance between public and private interests, including by regulating the exploitation of IPRs beyond their grant by monopolists or dominant firms.

Chapter 7 by Frabboni continues this exploration of competition law as an external tool shaping IPRs to achieve distributive justice, here in the context of the collective exercise of IP rights, a unique and ironic convergence of issues. Using an economics approach, Frabboni evaluates the impact of an EU Commission competition law decision on collection societies in striking down their mutually reciprocal exclusivity clauses in light of online music distribution. The analysis highlights the ease with which an imbalance can be created within, or by accommodations made within, the IP framework itself where such changes as new forms of works or distribution channels providing access to works arise to tip the scales, suggesting that perhaps the IP framework alone cannot be left to discover the proper social dimension. Collection societies are historical structures created to facilitate fairness, equitable counterbalance and distributive justice in order to address the plight of the individual author versus powerful publishers and which still might be viewed as economically efficient. Now, however, as powerful national monopolies, their operations and arrangements are perceived to hinder the facile cross-border distribution of works online. As Frabboni notes, the Commission here uses competition law not to require actual competition among these societies, but to alter their practices impeding such online distribution, thus furthering a form of greater access to creative works. The use of competition law to further the EU information society goals of social and economic inclusion has underlined other Commission competition law decisions.[25]

Maggiolino in Chapter 8 continues the exploration of competition law as an external compensation in balance of the structure and exercise of IP rights by dominant firms to protect innovations, and analyses recent EU decisions imposing a duty to license, which arguably changes the scope of their national IPRs. She posits that fairness, equity and the protection of rivals' welfare, which might be labelled 'social justice' considerations, are no longer the stated guiding principles or objectives under EU or US modern competition law, if they ever were. Rather, it is only allocative efficiency that requires the deterrence of behaviour that harms innovation

---

[25]   See, e.g., Case No Comp/M.1845 AOL./Time Warner (2000); Case No. Comp/M.174 MCI orldcom/Sprint (2000) Identrus. Whether competition law should address such broad social policy dimensions is considered by Maggiolino, *infra* at Chapter 8.

promoting economic progress, wealth building and long-run consumer welfare. This chapter explores how recent EU Microsoft and other cases have, based on efficiency considerations, resulted in protection for rivals by ensuring their incremental follow-on innovation, and questions whether adding the social dimension to competition law is advisable. One of the noted reasons for the query is that the EU has sought to ensure broad-based consumer protection in another specific legal framework directed solely to that, the focus of the discussion in Chapter 9 by Ghidini and Falce. The Commission's stated aims for the Consumers Rights Directive, as it is called, are clearly those of economic efficiency, competitive market-place and consumer welfare, and must be seen as having an overlap with the aims of competition law. According to the Commission, the Directive 'ensures a high level of consumer protection and aims at establishing the real retail internal market, making it easier and less costly for traders to sell cross border and providing consumers with a larger choice and competitive prices.'[26]

This blurring of the lines here and as examined in some of the other chapters only reinforces the likely impossibility and possible undesirability of ringfencing any one body of law from the fuzzier and difficult challenges of setting the balances and benefits in any society to make it fair and just. The social justice issues are not going to go away. We are in a world where accelerating knowledge, innovation and technology with life and societal transfiguring potentials only serve to enhance the divide between the haves and the have-nots; the IP legal framework, therefore, will have to continue to, and better, address this growing imbalance. And also, while the uneasy and yet imprecise relationships between IP and other frameworks acting as external tools to compensate the former's disequilibria indicate a need to rethink the role of IP laws as a set of rules that goes beyond individual incentives to produce, it is unlikely that the work of meeting the growing calls for greater and fairer access to knowledge and products of knowledge can be left to IP legal frameworks alone. Indeed, such recent developments as emergent human rights' theory and law suggest that legal frameworks external to IP law will continue to develop and as applied exert an important counterbalance to perceived imbalances set by IP laws between the private and societal interests. The chapters of this book thus continue a dialogue that appears to have begun long ago.

---

[26] See Commission, Proposal for a Directive on Consumers Rights (DG Health and Consumers), available at: http://ec.europa.eu/consumers/rights/cons_acquis_en.htm.

1. Intellectual property, social justice and economic efficiency: insights from law and economics*

Giovanni B. Ramello

1. INTRODUCTION

Property rights have been a powerful device for promoting trade development, market existence and efficiency throughout human history. What is not owned cannot be traded. Hence, a well-defined set of property rights is central to the existence of trade.

In addition, commonly held resources cannot be divided without a specific set of rules assigning the various parts to individuals. Thus, the market as we define it today could not exist without property rights. On the other hand, a system of allocating goods that does not rely on market exchange – such as war, theft or gift – seems unable in most cases to achieve the attainment of maximum welfare through the allocation of a scarce resource to the one who most values it. Therefore, as confirmed by a long tradition of economic theory, a well-defined set of property rights can play a crucial role in promoting the efficient allocation of scarce resources and social welfare.[1]

Further, in Western culture private property has been the cornerstone of capitalist society, to the point of being considered to some extent the necessary condition for the freedom of its citizens and the existence of the market. It is hence an irrefutable component of individual liberty. These premises are quite inarguable, and the beneficial role of property rights should be duly acknowledged.

---

*   An earlier version of this chapter was published in Gosserie A., Marciano A. and Strowel A. (eds, 2008), *Intellectual Property and Theories of Justice* (London and Basingstoke, Palgrave). This paper was supported by the PRIN-MIUR research grant. The usual disclaimer applies.
[1]   Since Coase, there have been several streams of economic literature dealing with property. For references, see Ramello (2007) and the rest of the book in which that article is published.

However, the reverse cannot be equally endorsed: recognizing the virtues of property rights should not mechanically translate into a blank check, giving them the status of universal remedy for any issue.

From the perspective of demand, even when promoting productive efficiency, the market order can be (and very often is) unable to serve the criterion of social justice, and there is no denying that under many circumstances it leaves basic needs unsatisfied for a significant number of individuals.[2] This in turn puts serious limits on the exercise of individual liberty.[3]

From the supply standpoint, too, property rights do not always translate into the attainment of efficiency, mainly because productive milieus present idiosyncratic features requiring different regulatory frameworks. Property rights are 'genetically' conceived to manage economic resources, for which excludability plays a significant role in regulating their use or avoiding their depletion, as in the case of private goods or commons (a fishery stock, a pasture, and so on). In contrast, property rights do not apply in the same way or produce a similar result in domains with distinct characters, where excludability can directly influence productivity.

This chapter is an attempt to gain further insight into one such domain: knowledge, a distinctive realm that deeply characterizes human relationships and particularly the semantic sphere of human groups. Knowledge relies heavily on the sharing process, long governed by exchange mechanisms that are different from the market – mainly communication – but which is now broadly 'colonized' by the market paradigm through intellectual property rights.

The main rationale justifying this change and appropriation of this resource relies on the widely held belief that intellectual property rights promote efficiency, by providing the owner/creator with the proper economic incentive for producing the optimal level of new knowledge and knowledge-intensive products.[4] Noticeably, and in line with the above contrasting scenario, this stance ignores the specific features of knowledge and the consequences of the newly enforced excludability on its production.

Although not contesting the incentive effect provided to the owner by intellectual property rights, this chapter explores the ramifications of this

---

[2]   A definition of social justice and its discussion is addressed in Section 5 of this chapter.

[3]   Today, such instances permeate the core of economic debate. In corporate social responsibility, for example, aspects directly concerning efficiency seem to merge with those concerning social justice (Banerjee 2007).

[4]   For further explanation of this rationale see Ramello (2005a).

oversimplified assumption on knowledge. Using a selection of literature drawn from the disciplines focusing on knowledge, it attempts to expose some of the shortcomings of traditional economic theory as applied to intellectual property. It also seeks to elaborate an alternative economic model, from which policy implications can be drawn.

As will be shown, the main findings support the thesis that while limited appropriation via weak intellectual property rights can indeed provide some incentive for knowledge production, overly extensive appropriation by way of strong intellectual property rights will likely produce an adverse outcome for the total amount of knowledge feasible and for overall efficiency. Thus, it is crucial to preserve wide accessibility to knowledge in order to promote efficiency in this domain. Interestingly, this prescription seems to serve social justice equally well, once again confirming the idiosyncratic nature of knowledge as economic resource.

The chapter is organized as follows. Section 2 considers the standard thesis justifying intellectual property and the functional role of exclusion. Section 3 discusses the idiosyncratic nature of knowledge, which is simultaneously output, input and productive technology, and thus calls for a different analytical paradigm. Section 4 seeks to systematize this assertion by means of a simple descriptive model that illustrates the effect of varying the strength of intellectual property rights on knowledge. Section 5 argues that the paradigm is equally serving the goal of social justice; Section 6 concludes.

2. KNOWLEDGE, INTELLECTUAL PROPERTY AND MARKETS: THE ROLE OF EXCLUSION

Generally speaking, the traditional thesis advocated by the scientific literature depicts intellectual property rights as devices designed to encourage creative and inventive activity. From this perspective, patents and copyrights – and also trade secrets and trademarks, although with different flavors[5] – are essentially viewed as incentives to create, in accordance with the utilitarian tradition summed up in this well-known quote from Bentham (1962 [1839], p 71):

---

[5] In the case of trade secrets, appropriation is pursued by protecting the secrecy of the discovery, while in the case of trademarks the incentive is to produce information that does not represent per se the product – at least in the original rationale – but an ancillary device to the market and competitive process (see Ramello 2005a).

> [. . .] which one man has invented, all the world can imitate. Without the assist-
> ance of the laws, the inventor would almost always be driven out of the market
> by his rival, who finding himself, without any expense, in possession of a dis-
> covery which has cost the inventor much time and expense, would be able to
> deprive him of all his deserved advantages, by selling at a lower price.

Consistent with this argument, intellectual property rights are held to
address a specific market failure: the underproduction of knowledge
because of the lack of profitability for inventors/authors. Variations on
this theme abound (Ramello 2005a). This interpretation is highly conven-
ient for economics theory, as it likens knowledge production to a standard
manufacturing process. In this vein, the creator is represented as an economic agent aiming at maximizing his/her utility under the assumption
that 'he who has no hope that he shall reap, will not take trouble to sow'
(Bentham 1962 [1839], p 31). Hence, the pecuniary incentive obtained
thanks to intellectual property rights is needed in order to pay the opportunity costs of inventive and creative activity. Finally, the production
process is treated as a typical manufacturing function with knowledge as
the standard output.[6]

All in all, if this stylization is valid, intellectual property rights are a
good thing and the main critical concern is the exclusion of a number of
individuals from consumption of knowledge because of market power,
possibly introduced by the new rights and its consequent above-cost pricing.[7] The latter implies that the exclusion from knowledge enforced by
intellectual property rights is a necessary condition of the newly devised
economic mechanism. This point, however, requires further discussion.
Since Arrow (1962), the economic nature of knowledge has been identified
with that of a public good. Once an individual is part of a human group,
he/she cannot be excluded from the collective sharing of knowledge and
his/her access to it is not that of a rival.[8] Accordingly, from the standpoint
of allocative efficiency, no-market is the optimal solution.

Therefore, market can be introduced in order to promote the attainment
of productive efficiency, since, to borrow Bentham's words again, 'without
the assistance of the laws' a suboptimal quantity of knowledge would be

---

[6]   The same criticism has been raised by other scholars. Among them, Weitzman
(1998, p 332) asks whether '[. . .] production of knowledge [is] a process that can be
modeled by analogy with fishing new ponds or discovering new oil reserves' and
answers '[. . .] that something fundamentally different is involved here'.

[7]   For a further discussion of how market power can arise in knowledge
markets, see text accompanying notes 9 and 10, infra.

[8]   If the individual is excluded, this means that he/she is no longer part of the
human group. This happens for instance when he/she dies.

produced. This, at least, is the thesis supported by the incentive-to-create argument. Nonetheless, once the market is shaped, a positive price translates into exclusion of those consumers not able to pay it.

However, since in the knowledge domain the marginal cost of reproduction is close to zero, in perfect competition this would essentially mean no or very low exclusion. Unfortunately, as discussed further below, perfect competition is not the market structure that is likely to arise within intellectual property domain, because the proper working of the incentive mechanism requires market power, which in turn produces the exclusionary effect.

It is worth noting that although the mere existence of intellectual property rights, as with ordinary property rights,[9] does not necessarily confer significant market power to the right-holders per se – so rationing via above-cost-pricing is not always found – the success of a given item of knowledge on the market and its exclusive exploitation is likely to produce market power, hence exclusion. This is consistent with the reward mechanism set up by the intellectual property rationale. In fact, most knowledge protected by intellectual property rights must necessarily be difficult to replace, otherwise, there would be no need to set up such a complex system of incentives. If the protected fragments of new knowledge were near or perfect substitutes for one another – as would be necessary to cancel out market power – then the intellectual property system would make no sense, because it would be easier and cheaper to provide direct incentives to only one (or a few) inventors and creators. This notion is thus consistent with the concept of the welfare-enhancing effects of variety in ideas, but implies imperfect substitutability and consequently market power.[10]

Also, in order to be effective, the incentive to create demands a profit and therefore above-cost pricing. In general, this profit has been likened, since the earliest writings (Nordhaus 1969), with the concept of quasi-rent.[11] If this were not the case, the outcome would be exactly the same as that of a market without intellectual property rights and as Scherer (1980, p 444) puts it (on the subject of patents), 'If pure and perfect competition

---

[9] A land owner has an exclusive right over his/her parcels, but this does not imply that he/she is monopolist. Neighboring parcels can be almost perfect substitutes.

[10] As it is well known among economists, the imperfect substitutability is the feature that permits raising price above cost.

[11] A basic discussion of 'quasi rent' in contrast to 'rent' in economic theory can be found at Bryan D Caplan, 'What is a Quasi-Rent?' (George Mason University). Available at: http://www.gmu.edu/departments/economics/bcaplan/quasi-rent (accessed 2 February 2009).

in the strictest sense prevailed continuously [. . .] incentives for invention and innovation would be fatally defective [. . .]'.[12]

Further, the possibility for above-cost pricing brought about by intellectual property rights is easy to observe in the real world, where mark-ups on such property are significant. This is the case, for example, of trademarks and fashion, copyrights and music, patents and pharmaceuticals. Taking the last example, the exclusionary effects and tragic consequences of uniformly enforcing patent laws have been widely debated with reference to antiretroviral drugs and HIV/AIDS in South Africa, and clearly illustrate the extent of the problem (Attaran and Gillespie-White 2001; Scherer 2004).

On the whole, above-cost pricing and the consequent exclusionary effects are the outcome of the intellectual property rights system, but are also a major policy concern when it comes to distributive and egalitarian principles. Nonetheless, if the above justification holds, intellectual property rights are necessary and the exclusionary effects on knowledge can be, to a great extent, likened to those involving private property and restricted access to protected resources such as food, land, and water.[13] Knowledge is a valuable, scarce resource – although being a public good, it is scarce in production and not in consumption – and requires that enclosures be built to avoid free-riding and thus promote productive efficiency. This brings up the usual trade-off between efficiency and social justice, hence the discussion seems, at first glance, not to differ from those pertaining to private property in general.[14]

---

[12]   In accordance with antitrust literature and practice, intellectual property rights per se do not in fact confer any market power, as affirmed by the European Court of Justice (*Deutsche Gramophon GmbH* v. *Metro-SB-Grossmrkte GmbH*, 78/80 [8 June 1971] ECR 487) and by the US FTC and DOJ (*Antitrust Guidelines for the Licensing of Intellectual Property*, 1995). Intellectual property right-protected information, if not successful, will not allow the legal monopoly granted by intellectual property rights to translate into an economic monopoly. However, it is the prospect of securing supra profits (and therefore market power) that constitutes the incentive to create, since a perfectly competitive market would deliver no extra profits and therefore zero incentive. The logic behind intellectual property rights is thus to reward successful ideas with market power: to provide a monopoly, to a greater or lesser extent, as a private benefit in exchange for the creative effort/ investment. For an in-depth discussion see Ramello (2005a).

[13]   Of course, in the case of private property, prices are exclusionary in the competitive regime as well, because they must cover significant costs. By contrast, in the knowledge domain competitive pricing would imply prices close to zero since marginal costs are very low. It is the incentive mechanism that requires pricing above marginal cost.

[14]   For an economist's perspective on property and hunger see for instance Sen (1988). For general theory on property see, among others, Munzer (1990).

As discussed in the following sections, however, this is not the case. Intellectual property rights concern an idiosyncratic domain where the typical exclusionary effects they create are amplified in a way that affects not only the static efficiency, in the manner with which we are familiar – that is, by excluding those who are not able to pay the price for a good – but also the productive process (by causing the underproduction of a public good and the depletion of production technology). This, it will be argued, affects not only efficiency, but also social justice.

3. THE IDIOSYNCRATIC NATURE OF KNOWLEDGE

The standard economic argument about intellectual property rights works if we envision knowledge as a typical private good or a sum of private goods. As we will see below, however, this is actually not the case. Consequently, such perspective is also misleading when it comes to setting policy. Rather, in the knowledge domain, it will be argued that the criteria of both efficiency and social justice require substantial access to knowledge, which is only possible if intellectual property rights are weak.

3.1 Knowledge as a Social Entity

Indeed, while property exists in almost all human groups – although in distinct configurations – intellectual property is essentially a peculiar institutional outcome of Western culture. The recent proliferation of the literature justifying intellectual property rights demonstrates that, even in this specific legal culture, the concept behind it is not as trivial as it may seem. Rather, the design of a particular legal category for appropriating knowledge suggests that we are dealing with an idiosyncratic milieu: what is standard for other 'res' subject matter of property rights is not automatically transferable here. If one looks at the variety of intellectual property rights and the differences in design, one can infer that knowledge is so different from the typical property subject matter that it requires distinct paradigms for its appropriation, which must be finely tuned in order to obtain the expected outcome. In particular, the nature of knowledge and the specificity of its productive process must be duly taken into account.

Nonetheless, a detailed description is not a trivial task. Knowledge is not just an intangible good or resource defined and delimited like standard goods produced and exchanged on the markets, but a dynamic entity and a cognitive tool pertaining to social groups that is crucial to both the individual and to social action.[15] Knowledge essentially belongs to the collective context in which it is created. It is brought to fruition in the symbolic and semantic sphere defined by society, and renewed through sharing among individuals, which is thus an indispensable feature for creative activity.

Anthropology and social sciences have long generalized knowledge as follows: knowledge is public because meaning is, and obviously there can be no knowledge without meaning.[16] Accordingly, there can be no meaning without a human group to share it. Therefore, although knowledge fragments are often created by individuals, this can only happen embedded within the broader context of the collective semantic space to which the knowledge fragments are inextricably tied.[17]

Romney (1999, p 104) provides some enlightening insight into this idea:

> knowledge, found mostly in humans, arises from human inventions, is learned and handed down from one generation to the next, and usually varies from one society to another. [. . .] it is shared among relevant participants and [. . .] it is learned as part of our social heritage. [. . .] In short, careful reflection reveals that the very notion of [knowledge] involves sharing of ideas, concepts, behaviors, etc., by more than one person.

---

[15]   It is worth noting here that I avoid the term 'information' and the related 'information goods' in favor of 'knowledge', in accordance with extensive economics literature (for a survey see Carlaw et al. 2006). Although the two terms are sometime used interchangeably, they refer to distinct concepts. An item of information is a message containing structured data, while knowledge addresses the cognitive context of economic agents (Cowan, David and Foray 2000). It bears the expanded meaning commonly associated with 'the state or fact of knowing', and corresponds to the more general definition of 'the sum or range of what has been perceived, discovered' (4th edn American Heritage Dictionary of the English Language 2000). It is dynamic in nature, and can therefore never be entirely encoded or commodified as a whole. Although fragments can be encoded and somewhat appropriated, it is only an attribute of a collectivity of individuals (Cowan, David and Foray 2000; Rooney et al. 2003; Ramello 2005b). In effect, the dynamic character arising from the process of communication is necessary not only for the existence of knowledge, but also for the sustenance of human groupings (see Polanyi 1966).

[16]   See also infra note 17.

[17]   There is extensive literature on this point. One of the most illuminating is Geertz (1973). For example, speaking of culture as the collective knowledge of a certain human group, Geertz (1973, p 12) said 'Culture is public because meaning is. You can't wink (or burlesque one) without knowing what counts as winking or how, physically, to contract your eyelids, and you can't conduct a sheep raid (or mimic one) without knowing what it is to steal a sheep and how practically to go about it.' Clifford Geertz, 'Thick Description: Toward an Interpretive Theory of Culture', in *The Interpretation of Cultures: Selected Essays* (Basic Books, New York 1973) 3–30.

On the whole, the above demonstrates two important features of knowledge: knowledge is both input and output as recognized though not developed by selected articles in economics;[18] and the sharing process is necessary in order to make any creative effort effective, constituting, from this perspective, a sort of 'technology' of production (Weitzman 1998; Rooney et al. 2003; Ramello 2005b).

Consistent with its social and dynamic nature, knowledge presents another puzzling feature not possessed by ordinary commodities: its 'indivisibility'. This implies two kind of difficulties somehow connected to one another: first, defining what can and cannot be appropriated by an intellectual property right is not trivial; and second, the appropriation of a part always entails the whole entity (Rooney et al. 2003).

The first such concept, according to nineteenth century English legal scholar Augustine Birrell, is easily explained: while it is simple to draw the boundaries of a physical asset – a leg of a mutton, in Birrell's example – it is altogether impossible to determine (for example) how much a book truly belongs to an author, because any creative endeavour contracts a significant and indissoluble debt with its precursors, and with the context in which it is generated (Goldstein 1994). This, of course, is consistent with the nature of knowledge as a public good.

Hence, the knowledge fragmentation process into single property items enforced via copyright, and via intellectual property rights in general, is just a rough approximation of the division of physical assets – land, cattle, and so on – while any appropriation in the knowledge sphere will be more extensive than in physical property domain, generally appropriating parts that are socially owned or that have been created by someone else.

The second implication, again linked to its nature as a public good, is that because knowledge is a collective and dynamic entity, appropriation cannot concern only a specific number of bits, but also the process itself.

Taken together, these two notions can easily lead the intellectual

---

[18]   There are few economics papers that take this feature into account. They generally emphasize appropriability over accessibility, with one notable exception being Arrow, who in his seminal paper (1962) warned that if this is the case, then private appropriation procured by intellectual property rights may seriously compromise the incremental accrual of knowledge and, consequently, the collective well-being. Unfortunately, Arrow does not follow up on this observation. More recently, Landes and Posner (1989) stressed that when enforcing copyright, there are two opposite effects: an increase in the supply of new works brought about by the statutory economic incentive, versus a decrease in supply brought about by the exclusionary effect of copyright. The resolution of this trade-off is the key to determining what the overall consequences of copyright will be. Nonetheless, they rely on some specific assumptions considering that the first effect will always prevail.

property rights system into what can be termed a 'hyper-appropriation,' where the typical exclusionary effects generated by property rights are amplified, since they simultaneously affect 'the product and the process.'

The main reason for this outcome is the stylization and over-simplification procedure, in general, endorsed by economic analysis representing human activities. This procedure, according to its critics, has the effect of can-celling from view all that which cannot be directly attributed to single individuals, and which resides instead in the relationships between them (Granovetter 1985).[19] On the whole, this over-simplification leads to a misrepresentation of knowledge viewed as a sum of discrete bits of infor-mation, thus neglecting the social dimension and its role in the productive process.

3.2   Codified and Tacit Knowledge

A further elaboration is possible via the analytical framework introduced by Polanyi in his seminal work *The Tacit Dimension* (1966). This mainly addresses the role of knowledge in the scientific domain but is widely referenced in the literature for its accurate description of the multifaceted nature of knowledge.[20]

Polanyi represents knowledge essentially as a dyadic structure, made up of two distinct but complementary components: 'codified knowledge' and 'tacit knowledge'. The former can be articulated and encoded; the latter is an immanent form of knowledge, which does not lend itself readily to articulation or codification but which is nevertheless communicated, and therefore exists in interpersonal relations.[21]

Codified knowledge is any fragment of knowledge encoded in any of the various media made available by society such as language, writing, repro-duction technologies, and so forth. Because it can be encoded in discrete units (for example, a book, a CD, and so on), it can also be commodified, appropriated by means of intellectual property rights and exchanged,

---

[19]   This representation of human action 'disallows by hypothesis any impact of social structure and social relations on production, distribution, or consumption' and thus produces a poorly descriptive picture (Granovetter 1985, p 483).

[20]   For a survey on economics literature see Cowan, David and Foray (2000).

[21]   For an overview see Cowan, David and Foray (2000). The fact that tacit knowledge is physically held by individuals does not negate its social nature, since, generally speaking, there is no such thing as a physical entity called 'social relation-ships'. In other words, individuals are the 'bearers' of this type of knowledge, but the expression and transmission of tacit knowledge nevertheless requires interac-tion between individuals to take place.

giving rise to knowledge markets. Note that through the encoding process, knowledge becomes a static entity and can be more or less likened to traditional private property, such as a parcel of land or a can of beer.[22] After all, the very purpose of the label 'intellectual property' is to bring appropriated knowledge into the realm of property.

On the other hand, the tacit form of knowledge is by nature a dynamic entity, and as such can never be entirely encoded and commodified. Consequently, as we shall see below, it cannot be produced and directly exchanged on the markets, thus giving rise to specific property rights on it, but depends instead on interpersonal relationships for its production and dissemination.[23] This is supported by various studies on technology transfer, which have stressed the difficulty of transferring the tacit portion of knowledge as compared with its codified portion, due precisely to the necessity of moving individuals as well as physical goods (that is, of establishing ad hoc social relations), while demonstrating the inevitable need to promote both types of transfers if the policy is to have a favorable outcome (Williams and Gibson 1990; Takii 2004).[24] In effect, tacit knowledge grows out of the dynamic sphere of the communication process, a prerequisite for the very existence of knowledge as well as for the sustenance of human groupings.

It is worth noting that in view of the dyadic structure, the knowledge set encompasses the sum of codified knowledge fragments and their exchange does not per se imply the transmission of the tacit dimension. Given its nature, tacit knowledge can only be transmitted within a context of social interaction. This explains, for example, the rationale behind typical educational systems: books are generally used to provide information, but the presence of a teacher is necessary to impart learning and, in general, to communicate those aspects of knowledge that cannot be statically

---

[22] Interestingly, Thomas Alva Edison used the term 'canned sound' to discuss the possibility of recording sound in a wax cylinder thanks to his 1877 invention, the phonograph (Silva and Ramello 1999).

[23] The dyadic nature of knowledge is also recognized by von Hayek (1945, pp 521–2), who distinguished the portion of scientific knowledge that can be encoded as 'unorganized knowledge [. . .], the knowledge of the particular circumstances of time and place', which is essentially inalienable and demands the participation of several individuals in order to be exploited.

[24] This assertion does not deny that in specific cases, intellectual property rights can play some role in transferring both codified and the related tacit knowledge by facilitating contracting and interpersonal interaction. However, this can be seen as more an exception than a rule and strengthens the argument that in intellectual property, a more conscious balance should be considered between various effects (Arora and Merges 2004; Ramello 2005c).

encoded. Accordingly, Nelson (2003, p 917) asserts that any 'classroom equipment [. . .] [is a] complement not a substitute for an effective teacher working with students'. What is missing, in fact, is the imparting of that tacit knowledge, which books alone are unable to convey.[25]

On the whole, the above has serious implications for knowledge production: tacit knowledge and the related social relationships are not only an important part of knowledge, but also a crucial determinant for the productivity of the creative process.[26] In other words, the existence, transmission and development of knowledge, simultaneously representing the productive technology, require as a necessary condition the social interactions, which in the knowledge domain are called 'sharing', and what elsewhere has been termed 'some kind of cumulative interactive process' (Weitzman 1998, p 332). This is tantamount to asserting that knowledge, when construed as a productive technology, presents increasing returns in the access of users, since this is the necessary condition for letting the cumulative process work. Several studies in fields as diverse as medical sciences, organizational sciences and economic growth essentially confirm this claim.[27]

4.   ACCESS TO VS. EXCLUSION FROM KNOWLEDGE: A SIMPLE ECONOMIC MODEL

Further to the above, the effects of intellectual property rights are various and should all be properly taken into account in order to evaluate the overall outcome in terms of welfare that, as the reader will remember, represents the reference for their economic justification. In particular, considering the combined nature of knowledge as an output, an input and a productive technology, the appropriation set up by intellectual property produces three categories of consequences:

---

[25]   Nelson and Winter (1982, p 78) further argue that '[. . .] a trait that distinguishes a good instructor is the ability to discover introspectively, and then articulate for the student, much of the knowledge that ordinarily remains tacit'.

[26]   Nelson and Winter (1982) explicitly introduce the productive role of tacit knowledge.

[27]   In biomedical sciences, e.g. Willison and MacLeod (2002) and Liebeskind et al. (1996); on theoretical model on economic growth Romer (1990), Weitzman (1998). The adoption of specialized knowledge such as judge-made law governed by an open access model is essentially rooted in the need to preserve the collective dimension of creation, and can be interpreted in the same vein (Harnay and Marciano 2007).

1. First is the pecuniary incentive that can play the useful role of attracting individuals to the inventive process; this is not challenged here per se. Of course, for anyone who has to earn a living, expecting economic benefits to exceed opportunity costs thanks to specific property rights can make knowledge production an attractive endeavour. This is not the only feasible incentive, but is certainly an important one.[28]
2. Secondly, as pointed out by Arrow (1962) and less strongly by Landes and Posner (1989), the incentive mechanism will likely increase the cost of knowledge as an input. Hence, the total incentive effects will be discounted by the increase in production costs.
3. Finally, the exclusion enforced via intellectual property rights will impair the sharing process and thus, according to what has been discussed in the previous section, the productivity of knowledge as a technology.

The net balance of the three effects is not obvious and must be adequately considered when setting policies. In particular, the last feature is crucial for understanding the overall consequence of exclusion; it provides an important new argument for preserving extended access to knowledge in view of efficiency. This, in turn, suggests a convergence between the promotion of efficiency and the pursuit of social justice in the knowledge domain, as further investigated in the next section.

The model shown below tries to capture this view by proposing a bridge between standard economic reasoning and the hypothesis concerning the idiosyncratic nature of knowledge. Figure 1.1, highlights the consequence of neglecting the nature of knowledge as a productive technology. It starts from a standard representation of the 'incentive to create', then introduces the changes occurring once the effect on the production side are considered, by overlapping a number of different pictures corresponding to varying levels of appropriation via intellectual property. Figure 1.2 presents the new setting once all the knowledge features are considered, and is useful for normative purposes.

Let us imagine, for the sake of simplicity, that the production of new knowledge depends only on a variable θ representing the strength of the intellectual property right and thus negatively affecting access to knowledge.[29] In other words, θ measures the degree of appropriation

---

[28] For an in-depth discussion of different incentives see, e.g., Nelson (2003).
[29] Remember that the exercise of the exclusive right granted by intellectual property rights, as discussed in Section 2, implies above-cost pricing and by consequence exclusion.

permitted by an intellectual property right. Let us assume $0 \leq \theta \leq 1$, though this assumption will be more practical in Figure 1.2. Thus, $\theta=0$ means no appropriation; $\theta=1$ implies the strongest level of appropriation and, in accordance with incentive theory, should stimulate greater revenue for the owners of the rights.

The value of θ depends on numerous variables such as the right duration (time span) and scope (breadth of appropriation), the strength of law enforcement (hence the infringer's likelihood of being caught), the extent of fines and criminal sanctions, the selectiveness of entitlement criteria, the extension of spill-over spaces intended as derogation of property rights on knowledge (for example, the case of fair use doctrine in copyright domain), and so forth.[30] Consequently, while the definition of θ is easy in abstract, it is difficult as a matter of practice, meaning that it is simple to talk about weak or strong appropriation but is hard or even impossible to define a precise (for example, optimal) level. This observation, as discussed further below, is useful for policy prescriptions.

The F_i curves with $i=1,2,\ldots n$ in Figure 1.1 represent a set of knowledge production functions – roughly speaking, productive technologies – such as $q=F_i(\theta)$ where q is the level of knowledge produced and $q^*=F_i(0)$, with $q^*>0$, the level of knowledge freely produced in a given state of nature. The latter value is easily demonstrated by the observation that knowledge production exists throughout human history and societies, even in their absence. It takes into account that for any given human group there is a certain level of knowledge sharing and productivity.

The slope of F_i production functions is determined by the ratio between the incentive effect and the increase in production costs determined by appropriation via IPRs: the stronger the appropriation, the higher the cost of knowledge as an input. Accordingly, the incentive effect along a given curve (for example, F_1) diminishes with the increase in θ.

Nonetheless, it has been argued that appropriation will also affect the productivity of knowledge by decreasing θ due to the negative effect on the sharing process. Hence, a significant increase in θ will negatively impact the creative technology; this can be taken into account by the shift from a given production function, say F_1, to another to the left, say F_2, where any given level of θ will generate a lower level of q.

This impairment process will go on as long as appropriation is strengthened, and for a certain level of θ, the effect will become totally negative and

---

[30]   The strength of appropriability is linked to the design of the law and other law enforcement variables. For a discussion of distinct intellectual property rights and references to further literature see Ramello (2005a).

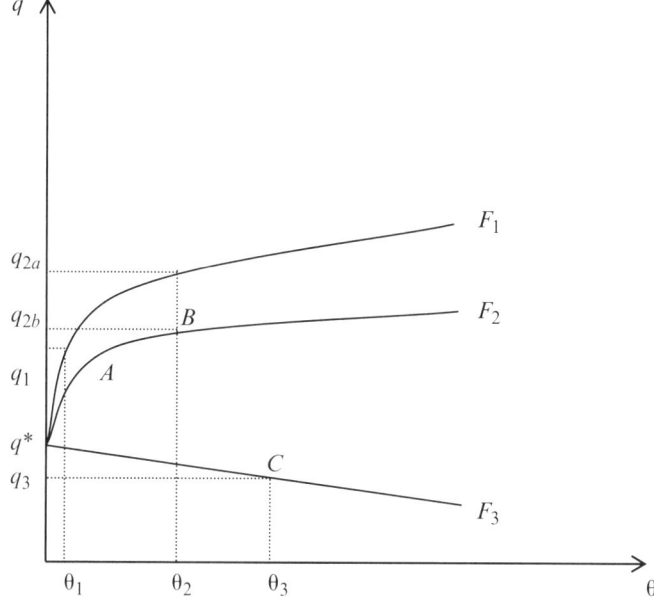

Figure 1.1   The puzzling issue of appropriation, incentives and productivity in knowledge domain

the production function will be downward sloping, as in the case of F_n thus always undermining q^*.

This contradicts the standard incentive theory, for which the production of knowledge is always positively related to appropriation; hence the production function should not change. The idea behind the incentive rationale is therefore that if one raises the level of θ, q will likewise increase. For a low intellectual property right strength, say θ_1, the production function in a given time will be described, for instance, as F_1 and the level of knowledge produced will be q_1 which is greater than q^*. Hence, intellectual property rights have the desired incentive effect on the production of knowledge.

By this reasoning, a stronger appropriation regime θ_2 should thus produce a higher quantity of new knowledge, say q_{2a}, and accordingly exclusion will always enhance the welfare.

As discussed above, however, this does not actually happen if we introduce the idiosyncratic nature of knowledge. Expectations will be only partially fulfilled because the stronger intellectual property right regime will negatively affect the sharing process, hence productivity.

In Figure 1.1 this effect causes, for instance, the shift from F_1 to F_2, the new production function characterized by lower productivity.

Consequently, there will be significantly less new knowledge, since q_{2b} < q_{2a}.

Nevertheless, in this case the incentive still seems to work as the quantity of knowledge still increases in θ. Things change when θ grows even stronger, up to $θ_3$ for example, the production function will continuously shift to the left: let us assume this has become F_3. Clearly, in this case the knowledge produced will be less than in the absence of intellectual property rights, because $q_3 < q^*$.

Taking this to an extreme, when intellectual property right strength is high enough, the quantity of new knowledge produced will tend toward zero, meaning that the entire sharing process will be impaired, that is to say tacit knowledge will be erased, and creative activities will come to a halt. This outcome is essentially the effect of an excessive appropriation of intellectual property on knowledge as a technology and corresponds to an extreme situation (θ=1), which is difficult to verify since no law yet designed permits total appropriation.[31] In a sense it represents the upper boundary of appropriation.

The pattern for productivity described above can be further clarified by linking all the points corresponding to different pairs of (q, θ) – q*, A, B, C, and so on – as shown in Figure 1.1. The outcome will be the curve presented in Figure 1.2.

It is straightforward to note that q increases with appropriation at lower levels and decreases when appropriation is greater. In particular, the figure shows that below a certain level θ, corresponding to weak appropriation, intellectual property rights indeed produce a positive effect on knowledge production; though for higher levels the overall effect will be negative.

In other words, appropriation by means of intellectual property, similarly to what happens with trade tariffs or taxes, acts as a sort of tax on the production of knowledge: a certain level of appropriation has positive effects on productivity up to a given threshold, after which the effects will be negative.

At this juncture, the next logical step for economists would be to find the optimal level of appropriation by means of the usual mathematical tools, which in Figure 1.2 happens to be θ. Unfortunately, this is easy to do in theory and almost impossible in practice, because the model presented above indicates just the essence of what happens in the real world.

---

[31] The best example of the described outcome is brought by what happens when all the individuals belonging to a specific culture die. It is possible to preserve objects and relics, cultural products and literary texts, that is, codified knowledge, but the elements pertaining to interactions among individuals are lost and no new knowledge is produced.

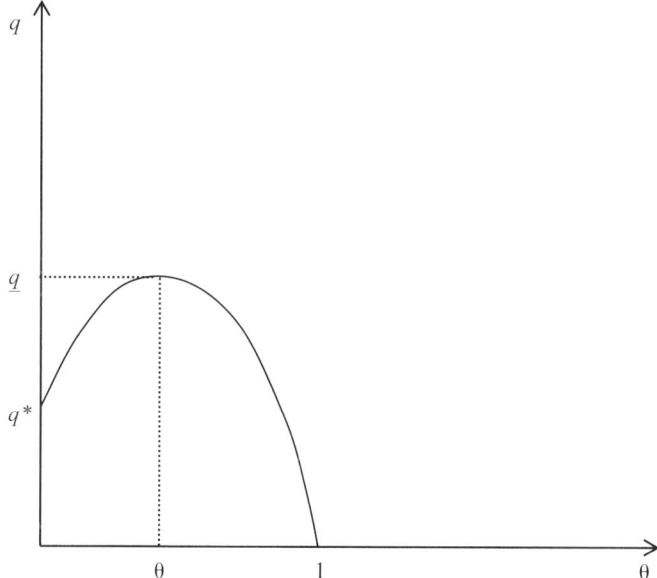

Figure 1.2   Appropriation and knowledge productivity

Considering the high variability of creative and inventive environments, the differences in knowledge produced in distinct domains and the number of all variables defining θ, the search for this figure could be fruitless.

Nonetheless, from a qualitative perspective the previous result has an important consequence in terms of normative implications. Indeed, at least one important policy prescription can be inferred: the total appropriation of knowledge will never lead to an efficient outcome. Accordingly, the general rule that emerges is that weak intellectual property rights will likely have a more efficient outcome than strong ones.

All in all, if intellectual property can do some good, this will occur in a region of limited appropriation which implies, of course, lower productive costs for follow-on creators, wider access to knowledge, and the possibility of free-riding, understood as unpaid access to knowledge for a considerable number of individuals.[32] Stated differently, efficiency in the knowledge domain requires the preservation of broad access.

---

[32]   To put it differently: '[a] culture could not exist if all free riding were prohibited within it' (Gordon 1992, p 167). This is consistent with a significant stream of literature claiming the central role of free-riding and knowledge spill-over in its production.

5.   SOCIAL JUSTICE MEETS EFFICIENCY

The policy-setting concept described above has another interesting feature, as it also serves the aim of social justice with regard to the provision of a range of welfare rights outside the sphere of income and the satisfaction of basic needs, regardless of individual merit (Stapleton 1998).[33]

As economic theory broadly attests, entitlement to property rights affects the distribution of resources and is essentially geared toward promoting efficiency. The idea is that property rights attempt to achieve the optimal allocation of scarce resources in order to enhance social welfare, roughly interpreted in the Pigouvian tradition as the maximum production of wealth. In other words, the only distributive principle in economics asserts that a given resource should be allocated by the most efficient user, regardless of other individuals or fairness.

From an egalitarian perspective, however, the concept of social justice demands that the distribution of scarce resources preserve the equal right of individuals to 'the most extensive total system of equal basic liberties compatible with a similar liberty for others' (Rawls 1971).

Clearly, although both principles deal with the allocation of scarce resources, they are guided by distinct and somewhat divergent goals. While the former essentially aims to determine the optimal use of a given (scarce) resource in order to achieve a higher level of wealth, no matter who benefits, the latter hinges on the principle of equality among individuals, and thus specifically takes into account the distribution of that resource and the provision to every individual of a range of welfare rights (Barry 1989; Munzer 1990).

In other words, while economic theory trusts in the mere assignment of rights and in the power of the market to produce efficient outcomes, completely disregarding the issue of distribution, the social justice rationale focuses on distribution and on the asymmetries created by economic mechanisms, possibly recognizing the need for an authority to take action on distributive matters.

Generally speaking, the two principles produce a trade-off that can be solved only on the basis of political considerations. This is the typical dilemma raised, for instance, by the general equilibrium theory, where most efficient solutions (almost) never meet the criterion of social

---

[33]   Of course the concept and the definition of social justice have been disputed and questioned ever since Plato's Republic. I am endorsing here the modern thesis that social justice 'has less to do with individual conduct than a "fair" distribution of material benefits and burdens in society and in this perspective it represents a major function played by states' (Stapleton, pp 468–9).

justice.[34] What's more, economic theory is totally unequipped to deal with this.[35] Given the considerable number of efficient solutions lying on the contract curve, economics has no guiding principle for choosing a specific solution. Even a very asymmetric distribution of resources – for example, one party has all and the others nothing – is acceptable on the grounds of efficiency.

Social justice sets a different condition: the choice should be guided by the achievement of a common level of 'wellbeing', that is, the satisfaction of basic needs, regardless of personal merit, that are deserved simply because one is a human being living in a given society (Rawls 1971; Miller 1976). This principle relates neither to the claim of an identical level of material resources, nor to a minimal standard of living, nor to the goal of efficiency. Rather, it concerns 'the willingness to recognize the rights and liberties of others and to share fairly in the benefits and burdens of social co-operation' (Rawls 1971, pp 60–61).

Obviously, then, the creation of new property rights for a social entity such as knowledge addresses the concept of social justice, since it impacts not only the distribution of knowledge and rights over knowledge, but also the social relationships, communication processes and self-expression that access implies. All in all, appropriation and the resulting exclusion conflict with social justice.

It is worth noting that the feasibility of a higher level of knowledge does not imply per se an increase in social justice. Referring to Figure 1.1, for instance, the q_1 quantity of knowledge produced is in economic terms better than q^*. However, since it is achieved by increasing the property of a few individuals and consequently prejudicing access to knowledge by a large number of individuals, it can negatively affect distribution, increase exclusion and thus hinder social justice. This effect is more likely when the level of appropriation θ is higher. Nonetheless, since in terms of efficiency there is an upper boundary to appropriability, the previous equals to preserve a significant degree of accessibility thus serving indirectly social justice.

When appropriation is excessive, the outcome is a reduction in the total amount of knowledge that is socially feasible ($q<q^*$ in Figure 1.2). This

---

[34]   For a survey on general equilibrium theory see any textbook on microeconomics.

[35]   Naturally, this assertion refers mainly to the mainstream neoclassical tradition and does not consider the heterodox perspectives that attempt to solve the conundrum. Thus far, however, there is a widespread idea that the needs of many, if not most, individuals are unmet in the market order and in the theoretical representation of it (Stapleton 1998).

of course renders the impairment of social justice more likely as it signifi-cantly reduces not only the access, but also the total amount of resources. It also violates social justice from an inter-temporal perspective, because appropriation by a given generation depletes the resource for the next gen-eration, again, now accessing a stock of knowledge $q<q^*$. It is intuitively clear that from an economic viewpoint, the society in time t produces an externality over $t+1$ and subsequent generations. Accordingly, extended appropriation at time t not only impairs social justice for the current gen-eration, but can prejudice the attainment of it for any future generation. Indeed, the egalitarian principle embedded in social justice dictates that no generation has a greater right to a given resource, so 'each genera-tion accepts the dual role of beneficiary and trustee' (Frischmann 2005, pp 464–5). This means that individuals are prohibited from compromising the interests of future generations in a given resource, intended as their right to inherit the resource in at least the same conditions as previous generations have had.[36]

On the whole, the social justice rationale argues again, although on different grounds, for as little appropriation as possible. As discussed in Section 4 of this chapter, this is also valid from the perspective of effi-ciency: given the idiosyncratic nature of knowledge as a dynamic entity, its existence requires the preservation of sufficiently wide accessibility, while extensive appropriation impairs the resource and its productivity. When increasing returns in the number of users do matter, as in the case of knowledge, the scarcity concept is simply reversed (Ramello 2005b). Then the exhaustion of knowledge is caused by under-exploitation, which calls for weak propertization. Hence, in the knowledge domain, efficiency seems to shake hands with social justice.

The earliest structure of intellectual property rights appeared to be con-sistent with the enounced rationale, as the rights were originally conceived to give individuals incentive and entailed marginal private appropriation. This feature kept the impact on the public dimension and the sharing process as low as possible. Copyright, for example, was originally drafted to expire 14 years after the publication date. The fair use doctrine, again

---

[36]   It goes without saying that this concept should be equally applied to other resources such as the environment. However there is a significant difference in the case of knowledge relying on the concept of scarcity, again highlighting its distinc-tive nature: while in the former, depletion of the resource stems from its overutili-zation – this is the typical case of commons that exhibit diminishing returns with a growing number of users – in the latter, depletion is caused by underutilization, since the creative commons present increasing returns with number of users. For an in-depth discussion of this point see Ramello (2005b).

concerning copyright, permitted several exceptions to the exclusive right granted to the owner. In science, wide swaths of public domain were recognized in order to preserve the basic tools of research.

The current extension of copyright to 70 years after the author's death, the progressive erosion of fair use space, and the possibility to copyright and patent an increasing number of subject matters is now changing the entire framework, with apparent disregard for the original criteria. Analogous dynamics characterises other IPRs.[37]

6.   CONCLUDING REMARKS

The main rationale for justifying intellectual property relies on the thesis of the incentive to create. Creators and inventors are economic agents attracted by the returns they expect from their effort. This depiction is practical and widely endorsed by law and economics theory, but does not give due weight to the complexity of knowledge production.

This work does not contest the potential benefit of the opportunity for creators and inventors to reap some profit from their work. Rather, it considers the idiosyncratic nature of knowledge, which is simultaneously input, output and productive technology, and is closely linked to the social dimension. This provides further insight into the production process and suggests a significantly different framework for policy.

More specifically, because of the increasing returns governing creative technology, the efficiency criterion used to guide economic choice calls for weak intellectual property rights, thus preserving wide access to knowledge. A stronger appropriation regime would significantly impair the total outcome of the creative processes. Interestingly, this appears to apply equally from a social justice perspective, perhaps in an effortless solution to the age-old trade-off between economic efficiency and social justice.

REFERENCES

American Heritage Dictionary of the English Language, 4th edn (Houghton Mifflin, Boston 2000).
Arora, Ashish and Robert P Merges, 'Specialized supply firms, property rights and firm boundaries' (2004) *Industrial and Corporate Change* 13 (3), 451–75.
Arrow, K, 'Economic welfare and the allocation of resources for inventions',

---

[37]   See for instance Ramello (2005b).

in RR Nelson (ed.), *The Rate and Direction of Inventive Activity* (Princeton University Press, Princeton 1962).

Attaran, Amir and Lee Gillespie-White, 'Do patents for antiretroviral drugs constrain access to AIDS treatment in Africa?' (2001) *Journal of the American Medical Association* 286, 1886–92.

Banerjee, Subhabrata, *Corporate Social Responsibility: The Good, the Bad and the Ugly* (Edward Elgar, Cheltenham 2007).

Barry, Brian, *A Treatise on Social Justice* (Harvester-Wheatsheaf, London 1989).

Bentham, Jeremy, 'A manual of political economy', in *Works of Jeremy Bentham*, vol. 3 (Russell & Russell, New York 1962).

Carlaw, Kenneth, Leslie Oxley, Paul Walker, David Thorns and Michael Nuth, 'Beyond the hype: intellectual property and the knowledge society/knowledge economy' (2006) 4 *Journal of Economic Surveys* 20, 633–90.

Cowan, Robin, Paul A David and Dominique Foray, 'The explicit economics of knowledge codification and tacitness' (2000) *Industrial and Corporate Change* 9, 211–53.

Frischmann, Brett, 'Some thoughts on shortsightedness and intergenerational equity' (2005) Loyola University Chicago LJ 36, 457–67.

Geertz, Clifford, *The Interpretation of Cultures* (Basic Books, New York 1973).

Goldstein, Paul, *Copyright's Highway* (Hill and Wang, New York 1994).

Gordon, Wendy, 'On owning information: intellectual property and the restitutionary impulse' (1992) Vanderbilt LR 78, 149, 167.

Granovetter, Mark, 'Economic action and social structure: the problem of embeddedness' (1985) *American Journal of Sociology* 91, 481–510.

Hardin, Garrett, 'The tragedy of the commons' (1968) *Science* 162, 1243–8.

Harnay, Sophie and Alain Marciano, 'Intellectual property rights and judge-made law: an economic analysis of the production and diffusion of precedent', in D Porrini and GB Ramello (eds), *Property Rights Dynamics. A Law and Economics Perspective* (Routledge, London 2007).

Landes, William M and Richard A Posner, 'An economic analysis of copyright law' (1989) *Journal of Legal Studies* 18, 325–63.

Langlois, Richard N, 'Knowledge, consumption and endogenous growth' (2001) *Journal of Evolutionary Economics* 11, 77–93.

Liebeskind, JP, A Lumerman Oliver, L Zucker and M Brewer, 'Social networks, learning, and flexibility: sourcing scientific knowledge in new biotechnology firms' (1996) *Organization Science* 7, 428–43.

Miller, David, *Social Justice* (Clarendon Press, Oxford 1976).

Munzer, Stephen, *A Theory of Property* (CUP, Cambridge 1990).

Nelson, Richard R, 'On the uneven evolution of human know-how' (2003) *Research Policy* 33, 909–22.

Nelson, Richard R and S Winter, *An Evolutionary Theory of the Economic Change* (Belknap Press, Cambridge Mass 1982).

Nordhaus, William D, *Invention, Growth and Welfare* (MIT Press, Cambridge Mass 1969).

Polanyi, Michael, *The Tacit Dimension* (Doubleday, New York 1966).

Ramello, GB, 'Intellectual property and the markets of ideas' (2005a) *Review of Network Economics* 4, 68–87.

Ramello, GB, 'Private appropriability and knowledge sharing: contradiction or convergence? The opposite tragedy of Creative Commons', in L Takeyama,

W Gordon and R Towse (eds), *Developments in the Economics of Copyright* (Edward Elgar, Cheltenham 2005b).

Ramello, GB, 'Property Rights, Firm Boundaries and the Republic of Science' (2005c) *Industrial and Corporate Change* 14 (6), 1195–204.

Ramello, Giovanni B, 'Property rights dynamics: current issues in law and economics', in D Porrini and G Ramello (eds), *Property Rights Dynamics: A Law and Economics Perspective* (Routledge, London 2007).

Rawls, J, *A Theory of Justice* (Belknap Press of the Harvard University Press, Cambridge Mass 1971).

Romer, P, 'Endogenous technological change' (1990) *Journal of Political Economy* 98, 71–102.

Romney, AK, 'Culture consensus as a statistical model' (1999) *Current Anthropology* 40, 103–15.

Rooney, D, G Hearn, T Mandeville and R Joseph, *Public Policy in Knowledge-Based Economies* (Edward Elgar, Cheltenham 2003).

Scherer, FM, *Industrial Market Structure and Economic Performance* (2nd edn Houghton Mifflin, Boston 1980).

Scherer, FM, 'A note on global welfare in pharmaceutical patenting' (2004) *World Economy* 27, 1127–42.

Schumpter, Joseph A, *The Theory of Economic Development* (Harvard University Press, Cambridge Mass 1934).

Sen, Amartya, 'Property and hunger' (1988) *Economics and Philosophy* 4, 57–68.

Silva, F and GB Ramello, *Dal vinile a Internet. Economia della musica tra tecnologia e diritti* (Edizioni della Fondazione Agnelli, Torino 1999).

Stapleton, J, 'Social justice', in P Newman (ed), *The New Palgrave Dictionary of Economics and the Law* (Macmillan, London 1998), 3, 468–76.

Takii, Katsuya, 'A barrier to the diffusion of tacit knowledge' (2004) *Review of Development Economics* 8, 81–90.

von Hayek, Friedrich, 'The use of knowledge in society' (1945) *American Economic Review* 25, 519–30.

Weitzman, Martin L, 'Recombinant growth' (1998) *Quarterly Journal of Economics* 113, 331–60.

Williams, F and DV Gibson (eds), *Technology Transfer: A Communication Perspective* (Sage Publications, Newbury Park 1990).

Willison, DJ and SM MacLeod, 'Patenting of genetic material: are the benefits to society being realized?' (2002) *Canadian Medical Association Journal* 167, 259–62.

2. Copyright default rule: reconciling efficiency and fairness*

Federico Morando

1. INTRODUCTION

Information and communication technologies – and the Internet in particular – make everybody a potential author and self-publisher. Instead of following the traditional 'long route' and passing through several professional intermediaries, new authors are able to reach the public directly or through new 'lightweight' service providers (offering a technological infrastructure, but essentially no editing or other gatekeeping functions). The revolution represented by the so-called Web 2.0 makes the phenomenon of authors publishing through new 'short routes' even more significant.[1] Users considered as passive consumers of content in the context of Web 1.0 generate a growing percentage of the virtual goods circulating on telecommunication networks. In other words, the distinction between authors and their audience becomes increasingly blurred and everybody

---

*   A preliminary version of this chapter (titled 'Creative Menus: Applying Some Considerations about Default Rules and Contractual Menus to the Case of Creative Commons Licenses') was presented at the 3rd Annual Workshop on the Law and Economics of Intellectual Property and Information Technology, (5–6 July 2007), Queen Mary, University of London, UK. A more advanced draft was presented at the Society for Economic Research on Copyright Issues Annual Congress, (10–12 July 2008), Geneva, CH. I thank all the participants to both events for their insightful comments and critiques.

[1]   See M Ricolfi, 'Copyright policy for digital libraries in the context of the i2010 strategy' 1st COMMUNIA Conference on the Digital Public Domain (Belgium, 30 June 2008) <http://communia-project.eu/node/110> accessed 10 June 2009. See also M Ricolfi, 'Gestione collettiva e gestione individuale in ambiente digitale' in ML Montagnani and M Borghi (eds), *Proprietà digitale: diritti d'autore, nuove tecnologie e digital rights management* (Egea, Milano 2006), 215–21, or, from the same author, 'Individual and collective management of copyright in a digital environment', in P Torremans (ed), *Copyright Law. A Handbook of Contemporary Research* (Edward Elgar, Cheltenham 2007) 282–5, 308.

may become a publishing author with negligible technological and financial means.

This chapter looks at this scenario through the lens of law and economics reasoning, discussing whether the existing copyright system, devised to handle the economic and creative setting prior to the Web 2.0 revolution, is still appropriate today. In particular, I will investigate the appropriateness of the current default level of protection offered by copyright law to creators. To do this, I will first briefly sketch that which I label as the 'copyright default', which is the set of rights that the current regime of copyright protection grants and automatically reserves to authors. This section will also introduce some alternative default regimes, which this chapter will compare with the current copyright default. In Section 3, I will briefly analyse the rationale behind this present default setting. For a specific comparison, in Section 4 I will describe the alternative legal regime that Creative Commons licenses offer to authors who want to make it easier to circulate and share their works. Section 5 will compare – in terms of economic efficiency and fairness – the effects of protecting intellectual creations through the current 'all rights reserved' copyright default with the alternative legal regime offered by Creative Commons licenses. In Section 6, I will show that the alternative regimes offered by Creative Commons licenses represent preferable default rules in terms of efficiency and without appreciable negative impact in terms of fairness and social justice.[2,3] Overall, this chapter will conclude that both principles of efficiency and fairness[4] would suggest some

---

[2] This chapter adopts a definition of social justice loosely consistent with that proposed by John Rawls in his seminal book, *A Theory of Justice* (Belknap Press of HUP, 1971). Following Rawls' definition, social justice requires that access to scarce resources be managed to preserve the right of individuals to 'the most extensive total system of equal basic liberties compatible with a similar liberty for others.' For a fuller description concerning how to decline the concept of social justice in the field of intellectual property, see generally, G Ramello, 'Intellectual property, social justice and economic efficiency: insights from law and economics' in Chapter 1 of this book.

[3] That, as I will discuss, holds true as long as full copyright protection remains an option that can be chosen at negligible cost (from the point of view of the rightholder). Under such a condition, this chapter reaches conclusions that are fully consistent with those of Ramello.

[4] I use 'fairness' according to its ordinary meaning in plain English. As far as the relationship with social justice is concerned, the two terms cannot be considered as synonyms. In particular, some may think something that is socially just will typically also be fair. However, fairness – within this chapter – will be evaluated from the point of view of a single author and not from the point of view of society at large. Several authors will likely think that fairness implies rewarding authors for their work and not letting others reap what has not been sown, while social

modifications of existing default rules of copyright protection. Moreover, because I submit that operating these modifications unilaterally at national level would violate the Berne Convention,[5] I will suggest some 'second best' (and more feasible) alternatives, which are able to ease existing inefficiencies while empowering access to knowledge and culture and hence social justice.

Before moving on, though, a few introductory words about default rules are appropriate. Lawyers and law and economics scholars have long recognized that default rules are a powerful device to reduce transaction costs and 'fill the gaps in incomplete contracts'.[6] More recently, the literature about default rules has (theoretically and empirically)[7] shown lawmakers that it is possible to influence economic equilibria without restricting the freedom of contract of private parties by enacting different default rules. The so called 'iron law of default inertia',[8] in fact, predicts that, all other things being equal, the statutory default option will have a much higher chance of being applied (or even explicitly chosen) than any other option.

Insights from the default rules literature have already been applied to the field of copyright law,[9] leading to the conclusion that the existing 'full rights reserved' default may be economically suboptimal. This chapter reaches this same conclusion as far as economic efficiency is considered, but will cast new light on the discussion by analysing the further dimension of fairness and social justice.

---

justice – at least according to the definitions to which I have made reference, see supra note 2, – may likely imply some degree of redistribution (which some people contest as unfair).

[5] Berne Convention for the Protection of Literary and Artistic Works, <http://www.wipo.int/treaties/en/ip/berne accessed 10 June 2009>. I will argue that changing the 'default rules' governing copyright acquisition is likely to collide with the principles stated in the Berne Convention and in other international treaties. Hence, national legislators would risk being unable to follow any policy recommendation concerning a direct modification of these norms.

[6] I Ayres and R Gertner, 'Filling gaps in incomplete contracts: an economic theory of default rules' (1989) 99 *Yale LR* 87.

[7] See, in particular, Yair J Listokin, 'What do corporate default rules and menus do? An empirical examination' Yale Law & Economics Research Paper No. 335 <http://ssrn.com/abstract=924578> accessed 10 June 2009.

[8] See Ayres and Gertner (note 6).

[9] C Sprigman, 'Reform(aliz)ing copyright' (2004) 57 *Stanford LR* 485. The author suggests (in so many words) using 'transaction costs' related to copyright formalities in order to discourage the use of copyright to protect works with low or no commercial value (in the expectations of the author), so that the public domain is de facto expanded. This is an application of the 'default inertia'.

2. FROM THE COPYRIGHT DEFAULT TO ALTERNATIVE MENUS

In the field of copyright, the current 'default rule' is full protection for the maximum possible duration allowed by the law (typically the life of the author plus 70 years) and with 'All rights reserved'. As a typical feature of copyright law, no formalities are required to enjoy property rights on one's intellectual creations, not even a statement that a certain work is protected by copyright.[10] This boils down to saying that the 'iron law of default inertia' works in the direction of favoring the adoption of the most restrictive form of copyright available in the legal system.

The default rule granting full copyright protection, without requiring any formality, has been generalised as a characteristic of all legal systems compliant with the Berne Convention[11] (which has been incorporated in the WTO's TRIPS Agreements).[12] In the field of international law, the mandatory adoption (for Member States) of a 'no formalities' approach had a precise target: it was an anti-discrimination norm, introduced to avoid any kind of (more or less) hidden disadvantage for foreign authors, with respect to domestic authors.

However, it is likely that the desirability of a 'no formalities' approach has been reduced by the growing importance of intellectual creations published (on the Internet) by non-professional authors who may not seek, intend or need such protection. As suggested with great clarity by Sprigman,[13] a possible alternative default rule here for copyright protection could be a setting in which published works[14] are not copyrighted,

---

[10]   The widespread diffusion of the 'All rights reserved' statement is a remnant of the Buenos Aires Convention of 1910 Article 3, which required an explicit statement of reservation of rights. (An unofficial English version of the text is available online at: http://en.wikisource.org/wiki/Buenos_Aires_Convention.) All the member of this Convention are nowadays (since the year 2000) also signatories of the Berne Convention.

[11]   See Article 5(2) of the Berne Convention.

[12]   See TRIPS Article 9, <http://www.wto.org/english/docs_e/legal_e/27-trips_01_e.htm> accessed 10 June 2009.

[13]   See Sprigman, *supra*, note 9.

[14]   Full copyright would protect unpublished works in any case, at least before the death of the author. Discussing this point is beyond the scope of the present work, but I consider a basic human right to be the one of choosing when and how one's intellectual creations should be published. The common law followed a similar approach, providing perpetual copyright protection for unpublished works. See Sprigman, note 9, 503. Where existing, the moral right of 'divulgation', 'disclosure' or 'first publication' guarantees the author's control on the first publication of his or her works.

unless the authors comply with some (very simple and cheap) 'formality', that is, a rule similar to the one in place in the USA before the adoption of the Berne Convention. Sprigman's proposal, can be deemed to represent an economic 'first best'. However, it is likely that these formalities would still violate the literal text of the Convention. For this reason, as I will discuss below (see Section 5), enacting Sprigman's proposal would require a revision of international treaties and the political feasibility of such a modification of the equilibrium, achieved as a result of the Berne Convention, cannot be easily guaranteed.[15] Fortunately, as my discussion in Section 6 shows, there are 'second best' alternatives that do not require amending international treaties. Before discussing all these alternatives, however, a bit more discussion about the existing 'copyright default' is needed.

3.   SOME BASIC LAW AND ECONOMICS OF COPYRIGHT

It is well known that one of the main goals of intellectual property rights is to provide incentives to create intangible goods:[16] author's economic rights carry out this task in particular. At the same time, intellectual property rights also impose costs on society in terms of reduced availability of a certain intellectual creation, increased costs of new creations, transaction costs, costs of monitoring, enforcement costs and litigation costs.[17] All these *ex post* costs (with respect to the creation of the intellectual asset) may be justified *ex ante* as necessary to provide powerful incentives. In fact, without intellectual property rights, incentives to create literary and artistic works, and certain kind of innovations, would be lower or, at least, related to factors that are different from the judgement of the public (that is, authors would be dependent on their 'patrons' or on the preferences of the political powers, etc.). In general, the incentive mechanism

---

[15]   There are several reasons for which an international treaty may be difficult to ratify, the discussion of which is far outside the scope of this chapter: for instance, some members could have signed the treaty in the context of a broader negotiation, involving issues linkage, and a similar situation may be difficult to recreate.

[16]   See, among others, WM Landes and R Posner, 'An economic analysis of copyright law' (1989), 18 J Legal Studies 325. See also MA Lemley, 'Ex ante versus ex post justifications for intellectual property' (2004) 71 U Chi L Rev 129.

[17]   All these costs are not completely supported by the right owner, since when a 'right' is established, the government accepts to 'subsidize' (at least partially) the costs of monitoring, enforcement, litigation and other costs related to the administration of justice.

generated by intellectual property is also likely to be superior to other reward systems which could not provide incentives to produce the best possible intellectual good. For instance, in the case of public procurement or public prizes, once the initially defined goals and standard of quality has been reached, the author cannot fully internalize the benefits of any additional improvement since, at most, he or she can receive a fraction of these benefits in the form of improved reputation. This is one of the reasons why it can be argued that, even if it is possible to devise sophisticated reward-based incentive schemes, the market-based system constructed around intellectual property rights is likely to be superior, both for reasons of economics and socio-political ideals (in particular, higher freedom of speech).[18]

Other functions of intellectual property rights are related to the reduction of transaction costs in contracting with third parties (that is, solving the so-called 'paradox of information').[19] This function is especially relevant when the producer of a piece of information is not the best user of it (that is, when a creator needs to sell his or her creation, or to find a partner or financier in order to commercially exploit it). Moreover, intellectual property can be seen as a natural right of the creator to be recognized as such and to control certain uses (and abuses) of the fruit of his or her work: in particular, in the systems of *droit d'auteur*, these tasks are carried out by the author's moral rights.

The question that herein arises is whether the above-discussed functions of intellectual property rights are better carried out using a default rule granting the maximum available level of protection. Let me emphasize here that I am not discussing the optimal 'maximum level of protection' allowed by a legal system; it is just the optimal 'default level' that is discussed. This is the level of protection granted to an author who does not specify anything concerning the intellectual property rights attached to his or her work.

Before tentatively trying to answer this previous question, some

---

[18]   One could actually argue that the dictatorship of patrons ('maecenas') would be substituted with the one of the large public: I am not sure about which of these tyrants is worse, but notice that patrons are free to sponsor authors under a copyright system as well.

[19]   See Kenneth Arrow, 'Economic welfare and the allocation of resources of invention', in RR Nelson (ed), *The Rate and Direction of Inventive Activity: Economics and Social Factors* (Princeton University Press for the National Bureau of Economic Research, Princeton 1962) 609–25. For the purposes of this chapter, the paradox of information can be rephrased in this way: undisclosed pieces of information have no value because of lack of credibility; disclosed pieces of information have no value because of lack of control/excludability.

alternative 'levels of protection,' such as those implemented through the Creative Commons licenses, ought to be discussed.

4. CREATIVE COMMONS LICENSES

Instead of the detailed analysis of the menu of solutions proposed by Creative Commons (CC) Corporation,[20] it is more interesting for the analyses that will be carried out to describe the different 'items' (or 'modules') that right holders can pick from the 'menu' offered by CC in order to create one's license.

1. 'Attribution': in each CC license, users 'must attribute the work in the manner specified by the author or licensor'.[21]
2. 'Non-Commercial': authors can choose if other parties may or not 'use the work for commercial purposes'.[22] Verbatim copies may always be distributed for non-commercial purposes.
3. 'No Derivative Works' (or 'No-Derivs'): authors can choose whether licensees may or not 'alter, transform, or build upon the work'; in other words, they can authorize (or not) the creation of derivative works.[23]
4. 'Share Alike': authors can require the creators of derivative works to 'distribute the resulting work only under a license identical' to the one adopted by the original author. This is the so-called 'viral effect' of the license, making it 'persistent'.

Using the words of Lawrence Lessig, '[i]f the default rule of copyright is "all rights reserved", the express meaning of a Creative Commons license is

---

[20] You may find more practical information about the licenses at www.creativecommons.org: in fact, a significant part of the efforts of Creative Commons Corporation concern divulgation and other communication-related activities. For a more theoretical and impartial commentary about CC licenses, see (the first part of) Niva Elkin-Koren, 'Exploring creative commons: a skeptical view of a worthy pursuit' in Lucie Guibault and P Bernt Hugenholtz (eds), *The Future of the Public Domain* (Kluwer Law International 2006) <http://ssrn.com/abstract=885466> accessed 10 June 2009.

[21] In older versions of the licenses, the 'attribution clause' was optional, but it is currently included in all CC licenses.

[22] See Creative Commons, Summary of Attribution Non Commercial License 3.0, available at: <http://creativecommons.org/licenses/by-nc/3.0/>.

[23] Obviously, people interested in the creation of derivative works are always free to contact the original author(s) and ask for an explicit permission (completely independent from the CC license).

that only "some rights [are] reserved".'[24] In other words, CC licenses allow creators to easily decide which rights they want to reserve to themselves and at which conditions.

This short description of Creative Common's licenses merely describes the purpose of each 'module' forming a CC license. That such a purpose can be attained and enforced in any given legal system is likely but has yet to be fully demonstrated. That said, the reader should be aware that this chapter is premised on an assumption of full enforceability of CC licenses, which seems to be supported by the (limited) existing case law.[25]

5.   IS THE COPYRIGHT DEFAULT EFFICIENT?

If the main functions of authors' rights are those identified in Section 3, it may be difficult to justify the choice of the highest level of protection available in the legal systems as a socially optimal default rule. This holds true when the 'All rights reserved' default rule is compared with an alternative default rule inspired by the CC 'Attribution' license.

Realistically, no author is likely to have their incentives lowered by a 'formality' of asking for full protection, since all that is needed to receive the current standard of full protection for one's published works is to state explicitly 'Copyright: all rights reserved'.[26] In particular, professional authors and firms active in the field of copyrighted work production would not even need to change the copyright notice they already use. In other words, a very simple 'formality' – requiring an explicit statement that one claims full 'Copyright: all rights reserved' – would probably not create any transaction costs for professionals of copyright-based industries using the

---

[24]   L Lessig, 'CC in Review' (Blog post launching the first Creative Commons fund-raising campaign 2005), <http://creativecommons.org/weblog/entry/5661>, accessed 10 June 2009.

[25]   In March 2006, the District Court of Amsterdam handed down its decision in *Adam Curry* v. *Audax Publishing B.V.*, a preliminary ruling where a Creative Commons Attribution Non-commercial Share Alike 2.0 license has been deemed enforceable. This case and another Spanish case implicitly dealing with CC licenses are briefly discussed in M Travostino, 'Alcuni recenti sviluppi in tema di licenze Creative Commons' (2006) *Ciberspazio e Diritto* VII(II), 253–70. See also AG Gonzales, 'Viral contracts or unenforceable document? Contractual validity of copyleft licenses' EIPR, 26(8): 331–9.

[26]   To prevent the risk of misappropriation of 'works in progress,' drafts and the like, unpublished works could be granted the maximum available level of copyright protection, with 'All rights reserved'. This is what happened also under US common law when registration of copyright was still required (note 14).

traditional 'long route' (that is, from authors to consumers, via editors and other professional intermediaries) to disseminate works of authorship.

In further analysis of this point, recall that one of the criteria to establish a default rule may be the so-called 'majoritarian' one: if a rule is selected by the majority of people, transforming it into a default may be a good way to economize on transaction costs.[27] Hence, if everybody publishing a work wanted to receive full protection, the choice of eliminating any kind of formalities could be a wise one. Indeed, this was probably the case at the time of the adoption of the Berne Convention.[28] In other words, it may then have been the case that few publishing authors were uninterested in 'full copyright protection,' so that it was likely to have been more efficient to make only this minority state its 'peculiar' choice, while ridding the majority of authors of formalities. This could have been true, in particular, because publishing a work almost invariably implied significant financial investments, generally supported at least in part by professional publishers. However, we no longer live in that era; the GNU General Public License and the Creative Commons efforts flourish, rather, in the Internet era. In this context, a huge amount of texts, images, music or other creations are released to the public on the Internet. Works 'published' in this new way are released by authors who are likely to be fairly ignorant about copyright and not altogether interested in it, possibly excepting as it relates to moral rights (with particular reference to the right of attribution). This would encompass many bloggers, participants in social-networking platforms and Internet forums, or non-professional webmasters.

The growing use of the Internet as a powerful means to distribute information directly to the public (along the so called 'short route')[29] has dramatically increased the number of creators who are not interested in (or, at least, do not feel the need for) copyright, because they have other incentives to 'create'. This new balance between professional and non-professional – but 'publishing' (along the short route) – authors exacerbates problems coming from an 'all rights reserved default,' because thousands of people, who would be happy to see their works as wide-

---

[27]   I Ayres and R Gertner, 'Majoritarian vs. Minoritarian Defaults' (1999) 51–6 Stanford LR 1591.
[28]   By 'the time of adoption of the Berne Convention,' I refer to the long period starting from the drafting of the Convention (before the first signature of 1886, followed by several revisions between 1896 and 1979) and ending with the late ratification of the US (Berne Convention Implementation Act of 1988).
[29]   See Marco Ricolfi, 'Gestione collettiva e gestione individuale in ambiente digitale', in ML Montagnani and M Borghi (eds), *Proprietà digitale: diritti d'autore, nuove tecnologie e digital rights management* (EGEA, Milano 2006) 215–21.

spread as possible, are victims of their ignorance about the existing 'copyright default'. Sprigman describes this same situation, highlighting the costs for follow-on creators:

> Today copyright law has emerged as the principal barrier to the creative reuse of a large amount of material that under the former [US] conditional copyright regime [requiring formalities and renewal] would not have been subject to copyright in the first place. The majority of creative works have little or no commercial value, and the value of many initially successful works is quickly exhausted. For works that are not producing revenues, continued copyright protection serves no economic interest of the author. But in an unconditional copyright system, commercially 'dead' works are nonetheless locked up. They cannot be used as building blocks for (potentially valuable) new works without permission, and the cost of obtaining permission will often prevent use. In such instances copyright is radically unbalanced: its potential benefits are depleted, and it therefore imposes only social costs.[30]

Similar arguments apply to orphan works, whose number may increase in the Internet era,[31] because a growing quantity of digital content is made available without reference to any traditional 'publisher' and/or using pseudonyms (or nicknames), which cannot be easily traced back to the actual author.

Despite such considerations, one could still be tempted to argue that this is a false problem, since these new authors will not complain if someone violates their copyright in any way as they do not even know or care about their rights; thus, the default level of protection does not matter at all.[32] However, this critique is not conclusive, since – *ex post* – the same authors could understand that their rights have been violated and – for opportunistic reasons or as a matter of principle – this could create an incentive to litigate. In particular, claiming one's rights *ex post* may have a certain strategic value, even if no incentive to create was necessary in the first place. For instance, assuming that I am a blogger, *ex ante* I could have been willing to (enthusiastically) agree to the publication (without any remuneration, if that is the only available option) of some of my works in a book about the best blogs on the Internet. In fact, I simply derive a high level of personal satisfaction from the

---

[30]   See Sprigman (note 9) 489–490.

[31]   About orphan works, see J Brito and B Dooling, 'An orphan works affirmative defense to copyright infringement actions' (2005), 12 Michigan Telecommunications and Technology LR 75 <http://www.mttlr.org/voltwelve/brito&dooling.pdf> accessed 10 June 2009.

[32]   See Elkin-Koren (note 20) proposing a far more elaborated and nuanced version of this argument.

fact that my effort is being appreciated and I also enhance my reputation. However, consider what would happen, *ex post,* were I to discover
that someone has printed a book containing some of my creative works
without my permission. Once the book has been printed and promoted
without my explicit permission, I may discover that the threat of using an
injunction to stop the distribution of the infringing book has a strategic
value of several thousands dollars, which I will ask as a remuneration/
compensation. In practice, I can be paid in order not to start a lawsuit
that I am likely to win, maybe without being awarded significant
damages, but imposing relevant costs on my counterparts who could be
forced to leave the business and destroy the infringing book. More generally, the feeling of having been expropriated of one's own rights could
increase willingness to litigate *ex post*, even in cases in which a lawsuit
would not be financially opportune.

In other words, the existence of an 'All rights reserved' default level of
protection creates scope for significant transaction costs and increases
the likelihood of litigations, without increasing incentives to create (and
reducing incentives to disseminate creative works).

5.1   Putting Fairness into the Picture

Previous arguments concerning the (in)efficiency of the existing 'All rights
reserved' copyright default rule may surely be expanded. However, it is
already possible to argue that, from an efficiency point of view, substitut-
ing the current copyright default with a 'CC Attribution default' or an
analogous rule could likely increase social welfare and would be unlikely
to create significant social costs as long as the cost for claiming full
copyright is negligible, as previously described. Nonetheless, even if one
concurred with this point, the 'alternative default' could raise concerns,
particularly with respect to fairness and moral rights.

For instance, consideration must be given to the unplanned commercial
potential of a creation; that is, a work – released as an amateur exercise –
that becomes so successful to be interesting for commercial publishers or
similar firms. Since the work has already been created (when the author
did not believe it was worth the effort of putting a copyright notice on it),
it is likely that no efficiency problem would be encountered in allowing any
kind of commercial use by third parties. In fact, efficiency could actually
be increased by third parties being able to use the work better than the
author. Nevertheless, if a third party is able to extract a profit from a work
without sharing it with the author, the latter, or society in general, may
perceive such economic free riding as being 'unfair' or 'unjust'. Moreover,
this perception of unfairness may detract from the original author's will-

ingness to create additional works or impose other significant psychological costs.

If fairness problems are deemed relevant (and it is likely that they are), the optimal 'default rule' should possibly include a 'Non-Commercial' clause. Thanks to this item of the CC's menu, the contractual power of the author with respect to potential 'commercial' users of the work would be similar to the one available under the current default. In other words, under such a clause no 'unjust enrichment' will directly come from the exploitation of someone else's intellectual work.

To sum up, if we care not only about the 'incentive function,' but also about the 'contracting function' of the 'alternative default,' a simple 'Attribution-like' license may not be appropriate. However, the 'Attribution, Non-Commercial' license is not likely to be dramatically worse (for the author's interests) than the current 'All rights reserved' default.

An additional economic/institutional consideration in evaluating the introduction of a 'Non-Commercial' clause in a possible 'alternative default,' is the compatibility between 'open' licensing of one's works and membership in collecting societies. Discussing the relationship between collecting societies and CC licensing is far outside the scope of this chapter. However, it is worth mentioning that the coexistence between the two institutions is problematic; possible solutions under examination and experimentation suggest that members of collecting societies may leave to their organization the task of managing commercial uses of their rights, while directly licensing some of their works for non-commercial uses under CC licenses.[33] Hence, it is likely that an alternative copyright default including a Non-Commercial clause would facilitate the task of making this new regime seamlessly interact with the collective management of intellectual property rights.

If the problem with a simple 'Attribution-like default' is just related to fairness (that is, to the fact that money is being made without sharing it with the person whose work created a significant part of the value being exchanged), an alternative to the introduction of a 'Non-Commercial' clause may be the use of the 'Share-Alike' module. Using this clause, any subsequent derivative user cannot simply 'appropriate' the value coming

---

[33]   In the Netherlands, Buma/Stemra (www.bumastemra.nl) and CC Nederland (www.creativecommons.nl) have launched a pilot project concerning the compatibility between CC and collective management. The agreement enables members of that organisation to have the remunerations for commercial use of their work collected by Buma/Stemra, while licensing non-commercial uses for free under Creative Commons licences. Similar projects are being studied in Italy as well (and possibly in other countries).

from the original work, but must also share with the entire society any added value that is created on the basis of the original creative effort.[34]

To be sure, it is also possible to mix the clauses discussed above, in order to create an 'Attribution, Non-Commercial, Share-Alike' license. In fact, this license is one of the most adopted CC licenses, suggesting that authors who willingly decide to 'open' some of their creations to the public may indeed share some of the aforementioned considerations, either for economic or fairness-related reasons.

A final possibility is worth discussing: could the use of a 'No-Derivative Works' clause be desirable because of fairness-related reasons? In fact, some users of CC licenses may feel that the 'No-Derivs' clause also represents a safeguard against possible threats to their own reputation, coming from the creation of somehow inappropriate works. In other words, some kinds of derivative works (which are not banned by moral rights in the strict legal sense) may have 'negative externalities' for the author (that is, the author may dislike the existence of some derivative works, even if they are not obscene, offensive, etc.).[35] That said, it should be clarified that the right of having attributed one's works, along with the right of not having attributed that of someone else, are fundamental moral rights of creators that, strictly speaking, are not reduced by any of the 'alternative' defaults I am proposing, since CC licenses do not seek to (and normally cannot) alter this system of (inalienable) rights. Overall, as the restrictive No-Derivs option risks nullifying the majority of the benefits, arising from legitimate uses of a work, its adoption cannot be recommended. Nonetheless, it may still be considered a 'third best' option, being likely – in any case – to be socially superior to the current 'All rights reserved' default.

Summing up, this analysis suggests that either a CC 'Attribution, Share

---

[34] For instance, A may be a professor creating a math book and putting it online for the enjoyment and learning of her students or everybody else. Then, B may add appropriate exercises and transform A's book into a much more effective textbook, for which he claims full copyright. Without a 'Share-Alike' clause, A could not make photocopies of B's textbook to teach her students: B would have to 'make proprietary' A's work, in the sense that a derivative work based on it cannot be used anymore by A herself (a situation that A is likely to perceive as unfair). However, a 'Share-Alike' clause would imply that B could not prevent A from using B's work at her turn, hence everybody could appropriate part of everybody's else work, in a situation the symmetry of which increases fairness. All that, of course, is unless B decides to contract directly with A, in order to receive a specific license on the original creative work, enabling him to sell a derivative work under full copyright protection.

[35] See Lemley (note 16) 15–20.

Alike' licence or a CC 'Attribution, Non-Commercial' license could represent an alternative default, which would be preferable to the existing copyright default. In fact, any of the proposed alternatives would address fairness problems almost as well as the current default 'All rights reserved,' but would allow for a greater circulation of works and reduced transaction costs, especially in the context of the creation of user-generated content. Finally, assuming that claiming full copyright has a very limited cost, creators who need more control on their works to have incentives to create could easily opt for a more 'proprietary solution'.

Overall, neither an 'Attribution, Share Alike' or an 'Attribution, Non-Commercial' default would reduce economic efficiency, or would do so in a negligible way, because of the small transaction costs related to claiming full copyright. Yet, a social justice approach to intellectual property requires us to consider the positive effect, in terms of spread of knowledge created by a greater or lesser number of works that will be available under the new default regime of protection. In this sense, an 'Attribution, Share Alike' default may be the preferable one, since – in case of success of the works 'licensed' in this way – it would virally and persistently propagate through the market an open approach to the sharing of knowledge.

6.   THE 'EXPRESSIVE VALUE' OF THE CREATIVE COMMONS' MENU

Previous sections raised a reasonable doubt about the optimality of an 'All rights reserved' copyright default, at least as long as the maximum level of available protection is not reduced and can be claimed at almost zero cost by authors, simply saying [that] 'All [their] rights [on the work at hand are] reserved.' Indeed, similar concerns have already been raised in scholarly literature.[36] Regarding these, this chapter so far mainly adds the fairness arguments and moral rights concerns which may be of paramount interest for civil law countries.

However, despite the arguable inefficiency (and sub-optimality from a social justice point of view) of the current default level of copyright protection, one must concede that there could be high political costs in changing such a well-established legal setting. In particular, abandoning the 'no formalities' default rule for copyright acquisition would violate Article 5(2) of

[36]   See Sprigman (note 9) for additional and complementary arguments in this regard.

the Berne Convention and, more generally, amending such international treaty would impose significant 'transaction' costs.[37]

In the long run, international conventions are not written in stone and they may need to be amended, in particular when technological changes make their assumptions obsolete, as may have happened with the 'no formalities' provision. Indeed, the creation of a 'Copyright 2.0' legal regime,[38] built on assumptions including the new role of user-generated contents, needs to be encouraged. Hence, if the legal regime dictated by Article 5(2) of the Berne Convention needs to be changed, one should not be afraid of arguing so. However, the quest for a 'Copyright 2.0' legal regime is a major one and to be pursued at an international level.

In the short run, more modest reforms must be considered. Fortunately, some ways out of the existing inefficiencies of the 'All rights reserved' copyright default can be found, even at the relatively more modest scale of national law, indeed, even at the much more modest level of the design of a specific web portal, as I will show. Here, another strand of the literature – strictly connected to the one concerning default rules – may provide helpful suggestions. This field of study concerns the analysis of contractual menus and altering rules. According to the definition of Ayres, 'a menu is a contractual offer that empowers the offeree to accept more than one type of contract',[39] while 'altering rules tell private parties the necessary and sufficient conditions for contracting around a default'.[40] Thus, choosing from a given menu or creating a completely new contractual clause offers the possibility for such solutions.

In fact, an alternative to the adoption of a different default rule – which is likely to be much easier to reach in term of political costs – is the explicit statement of a menu of possible 'altering rules'. This 'second best' proposal

---

[37]   Sprigman, (note 9 at 554) is actually very optimistic about the compliance of some 'new style formalities' he defined with the Berne Convention and the TRIPS Agreements, but this is a highly debatable question. For a detailed critique of the compatibility of Sprigman's 'new-style formalities' with the Berne Convention, see J Brito and B Dooling (note 31).

[38]   See Ricolfi (note 1) foreseeing a promising roadmap toward a new copyright system ('Copyright 2.0'), which responds to many of the concerns raised herein.

[39]   I Ayres, 'Menus matter' (2006) 73(1) University of Chicago LR 3–16 and Lectio Magistralis of Stresa Lectures Series, 'A Theory of Default and Altering Rules in Contract Law' (July 2006). The above definition is usually stretched to encompass almost any kind of expressed list containing two or more options, not only in case the offeror actually proposes this list to the offeree, but also in cases in which this list is provided by third parties and its existence is simply known both by the offeror and the offeree.

[40]   Id.

has already been privately exploited in drafting some copyright licenses devised by non-profit institutions, such as Free Software Foundation, or the aforementioned Creative Commons Corporation. The existence and success of these initiatives make clear that no government intervention is strictly needed in order to take advantage of the usefulness of simply altering rules, possibly organized as menus of alternatives.

Hence, 'altering rules' changing the legal regime governing the circulation of a creative work may be devised using contract law, without any intervention from legislators. Nevertheless, a (more or less explicit) endorsement of these licenses by lawmakers and public institution could be desirable. In fact, a menu of altering rules may have greater effect on the market if it is provided either by the legislator as an effect of the so-called 'expressive value' of the law, or by some highly reputable institution, whether public or private. In fact, the law is clearly not only a set of constraints associated with various kind of incentives, for example, fines, but is also a cultural tool, modifying the meaning and understanding of the world for human beings.[41] Hence, the fact that an alternative regime of copyright protection – for instance a 'Creative Commons Attribution Share-Alike' type of legal regime – is recognised by the law may increase its desirability for some authors.

In other words, the literature about contractual menus and altering rules may be read as suggesting that, even without changing the default level of protection, the simple fact of stating a menu of alternative levels of protection is likely to change the choices of some agents. Moreover, the more highly regarded the reputation of the creating/endorsing agent or institution putting forward such 'menu', the greater the effect will be. This is, for example, what occurred in the field of open source software[42] and what seems to be occurring in the field of information freely released on the Internet and frequently using CC licenses[43] or produced by some not-for-profit institutions.[44]

---

[41] Both cognitive psychologists and empirical research confirm this intuition. See the empirical analysis of Listokin (note 7).

[42] Thanks to the existence of the GNU General Public License and of other open source licenses.

[43] The success of CC is, by now, a quite established fact. As of June 2006, Google reported more than 140 million web pages available under CC licenses, <http://creativecommons.org/weblog/entry/5936>. And in June 2007 more than 38.7 million CC licensed photos were available on the Flickr website, <http://wiki.creativecommons.org/License_statistics>.

[44] See, for instance, 'Final Report to the Common Information Environment Members of a study on the applicability of Creative Commons Licences' (10 October 2005), <http://www.eduserv.org.uk/research/studies/~/media/Foundation/pdf/CIE_CC_Final_Report%20pdf.ashx> accessed 10 June 2009.

Sometimes economists tend to see the advantage of a default rule only in terms of transaction costs. Since it is costly or difficult or time-consuming to 'opt out' from the default rule, this rule has an advantage. Other rules could be chosen if, and only if, they had greater advantages from the ego-istic and self-interested point of view of a *homo economicus*. One may think that this could hardly be the case with licenses that reduce the author's control over his or her works. Here, if our goal is to push non-professional authors using the Internet to release their works under less strict terms, the only feasible thing that we can do is change the default rule to obtain copy-right protection and introduce some formalities that serve as costs and, thereby, discourage the adoption of copyright when not strictly needed as an incentivizing device. In this way, works with zero-expected monetary value – or the works of authors who are not really aware of what copyright is, or who do not care – will fall in the public domain.

This strictly economic approach is certainly relevant and a significant part of the 'story'. However, it is not the 'whole story'. If it were, legisla-tive menus would have only minor effects, because it is only the default that would really matter. By contrast, a large number of non-professional authors do not choose, or stay with, full copyright simply because they do not want to sustain any kind of costs, including those related to acquiring information. An important element of their decision to keep 'All rights reserved' is precisely because they feel that the law is saying that this is the 'right and natural' thing to do; additionally, they feel the risk of being tricked by any alternative proposed by private parties with their own agendas. The perception of legality associated to the default may even carry a kind of presumption of fairness of such a legal setting, possibly making radically alternative options more difficult to enforce in front of the courts.[45] For instance, the GPL open source software license has been criticized as being unenforceable for various reasons, including being unconstitutional in the USA or against consumer law. Indeed, the origin of these criticisms may also be found in the GPL's revolutionary approach to copyright, more than in specific legal flaws of the license.[46]

The perception of unfairness or even illegality of rules which are very

---

[45]   Charles J. Goetz and Robert E. Scott (1985), 'The limits of expanded choice: an analysis of the interactions between express and implied contract terms', (Mar 1985) 73(2) California Law Review 261–322. The authors noted that legislatively created defaults may benefit of a kind of presumption of fairness.

[46]   See Jason B Wacha, 'Taking the case: is the GPL enforceable?' (Feb 2005) 21(ii) Santa Clara Computer & High Tech LJ 451; AG Gonzales, 'Viral contracts or unenforceable document? Contractual validity of copyleft licenses' (2004) EIPR 331–39.

different from the default could change if the law said that the default rule is still 'Copyright: All Rights Reserved', but also explicitly stated an altering rule such as simply saying that writing 'Copyright: Attribution-ShareAlike' is a sufficient way to opt into another kind of legally recognized regime. The fact of allowing such an easy way to alter the default would be perceived as proof of the favor of the law regarding a particular provision, for example, the Attribution Share-Alike license.[47] An additional and either complementary or alternative way to boost a legal regime as an alternate to full copyright could come from distributing intellectual works, created by several publicly-funded projects, within that 'alternative regime'.

A similar effect could come from an explicit encouragement to non-professional authors publishing on the Internet to use this regime (possibly incentivizing Internet service providers hosting blogs, forums and newsgroups to make it very easy for their users to choose 'open licences'). An interesting example of intermediaries encouraging the adoption of CC licenses through their technological platforms seems to be the one provided by Sony's eyeVio video-sharing service (for the Japanese market).[48] Also the well-known photo-sharing portal Flickr[49] makes choosing a CC license to release one's pictures easy: the website's default is 'All rights reserved', but users can change their own default for future uploads using a 'set default license' button.

Fortunately, Internet communities have already proved quite successful in encouraging non-professional authors, and even some professional ones, for at least part of their rights to opt out of copyright and choose CC licenses. The simple fact that a community will appreciate this decision, along with the satisfaction of participating in the creation of a public good, has been enough to convince several creators. The empirical success of the CC licenses, along with the more theoretical evidence against the

---

[47]   Even if one is skeptical about the 'expressive value of the law', the fact of explicitly recognizing some licenses in the law would be significant evidence about their enforceability.

[48]   G Duncan, 'Sony To Launch YouTube Competitor in Japan', (26 April 2007) *Digital Trends*, available at <http://news.digitaltrends.com/news/story/12831/sony_to_launch_youtube_competitor-in-japan> accessed 10 June 2009. 'Sony is throwing its hat into the video sharing arena – at least in Japan – with a new service called eyeVio. The new service enables users to upload and distribute their own videos [. . .] Sony plans to keep a pro-active, sharp eye on the service for copyright violations. [. . .] *By default, all content available on eyeVio will be offered under a Creative Commons license.*' (Emphasis added.)

[49]   See <http://www.flickr.com/>. See also the Frequently Asked Questions: <http://www.flickr.com/help/photos/#87> accessed 10 June 2009.

current copyright regime, should induce legislators to use at least the 'expressive value' of the law and/or other policy choices to encourage alternatives to full copyright.

7.   CONCLUSION

The existing 'All rights reserved' copyright regime has been devised for a creative setting much different from today's Web 2.0 world. As this chapter has shown, it is likely that changing the default level of copyright protection would not decrease economic efficiency and would increase the availability and re-usability of creative works, hence fostering the spread of knowledge and increasing social justice. While, unfortunately, changing the default rule of copyright protection is a decision that has to be made at an international level, some 'second best' policies are available and workable.

In the context of imperfect information and limited rationality, with problems arising from strategic behavior and significant transaction costs – in other words, in the real world – both private parties and legislators can change the outcome of a certain bargaining process, including the almost 'unilateral' bargain consisting in choosing a copyright license by simply stating a menu of possible alternatives.[50] In particular, if a certain menu of altering rules is provided – or at least backed – by the legislator, this can have a significant 'expressive value', encouraging the use of the contractual options proposed, even when the most complete freedom of contract is granted to the parties.

The simple existence of CC licenses is already changing the licensing choices of several authors and this will happen with increased frequency as these licenses become more well-known and their judicial enforceability is proven in courts (a special case of adoption by legislators, at least in common law systems). Moreover, legislators and reputable public institutions can use law, or lower level or even internal regulations, in order to economize transaction costs associated with the adoption of some of these licenses. In fact, there are transaction costs associated with the reading and understanding of a plurality of different licenses and contractual menus, and these transaction costs could encourage people to stick to the default

---

[50]   See Ayres (note 39) at 15 (maintaining that: '[p]rivate law theorists have known for a while now that lawmakers can change the world by imposing mandatory rules or changing defaults. But this chapter suggests that without doing either of these things, lawmakers might be able to change the world by regulating the existence and structure of menus.').

rules defined by the legal system. For this reason, legislators should be careful in choosing not only the system's default rule. They should also take into consideration the possibility of explicitly recognizing a certain, if very limited, number of contractual menus in the law,[51] without reducing the available level of freedom of contract, but thereby giving a certain 'imprimatur' to some selected 'menu items,' like some of those proposed by CC.[52]

Additionally, in the event that some of the clauses comprising CC licenses are not enforceable in certain legal systems, other policy recommendations emerge from the above analysis. Legislators should find legal and institutional frameworks in which these legal arrangements – which are welfare and social justice-improving with respect to the current copyright default – could be fully enforceable. What's more, and possibly more relevant in practice, policymakers should devote some effort toward making CC and similar licenses as compatible as possible with other legal tools and institutions, such as collecting societies that have been devised to reduce transaction costs in intellectual-property-related markets.

---

[51]   Legal systems are already offering 'menus' in the form of various typified contracts (for example, contract of edition).

[52]   The simple fact of using CC licenses to spread publicly funded research and similar documents could already be significant. See Beth S Noveck, 'The electronic revolution in rulemaking' (Spring 2004) 53 Emory LJ 433, 487–88.

3. The value of irrationality in the IP equation

Sharon K. Sandeen

1. INTRODUCTION

In the late 1980s and early 1990s, while working for the *Organisation Européenne pour la Recherche Nucléaire* (CERN), Tim Berners-Lee invented the World Wide Web and, in the process, forever changed the way that we communicate and conduct business.[1] Like other inventors, Berners-Lee could have sought patent protection but, instead, he made the conscious decision to freely distribute his invention so that it could benefit the world.[2]

Berners-Lee is not the first inventor to make the decision to contribute a valuable, ground-breaking invention to the public. Dr. Jonas Salk did the same thing when he developed a vaccine for polio in 1955, leading to the subsequent near eradication of a horrible and dreaded disease.[3] The famous American inventor and statesman, Benjamin Franklin, made a similar decision with respect to all of his inventions, including the important Franklin stove.[4]

---

[1]   For a history of how the World Wide Web was created, including the contributions of other individuals such as Robert Cailliau, see James Gillies and Robert Cailliau, *How the Web Was Born* (OUP, Oxford 2000).

[2]   Id., at 209 and 234.

[3]   In a famous interview with Edward R. Morrow, when asked 'Who owns the patent on the vaccine?,' Dr. Salk responded: 'Well, the people, I would say. There is no patent. Could you patent the sun?' *See It Now* (CBS television broadcast, 12 April 1955).

[4]   Benjamin Franklin, *The Autobiography of Benjamin Franklin* (Dover Publications, New York 1996) 92 ('Gov'r. Thomas was so pleas'd with the construction of this stove, . . ., that he offered to give me a patent for the sole vending of them for a term of years; but I declin'd it from a principle which ever weighed with me on such occasions, viz., That, as we enjoy great advantages from the inventions of others, we should be glad of an opportunity to serve others by any invention of ours; and this we should do freely and generously.').

Of course, the actions of Berners-Lee, Salk, Franklin and other like-minded inventors and creators are inconsistent with the predominant assumption underlying patent and copyright law (and to some extent trade secret law): that inventors and authors need strong intellectual property protection as an incentive to engage in inventive and creative activities.[5] In fact, devotees of rational choice theory might label the actions of Berners-Lee, Salk, and Franklin as 'irrational' because they were inconsistent with the assumed need for incentives and the perceived superior value of patent protection.[6]

Although the scope of law and economics literature concerning intellectual property rights (IPRs) has broadened in recent years to look beyond the incentive rationale, not much attention has been paid to inventors and creators who are motivated by factors other than wealth maximization.[7] This chapter addresses this deficiency by identifying and examining a broader array of behaviors that could be incentivized by IP laws.[8] Because the economic analysis of law is primarily based upon rational choice theory, this chapter begins in Section 2 with an explanation of how the concept of rationality is used in the field of law and economics. In

---

[5]   See Robert P. Merges, Peter S. Menell and Mark A. Lemley, *Intellectual Property in the New Technological Age*, Revised 4th ed. (Aspen Publishers, New York 2007) 11 (explaining that '[t]he principal objective of much of intellectual property law is the promotion of new or improved works. . . . Trademark and related bodies of unfair competition law focus primarily on a very different economic problem – ensuring the integrity of the market place.').

[6]   See Section 2 for a more detailed discussion of this point. For reasons that will become clear, while I use the term irrationality throughout this chapter, I disclaim the pejorative nature of the label to describe individuals who are not considered to be utility maximizers. Moreover, as the field of law and economics expands, it is possible that the neoclassical view of rationality will be replaced with a broader, more rational definition. See e.g., Claire A. Hill, 'Law and economics in the personal sphere' (2004) 29 Law and Soc Inquiry 219, 226 (defining rationality to mean: '. . . people are purposively seeking to maximize something – often (but not always) their own utility, as they appraise it—and that their purposive efforts are in general well suited to their ends.')

[7]   Robert Cooter and Thomas Ulen (eds), *Law and Economics* 5th edn. (Pearson Addison-Wesley 2008) 126 (generally describing the current state of the economic analysis of IP law and noting: 'Almost all questions regarding intellectual property law are open.').

[8]   In his article, 'Elementary and persistent errors in the economic analysis of intellectual property' (2000) 53 Vanderbilt LR 1727, Edmund Kitch called for a broadened economic analysis of IPRs, noting the failure of the literature on IPRs to consider the full range of policy variables. This chapter does not purport to offer the complete picture of IP policy variables but, rather, provides a glimpse into the value of seemingly irrational IP behavior.

Section 3, the narrow concept of rationality that is typically applied to IP actors is used to identify those behaviors that are likely to be considered irrational. Section 4 examines the potential value of irrational IP behaviors and makes some suggestions for how they could be encouraged by policy makers. The chapter concludes in Section 5.

2.   WHAT IS IRRATIONALITY?

In everyday usage, irrationality is typically equated with behavior that is outside the norm or is unexpected; that is, illogical. According to most dictionaries, the term irrationality means the quality of not being guided by reason.[9] The term 'reason' is defined as: '[t]he mental faculty which is used in adapting thought and action to some end'.[10] Thus, to act rationally means that some thought went into the decision to engage or not engage in a particular action, regardless of whether the thought that prompted the action is accurate.[11] To act irrationally, in contrast, means to act without thought.

In the field of economics the terms rational and irrational have special meanings, although there is an ongoing debate about the precise definition of those terms.[12] Generally, pursuant to rational choice theory, to act rationally does not simply mean to act in accordance with a thought process; it means to act with particular thoughts in mind.[13] Three key assumptions underlie this theory: (1) that individuals have preferences that are stable and can be predicted and ranked; (2) that given a choice, individuals will act to maximize their utility and firms will act to maxi-

---

[9]   *Shorter Oxford English Dictionary* (Vol 1, 2002).

[10]   Id., Vol 2.

[11]   This dictionary definition of rationality differs from the definition applied in the field of law and economics where Richard Posner has stated that '[r]ational choice need not be conscious or require a large cortext.' Richard A. Posner, *Frontiers of Legal Theory* (Harvard University Press, Cambridge Mass 2004) 252 (responding to the behavioral law and economics movement).

[12]   See Russell B. Korobkin and Thomas S. Ulen, 'Law and behavioral science: removing the rationality assumption from law and economics' (2000) 88 Ca. L Rev 1051, 1060–66 (describing the 'thick' and 'thin' versions of rationality). See also 'Roundtable discussion: must we choose between rationality and irrationality?' (2005) 80 Chi-Kent L Rev 1257, and Mark Klock, 'Are wastefulness and flamboyance really virtues?: use and abuse of economic analysis' (2002) 71 U Cin L Rev 181.

[13]   Hal Varian, *Microeconomic Analysis* 3rd edn (WW Norton & Company, London 1992).

mize their profits; and (3) that the examination of individual behavior (as opposed to collective behavior) is the best way to predict the behavior of economic actors. Thus, in economic terms, to act rationally means to act in a manner that is consistent with the predicted or assumed order of individuals' preferences.[14]

The field of law and economics, as currently dominated in the US by the 'Chicago school' of economics, uses rational choice theory as a key ingredient of its economic philosophy.[15] As explained by Posner and Parisi in *The Economic Foundations of Private Law: An Introduction*:

> Law and economics rely on the standard economic assumption that individuals are rational maximizers, and study the role of law as a means for changing the relative prices attached to alternative individual actions. Under this approach, a change in the rule of law will affect human behavior by altering the relative price structure – and thus the constraint – of the optimization problem. Wealth maximization, serving as the paradigm for the analysis of law, can thus be promoted or constrained by legal rules.[16]

Based upon the foregoing, to act irrationally means to act in a manner that is inconsistent with an interest in wealth maximization. However, as Chicago school economists are quick to point out, this does not necessarily mean that individuals will always act in a manner designed to increase monetary wealth.[17]

As explained by Cooter and Ulen: '[t]he construction of the economic model of consumer choice begins with an account of the preferences of consumers'.[18] Ideally, in order to determine the preferences of consumers, we would ask them. However, because empirical research is expensive,

---

[14] Claire A. Hill, 'The rationality of preference construction (and the irrationality of rational choice)' (2008) 9 Minn. J L Sci and Tech 689, 693 ('Preferences that are not as economists posit are not infrequently, and perhaps even typically, characterized as "irrational".').

[15] For a history of the 'Chicago school' of economics, see Nicholas Mercuro and Steven G. Medema, *Economics and the Law: From Posner to Post-Modernism* (Princeton Univ Press, Princeton 1997) 51.

[16] Richard A. Posner and Francesco Parisi (eds), *Economic Foundations of Private Law* (Edward Elgar, Cheltenham 2002) xi. As used by Posner, wealth maximization 'refers to weighting preferences for the things people want.' Richard A. Posner, 'Wealth Maximization Revisited' (1985) 2 JLEPP 85, 85–6.

[17] Richard Posner has stated that rationality to him means 'choosing the best available means to the chooser's ends.' Posner, *Frontiers of Legal Theory* (Harvard University Press, Cambridge Mass 2001) 252.

[18] Cooter and Ulen, *Law and Economics*, 22. See also, Edmund W. Kitch, 'Elementary and persistent errors in the economic analysis of intellectual property' (2000) 53 Vanderbilt LR 1727.

time consuming, and often messy (that is, it does not always reveal clear answers), economic analysis is usually based upon assumptions about human behavior.[19] Since these assumptions are developed by the individuals who are conducting the economic analysis, the application of rational choice theory necessarily involves value judgments about how so-called rational actors are supposed to behave. In other words, determining what consumers value is often in the eye of the economist.[20]

Recently, the field of behavioral economics and its progeny, behavioral law and economics, has focused attention on the need to question the assumptions about human behavior and preferences that underlie most economic models, including the wealth maximizing assumptions of the Chicago school of economics.[21] As this literature demonstrates, people are motivated to act (or not act) for all sorts of reasons.[22] This insight, in turn, has led to a re-examination of the meaning of rational behavior and to debate about which analytical methodology is superior: the traditional law and economics model based upon a utility maximizing model of rational choice, or a behavioral law and economics model based upon empirical evidence of actual human behavior.[23]

---

[19]   Cooter and Ulen, *Law and Economics*, 23 ('Economists leave to other disciplines such as psychology and sociology, the study of the source of [consumer] preferences.').

[20]   Mark Klock, 'Are wastefulness and flamboyance really virtues?: use and abuse of economic analysis' (2002) 71 U Cin LR 181 (arguing that if there is a problem with economic analysis based upon rational choice theory it is probably due to an error in the assumptions on which it is based and not because of the invalidity of rational choice theory).

[21]   See Cooter and Ulen, *Law and Economics*, Web Note 2.1, 16 (noting criticism of rational choice theory and citing the Nobel Prize-winning work of Daniel Kahneman who demonstrated that consumers do not always act as economists assume). See also, Francesco Parisi and Vernon L. Smith (eds), *The Law and Economics of Irrational Behavior* (Stanford University Press, Stanford 2005); Cass R. Sunstein (ed), *Behavioral Law and Economics* (CUP, Cambridge 2000); Russell B. Korobkin and Thomas S. Ulen, 'Law and behavioral science: removing the rationality assumption from law and economics' (2000) 88 Cal LR 1051; and Christine Jolls, Cass R. Sunstein and Richard Thaler, 'A behavioral approach to law and economics' (1998) 50 Stan LR 1471.

[22]   Jolls, Sunstein and Thaler identified bounded rationality, bounded will-power, and bounded self-interest as three reasons why individual behavior often deviates from the utility maximizing assumptions of rational choice theory. Jolls, Sunstein and Thaler, 'A behavioral approach to law and economics' (1998) 50 Stan LR 1471, 1476.

[23]   See Korobkin and Ulen, 'Law and behavioral science: removing the rationality assumption from law and economics' 88 Cal LR 1051, 1071–4 (summarizing the arguments of rational choice theorists against behavioral economics).

Generally, the disciples of traditional law and economics claim that their methodology is superior because it is more predictive of actual human behavior.[24] Those who favor a behavioral approach claim that their methodology is superior because it is based upon actual rather than hypothesized human behavior.[25] However, it is not necessary for policy makers to resolve (or even take sides in) this debate since both analytical models may reveal important insights about human behavior that can lead to the adoption of better laws. In the case of IP policy, if a principal goal is to encourage greater innovation, invention, and creativity, then it is important to understand all of the factors that motivate individuals to engage in such endeavors. For instance, the reasons why some IP actors choose not to secure or enforce their IPRs may provide useful information about the needed scope and structure of IP laws. It is to these seemingly irrational behaviors that this chapter now turns.

3. IRRATIONALITY AMONG INTELLECTUAL PROPERTY ACTORS

As the foregoing definition of irrationality reveals, what is irrational behavior among IP actors can only be defined in terms of those behaviors that are assumed to be rational. This is usually determined by considering the stories that are told about how IP actors are supposed to behave. As will be seen, the assumptions about how IP actors are supposed to behave are often defined by the IP laws themselves.

According to the predominant law and economics story about IPRs, inventors and creators are highly self-interested individuals who will not invent or create unless they are provided with sufficient incentives or who will aggressively guard the secrecy of their inventions and creations. Thus, in order to encourage investment in the development of IPRs and the disclosure of inventions, it is necessary for laws to provide sufficient incentives, most notably in the form of potential monetary gains.[26] Although

---

[24] See e.g., Posner, *Frontiers of Legal Theory*, 252.
[25] Jolls, Sunstein and Thaler, 1476 ('The task of behavioral law and economics, simply stated, is to explore the implications of actual (hypothesized) human behavior for the law.').
[26] See William M. Landes and Richard A. Posner, *The Economic Structure of Intellectual Property Law* (Harvard University Press, Cambridge Mass 2003) 9–10 (noting the emphasis on incentive theory but urging a broader economic analysis).

there are a number of ways to provide monetary rewards, the laws of the United States and most other countries rely primarily upon a model whereby inventors and creators can obtain exclusive rights in their inventions and creations. Underlying this story is the perceived connection between innovation and creativity and economic growth,[27] and the assertion by many that more IP protection will lead to greater innovation and creativity, and therefore more economic growth.

Another story ties IPRs intricately to property theory and the public goods problem.[28] According to this story, in the absence of patent, copyright, and trade secret laws, the transaction costs associated with using another person's inventions and creations would to be so low that the user of the invention or creation would be disinclined to bargain. Underlying this story is the value that the Chicago school of economics places on markets that are unrestrained by government regulation except, as is the case with respect to IP, where government regulation is needed to create, define, expand, or protect markets.[29]

Historically, the story of trademark law is not based upon property theory or a desire to create incentives for the creation of trademarks.[30] Rather, it was related to the tendency of some competitors to engage in acts that were deemed unfair (even though those acts might be considered rational in the absence of trademark laws).[31] Trademark laws specify that

---

[27] See e.g., Peter S. Menell and Suzanne Scotchmer, 'Intellectual property law' in A. Mitchell Polinsky and Steven Shavell (eds), *Handbook of Law and Economics* (2nd Vol, Elsevier, Amsterdam 2007) ('Economic interest in intellectual property grows primarily out of the critical importance of innovation to social welfare.'); Commission to the Council, 'Green Paper on Promoting Innovation through Patents: The Follow-up to The Green Paper on the Community Patent and the Patent System in Europe' (5 February 1999, COM (99) 42 final) 8 <http://ec.europa.edu/internal_market/indprop/docs/patent/docs/8682_en.pdf> accessed 9 February 2009 ('The patent system should no longer be conceived in isolation from the economic and industrial reality of which it is part.'); Commission to the Council, Green Paper on Copyright and the Challenge of Technology: Copyright Issues Requiring Immediate Action, (7 June 1988, COM (88) 172 final) 11–12, <http://ec.europa.eu/internal_market/copyright/docs/docs/com-88-172_en.pdf> accessed 9 Feb 2009 (noting the growing importance of copyright to industry and commerce).
[28] Landes and Posner, *The Economic Structure of Intellectual Property Law*, Ch 1; and Cooter and Ulen, *Law and Economics*, Ch 5.
[29] 'Today it is acknowledged that analysis and evaluation of intellectual property law are appropriately conducted with an economic framework that seeks to align the law with the dictates of economic efficiency.' Id. Landes and Posner, Ch 4.
[30] Id. Landes and Posner, Ch 7.
[31] See Menell and Scotchmer, 'Intellectual property law', 1537–8.

it is wrongful for a competitor to use a mark in a manner that is likely to cause confusion. A more contemporary story concerns the power of advertising and the assumptions about how consumers use trademarks in making purchasing decisions; namely, that consumers want to know the source of goods and services that they are purchasing, and trademarks give them shorthand references that allow them to reduce their search costs.[32] Increasingly, however, what began as a body of law focused on the needs of consumers has become a quasi-property regime designed to protect the branding of companies and their products.[33] Underlying these stories is the value that policy makers place in 'protecting the integrity of the markets'.[34]

Once IP laws exist, it is generally assumed that rational IP actors will be able to discern the value of their innovations, creations, and trademarks so that they can make the correct choices about whether to secure and enforce their rights. If an invention is within the scope of patentable subject matter, and has a reasonable chance of meeting the patent law requirements of originality, novelty, and non-obviousness (inventive step), it is also assumed that the inventor will seek patent protection.[35] Finally, given the perceived value of IPRs, IP owners are expected to act to protect their IPRs whenever and wherever necessary.

Pursuant to the foregoing narratives, you might be an irrational IP actor if:

1. You are willing to engage in innovative and creative endeavors without the availability of IP protection;
2. You do not feel compelled to hide your unprotected innovations and creations; that is, you are willing to freely share them with others;
3. You choose to forego IP protection when it is available to you;
4. If you are a consumer, you do not rely solely upon trademarks and service marks in making your purchasing decisions but, instead, take your time to carefully examine goods and services before deciding to purchase them; and
5. You do not take steps to enforce your IP rights.

---

[32] For a history of US trademark law as a tool of modern advertising, see Mark Bartholomew, 'Advertising and the transformation of trademark law' (2008) 38 New Mexico Law Review, 1.

[33] Id. at 12–16.

[34] See Menell and Scotchmer, 'Intellectual property law', 1536–44.

[35] See *Kewanee Oil Co.* v. *Bicron Corp.*, 416 US 470, 489–90 (1974).

The question that is examined in the remainder of this chapter is whether any of these seemingly irrational behaviors are of benefit to society and should be promoted by policy makers.

4.   THE BENEFITS OF IRRATIONAL IP BEHAVIOR

As noted above, the image that is created by the story of IP actors is of numerous self-interested individuals who prefer IP protection and the promise of personal financial gain over all other possible rewards. It is a story that is based upon the belief that innovation is the primary driver of economic development and that economic development should be the primary focus of policy makers. But there are other stories that can and should be told about the necessary components of economic growth and about the ways policy makers can help to enrich a society.[36]

4.1   The Benefits of Innovating and Creating without IP Protection

There are a lot of inventors and creators who contribute to the well-being of a country even though they may not profit directly from IPRs. In the United States, jazz musicians and other improvisational artists regularly create works of art that bring pleasure and happiness to their audiences, even though such works are not protected by copyright law if they are not 'fixed' in tangible form. In many countries, fashion designers expend creative capital to design works of style and beauty that help improve the appearance and self-esteem of their clients, despite the fact that copyright protection does not usually extend to their designs.[37] Individuals who engage in various labor and skill-intensive occupations – such as computer programmers, farmers, plumbers, and machinists – frequently devise solutions to problems that improve the efficiency of their business systems,[38] but which they never consider patenting. Retail stores create interesting and unique displays that make the shopping experience more enjoyable, but which do not result in the creation of IPRs. Even judges and law professors can contribute to the flourishing of a society through the (hopefully) cogent explanation of the law

---

[36]   See *e.g.*, Cass Sunstein, *Free Markets and Social Justice* (OUP, Oxford 1997).
[37]   French law is an exception to this rule. See Article L. 112–2 of the French Intellectual Property Code.
[38]   See Eric Von Hippel, *Democratizing Innovation* (MIT Press, 2005) (discussing user-generated innovation).

and related principles, even though their works may enjoy little or no IP protection or direct financial rewards.[39] Although the inventive and creative contributions of these individuals may not add directly to the GDP of a country through the sale or licensing of IPRs, they contribute in less tangible ways.

In explaining the foregoing activities, rational choice theorists are apt to argue that the individual actors were simply acting in accordance with non-IP driven preferences; that is, they acted rationally in accordance with other objectives. Alternatively, they might argue that the answer to the lack of IP-driven preferences with respect to certain inventive and creative efforts can easily be corrected by expanding the scope of IP protection.[40] However, both of these explanations miss a very important point: if individuals are willing to engage in inventive and creative activities without clear IP incentives, then something else is motivating their behavior. If we really care about incentivizing innovation and creativity, wouldn't we want to identify and understand all the factors that motivate inventors and creators?

What are the factors that motivate inventors and creators to invent and create without the promise of IPRs? In their article, *A Behavioral Approach to Law and Economics*, Jolls, Sunstein, and Thaler (collectively 'JST') identified bounded rationality, bounded willpower, and bounded self-interest as three possible (but not necessarily exclusive) reasons why individual behavior may deviate from the utility maximizing assumptions of rational choice theory.[41] Pursuant to bounded rationality, individuals may act in unpredictable ways due to cognitive difficulties; for instance, they might be unaware that IPRs are available or be unable to properly value the worth of their inventions and creations. The concept of bounded willpower

---

[39] For instance, in the United States of America, all works of federal employees, including members of the US judiciary, are not protected by copyright law. 17 USC §105. See <http://www.bitlaw.com/source/17usc/105.html>.

[40] France, for instance, has provided protection for dress designs for many years. See Jennifer Mencken, 'A Design for the Copyright of Fashion' [1997] 1997 BC Intell Prop & Tech F 121201 <http://www.bc.edu/bc_org/avp/law/st_org/iptf/articles/content/1997121201.html> accessed 9 Feb 2009; and Giorgio Bernini, 'Protection of designs: United States and French law' (1952) 1 Amer J of Comp Law 133.

[41] Jolls, Sunstein and Thaler, 'A behavioral approach to law and economics', (1998) 50 *Stanford Law Review* 1476. See also, Robert Frank, 'Departures From Rational Choice: With and Without Regret' in Parisi and Smith (eds) *The Law and Economics of Irrational Behavior*, Ch 1 (identifying three reasons for (seemingly) irrational behavior: (1) cognitive errors (also referred to as bounded rationality); (2) impulse-control problems; and (3) non-self interested motives).

refers to actions that are taken in conflict with an individual's long-term interests and are most relevant to decisions that have consequences over time.[42] Non self-interested behavior (or bounded self-interest) is attached to actions that deviate substantially from the usual or ordinary conduct under the circumstances.[43]

Although Berners-Lee, Salk, and Franklin may not have known the true value of their inventions and may have had some doubts about the patentability of their inventions, it appears clear that their actions were not motivated by bounded rationality; that is, cognition errors. They each knew that patent protection was potentially available for their inventions and that their inventions would be of great value to others. It also seems clear that their actions were not effected by bounded willpower. Instead, when viewed through the lens of how IP policy makers expected them to act – that is, to be motivated by IPRs and the promise of financial wealth – their actions were consistent with bounded self-interest. But what was it that motivated them?

Digging deeper into the motivations of Berners-Lee, Salk, and Franklin one sees a richer and more complex story about the motivations of inventors and creators that policy makers should consider. The story of Berners-Lee begins with his upbringing and his early exposure to, and intense interest in, mathematics.[44] Obviously, Berners-Lee would not have been in the position to invent anything if he did not have the requisite knowledge of computer science. Once educated and in a position where he could experiment, it was his intellectual curiosity and the challenge of improving existing systems that led him to develop the World Wide Web.

In making his decision not to patent his invention, Berners-Lee recognized that the invention of a valuable new technology was meaningless without its widespread adoption and that patent protection did not guarantee adoption.[45] The market can be a good judge of the worth of an invention, but the reality is that a lot of very valuable inventions never achieve commercial success. Often, businesses are reluctant to replace their incumbent technology with new technology before they have recouped their investment in the old technology. Also, when a business is

---

[42]   Id. The act of smoking, particularly in light of evidence that it is deleterious to one's health, is often cited as an example of bounded will power.

[43]   Id.

[44]   Tim Berners-Lee, with Mark Fischetti, *Weaving the Web: The Original Design and Ultimate Destiny of the World Wide Web* (Orion, 1999).

[45]   Gillies and Cailliau, *How the Web Was Born: The Story of the World Wide Web* (OUP, Oxford 2000) 234.

engaged in its own research and development activities, it is likely to prefer its own inventions if for no other reason than to justify the existence of the R and D department. For these and other reasons, it is not surprising that Berners-Lee found the academic and computer science communities to be most receptive to his ideas. Obviously, the members of those communities had the knowledge and skills necessary to understand his invention but, just as importantly, they shared an ethic of collaboration and a willingness to try new things. Rather than patenting his invention and relying on the market to place a value on it, Berners-Lee put his faith in the intelligence of a small group of individuals who, conveniently, were in a position to adopt his protocol.

Like Berners-Lee, Salk's inventive activities sprang from an intense intellectual curiosity that was fueled by his education, but with the added dimension of the reward of ending human suffering.[46] The way that his research was funded also played a role in Salk's decision not to seek patent protection for his invention. Because millions of people contributed to his research in the form of a grass-roots campaign known as 'The March of Dimes', Salk viewed the polio vaccine more as the product of collective action than as the property of one individual.[47]

Franklin's inventive activities were also due to his intense intellectual curiosity, but an intellectual curiosity that was fueled by problems he encountered in everyday life.[48] Frequently, his inventive efforts were simply designed to make his life easier and, in the process, he was willing to share his discoveries with others. Franklin was less interested in direct financial reward than in the indirect benefits he would derive in the form of an enhanced reputation and the inventions that others may be inspired to share with him.

What lessons could policy makers learn from the foregoing stories? First, education and intellectual curiosity are critical components of innovation and creativity. The corollary being that the more educated the citizenry of a country becomes, the more innovation and creativity that is likely to occur. Thus, countries that want to benefit from innovation

---

[46] See generally, David M. Oshinsky, *Polio an American Story: The Crusade That Mobilized the Nation Against the 20th Century's Most Feared Disease* (OUP, Oxford 2006).

[47] Id.,79–111 and 211–212 ('. . .Salk readily acknowledged that his vaccine quest, like so many scientific endeavors, had been built on ideas and techniques of others.').

[48] See generally, Benjamin Franklin, *The Autobiography of Benjamin Franklin* (first published in London in 1793).

and creativity must invest in the education of their citizens.[49] Second, the process of innovation and creativity is impacted (either negatively or positively) by the environment in which it occurs. The corollary is that the profit motive (particularly a short-term profit motive) can stifle successful innovation and creativity. Thus, countries can promote innovation and creativity by creating environments and institutions in which such activities can occur unrestrained by a profit motive. Traditionally, this was the role of research universities, but there are other places where such activities may occur (NASA and CERN being two obvious examples). Third, collaboration, like education, is a fuel for innovation and creativity. The corollary being that collaboration with one's peers may provide a better sense of the value of an invention than the market. Thus, if policy makers want to encourage the development of the best technologies, rather than the most commercially successful, they will create environments and institutions where peer-to-peer collaboration is facilitated. Fourth, policy makers should not forget the pure joy and pleasure that many people experience when sharing their inventions and creations with others. The corollary being that individuals are more apt to experience joy and pleasure if they perceive themselves as being a member of a community that will benefit from their contributions.[50] Thus, it is important to foster a culture that values innovation and creativity.

4.2   The Benefits of Sharing Information

As numerous studies have shown, innovation and creativity rarely occur in a vacuum. Innovators and creators need knowledge and information upon which to build.[51] This is one reason why the public domain is so

---

[49] 'It is now widely recognized that technological advancement and enhanced human capital are the principal engines of economic growth in the United States and other industrialized countries.' Menell and Scotchmer, 'Intellectual Property Law' 1476, citing F.M. Scherer and D. Ross, *Industrial Market Structure and Economic Performance* (3rd ed. Houghton Mifflin, 1990) 613–14.

[50] Johanna Gibson, *Creating Selves: Intellectual Property and the Narration of Culture* (Ashgate Publishing, 2006) 140 (noting that: '. . . the goods comprising intellectual property are not transacted in pure exchanges, but must be understood in terms of the political and ideological context of creativity, knowledge diversity, and the rich cultural and critical progress of a networked society.').

[51] See *e.g.*, Luis Suarez-Villa, *Invention and the Rise of Technocapitalism* (Rowman and Littlefield Publishers, 2000) 11–24 (discussing the importance of educational access and quality and the diffusion of new scientific knowledge); and Dov Greenbaum, 'Are we legislating away our scientific culture?: the database

important. Without a rich public domain, innovation and creativity is stifled.

US and international intellectual property policies recognize the importance of a rich public domain in a number of ways. First, the scope of IP laws is limited to exclude protection for information that is already publicly available. Second, as part of the patent bargain, inventors must fully disclose their inventions in a detailed specification, which is published a period of months after the patent application is filed. While publication of a work is not a requirement for copyright protection, it is assumed that most copyrightable works will be publicly disseminated or registered. Even trade secret law has a disclosure function by creating conditions under which inventors are more likely to share their information with others.[52] However, while the benefits of information disclosure are an important part of IP policy, they are typically cited as counter-weights to the grant of IPRs, rather than as important values in their own right.

The irony of the last statement should not be lost on those who know the history of patent and copyright law, and of higher education. All three systems were designed to add to the store of available knowledge and facilitate its distribution. Unfortunately, despite the obvious benefits of these systems, there remain impediments to the sharing of information. In Franklin's day (and in many countries today), there were few available books and only a small percentage of the population could read. Also, although education was highly valued, it was typically available only to the male elite. Today, while improvements in communication and the expansion of educational opportunities has greatly increased the dissemination of knowledge, there is concern that the incessant drum beat for IPRs has created a culture of information hoarders.[53] This is particularly true with respect to information that cannot be, or is not yet, protected by patent or copyright, such as: discoveries that do not fall within the scope of patentable subject matter; written content that is not protected by copyright (for example factual information); and ideas. Increasingly, the assertion of trade secret and contract rights is being used to restrict the free flow of information.

Of course, the narrative of law and economics counts on the market to fix the problem of insufficient information dispersal; if the information

---

debate' [2003] 2003 Duke Tech LR 22 (discussing the use and importance of the sharing of information in scientific research).

[52] *Kewanee Oil Co.* v. *Bicron Corp.*, 416 US 470, 485–6.

[53] See *e.g.*, Wendy Gordon, 'On owning information: intellectual property and the restitutionary impulse' (1992) 78 Va LR 149 (discussing the propertization of information).

is of value, then presumably someone will be willing to pay for it. There are, however, several problems with this explanation that policy makers who are interested in finding additional ways to encourage innovation and creativity should consider. First, as the previous story of the farmers, plumbers, and machinists reveals, individuals who do not see themselves as inventors (or, at least, persons who are not hired to invent) often devise ingenious solutions to problems that they encounter in their everyday lives. Although these solutions may, theoretically, be in the public domain because they are not patented or protected by trade secret law, they are not ordinarily captured in a manner that makes them accessible to others. Second, it is not just information that has a marketable value that should be the subject of distribution efforts; even information in the form of unprotectable ideas and facts can provide the spark of creativity and inventiveness. Third, market forces alone may not be sufficient to facilitate the optimal sharing of information.[54]

An example of an area that could benefit from new or improved laws designed to facilitate sharing non-IP information is the Open Innovation movement.[55] The underlying premise of the Open Innovation movement is that businesses can learn a lot from each other and may derive greater benefits from freely sharing their information than from hoarding it. The problem is that, given the nature of the innovative process (particularly in its early stages), businesses are unlikely to have sufficient knowledge of the value of their and their collaborator's information to enable them to make an accurate cost benefit analysis. Also, according to Arrow's information paradox, people who are inclined to share information face a dilemma: without some legal protection, the disclosure of secret information means that there is nothing left to sell; however, the prospective purchaser of the information is unlikely to buy the information without seeing it.[56] Patent law is often unhelpful in solving the Arrow paradox because the information that is proposed for exchange may not have reached a sufficient level of inventiveness to be patentable and, in any event, the parties may not

---

[54] See Menell and Scotchmer, 'Intellectual property law' 1502–3 (discussing the process of cumulative invention and the impediments to information and rights sharing that can impede improvements and adaptations).

[55] See Henry W. Chesbrough, *Open Innovation: The New Imperative for Creating and Profiting from Technology* (Harvard Business School Publishing, Boston 2006).

[56] See Kenneth J. Arrow, 'Economic welfare and allocation of resources for invention' in *The Rate and Direction of Innovative Activity* (National Bureau of Economic Research edn, 1962) 609, 615.

want to go to the expense of filing a patent application before they have more information.

In the United States of America, trade secret law serves the function of facilitating the exchange of information that is not protected by patent or copyright law and solving Arrow's information paradox. However, because the scope of trade secret law is limited, it does not cover all information that may be exchanged between parties. In the absence of clear IP protection, businesses that are inclined to share information will often engage in pre-disclosure bargaining that attempts to define both the parameters and the consequences of any disclosures. Typically, the entity who wants to receive information seeks to avoid making any binding promises, while the entity submitting information wants to exact a promise of compensation in the event the information is used. Unfortunately, as numerous cases demonstrate, the explicit and implicit bargaining that occurs between would-be information sharers often leads to costly and unsatisfying litigation regarding the scope and validity of alleged promises.[57] Without creating new IPRs, there may be ways for policy makers to reduce the incidence and cost of such litigation, while at the same time facilitating the sharing of information for the purposes of inventive and creative activity. For instance, governments could facilitate the creation of private institutions that are specifically designed to improve information sharing.[58] Or, based upon the example of the Uniform Commercial Code, perhaps a formal code of information sharing can be created that sets forth default rules that apply in open innovation settings similar to the informal code that has developed in the Open Source movement.[59]

4.3 The Benefits of Not Pursuing IP Protection

As noted in the introduction to this chapter, the most irrational behavior that an inventor might engage in is not to seek patent protection for an invention that is within the scope of patentable subject matter. However, for many inventors, the decision not to seek patent protection is completely rational for the simple reason that the prosecution and enforcement

---

[57] See *e.g.*, *Desny* v. *Wilder*, 46 Cal 2d 715 (1956) and *Faris* v. *Engberg*, 97 Cal App 3d 309 (1979).

[58] See *e.g.*, Robert P. Merges, 'Locke for the masses: property rights and the products of collective creativity' (2008) 36 Hofstra LR 1179; and Robert P. Merges, 'Of property rules, Coase, and intellectual property' (1994) 94 Colum L Rev 2655.

[59] For more information about the Open Source Movement, see the website of the Open Source Initiative available at: <http://www.opensource.org>.

of patent rights is very costly. Assuming that they have accurate information about the low commercial value of their invention and the costs to prosecute a patent (a big assumption), individuals and firms who elect not to obtain patent protection are acting in a manner that is consistent with wealth maximization. If the inventions have great commercial value – as they did in the case of the World Wide Web, the polio vaccine, and the Franklin stove – the inventors who choose not to pursue patent protection are often portrayed as being either stupid or altruistic.

Regardless of the intent of inventors who elect not to protect their inventions and creations, society benefits in at least two ways. First, there are obvious costs associated with establishing legal systems to protect IPRs. In the United States, these include the creation and management of the Patent and Trademark Office, the Copyright Office, and related judicial and administrative courts. Each time individuals and firms choose not to file patent applications or register their copyrights and trademarks, the costs incurred by the relevant governmental authorities is reduced.[60] The second way that society benefits from a decision not to pursue IP protection is in the enrichment of the public domain; if the decision not to pursue IP protection is coupled with a decision to disseminate information concerning the invention or creation, knowledge and the arts are enhanced. As noted previously, however, it is not a foregone conclusion that inventors and creators who elect not to pursue IP protection will disseminate their inventions and creations in ways that will lead to their capture by the public. They may keep them as trade secrets or, worse, put them on a shelf. As a consequence, there are a lot of good ideas and innovative solutions to problems that few people know about.

One of the reasons countries are willing to invest in IP institutions is because they believe that by granting IPRs the dissemination of knowledge will increase. Thus, it is ironic that some inventors and creators may elect not to utilize these services because they are too expensive. Of course, one answer to this problem is to reduce the costs associated with applying for patents and registering trademarks and copyrights. However, since the potential commercial value of an invention or creation enters into the equation of whether to pursue such efforts, reducing prosecution and application costs can only go so far in encouraging the dissemination of knowledge. In addition, policy makers should consider creating additional systems for rewarding information disclosure and sharing. Higher education is one system that rewards information disclosure and sharing, but it

---

[60]   These reductions in costs are offset to some extent by a reduction in the fees that are paid by applicants and registrants.

is not the ideal system for identifying the innovative activities that occur within commercial organizations, particularly in fields where knowledge of actual commercial practices is not highly valued. The numerous professional and industry associations that exist function, to some degree, as the facilitators of information dispersal, but more could be done to document and store such disclosures. Policy makers should also consider whether it makes sense to protect non-IP information that is submitted to the government when that information may be helpful to other innovators.[61]

4.4 The Benefits of Careful Purchasing Decisions

As noted above, the value of trademark law does not lie in its ability to incentivize innovation and creativity; rather, its purposes are to protect the integrity of the markets (that is, prevent unfair competition) and lower consumer search costs. Underlying the latter purpose is the assumption that it is better (that is, more efficient) for consumers to act quickly by relying on the presumed information value of trademarks than to expend time and energy to collect such information. Thus, pursuant to trademark theory, consumers act irrationally if they do not rely (at least in part) on trademarks when making their purchasing decision.

Under existing trademark law, as long as a mark is distinctive, we recognize trademark rights and leave it up to consumers to discern through their own experiences what a mark actually means. Although it is often stated that trademarks can have both positive and negative connotations, it takes time for either connotation to attach to a trademark and usually attaches only after multiple purchasing decisions have already been made. Moreover, through the use of advertising, trademark owners actively engage in efforts to build a positive image for their brands. If those efforts fail, or if their brand becomes attached to negative events, trademark owners can simply change their brand.[62]

While there are obvious temporal efficiencies to be gained by consumers from being able to select goods and services based upon trademarks, such efficiencies are not necessarily consistent with good public policy. As the recent meltdown of the US mortgage industry demonstrates, there are also benefits to be gained when consumers exercise deliberation and care.

---

[61] See *e.g.*, the 'data exclusivity' provisions of the TRIPS Agreement: World Trade Organization, 'Agreement on Trade Related Aspects of Intellectual Property' Article 39.3, available at: <http://www.wto.org/english/tratop_e/trips_e/t_agm0_e.htm> accessed 9 Feb 2009.

[62] For instance, after the Enron scandal, Andersen Consulting changed its name to Accenture.

Thus, it may be worth considering to what extent the strength or 'fame' of trademarks play a role in poor consumer decision-making and what governments could do about it. To pose the question in economic terms: To what extent do trademarks add to consumers' cognition errors?

Arguably, the greater the care that consumers should exercise in the selection of goods and services, the more important it is for cognition errors to be avoided. For instance, if we believe it is important for consumers to know that the institution where they are depositing their life savings is a bank that is insured by the US Federal Deposit Insurance Corporation (FDIC), then we should be concerned if a trademark leads them to believe that an institution is insured by the FDIC when it is not. In other words, we should care what information trademarks convey in addition to the source of goods and services. If we conclude that the use of certain trademarks in certain industries is too loaded with misinformation, perhaps we should limit the type of trademarks that can be used in those industries.[63] We should also consider other steps that governments can take to encourage care and deliberation by the consumer, including better consumer education.

4.5   The Benefits of Low Litigation Rates

For many of the same reasons that society benefits from the decision of IP owners not to pursue IP protection when it is available to them, society also benefits when IP owners choose not to sue to enforce their rights. A decision not to sue, or to settle soon after suing, reduces the burden that is placed upon the court system. The fewer IP cases that burden the courts, the more time judges have to spend on other cases, including other IP cases. The extent to which the decision of an IP litigant not to sue is beneficial to society, however, ultimately depends on whether the increase in innovation and creativity that results from the provision of IPRs outweighs the total costs associated with creating and maintaining an IP enforcement system. For most developed countries, the answer to the foregoing question is likely to be yes.[64] However, it would be interesting to

---

[63]   We already do this, in part, by restricting the registration of certain government symbols and misleading and disparaging marks. See *e.g.*, 15 USC §1052 (a)–(c).

[64]   Unfortunately, the answer is likely to be different for least developed and developing countries. In this regard, the requirements that are imposed on WTO member countries to institute effective means for IP owners to enforce their IPRs is very troubling when one considers that some countries do not have the means to provide all of their citizens with potable water.

consider how the benefits that are derived from increased innovation and creativity actually compare to the costs of an IP enforcement system.

Looking beyond the benefits of judicial efficiency, the decision of an IP owner not to sue for infringement of his IPRs reveals some potential flaws in the system. Of particular concern are the barriers that undercapitalized inventors and creators face when trying to use the IP enforcement system. Although some IP cases may involve a sufficient level of actual damages to be attractive to attorneys who are willing to represent a plaintiff on a contingency basis, IP litigation is usually a pay-as-you-go proposition. Thus, although in theory it is available to all inventors and authors, in practice it is largely the domain of large companies. The policy question that arises from this situation is whether people will value a system from which they are excluded. If a substantial number of people cannot benefit directly from a system of IPRs, how likely are they to engage in the inventive and creative endeavors that it is supposed to inspire? Of equal importance, how likely are they to respect the IPRs of others?

Once again, economists may explain away the barriers to the enforcement of IPRs as simply reflecting the low value that the market places on the subject innovations or creations. However, it is often the case that at the time of the alleged infringement, the innovation and creation has not yet been introduced to the market. In this regard, none of the IP regimes (except, to a small extent, trade secret law) requires proof of the worth or value of an invention or creation before IPRs will attach. If the invention or creation falls within the scope of protectable subject matter and otherwise meets the requirements for protection, IPRs attach and can be enforced with injunctive relief. It is this system of property-like entitlements that creates the market for IPRs in the first place; if it is not respected, the whole house of cards collapses. Thus, it should be in everyone's interest to understand why IP owners decide not to pursue litigation.

There are a number of ways that policy makers can reduce the costs of litigation so that it is easier for IPRs to be enforced and so that more members of society believe that the IP system is of potential benefit to them.[65] One large component of the costs relate to debates about the validity and scope of IPRs. Unfortunately, although most IPRs come with a presumption of validity, such validity remains a central issue in all IP litigation. One way to reduce these costs is to make sure that the examination

---

[65] See CJA Consultants Ltd, *Final Report, Patent Litigation Insurance: A Study for the European Commission on Possible Insurance Schemes against Patent Litigation Risks* (January 2003), available at: <http://ec.europa.eu/internal_market/indprop/docs/patent/studies/litigation_en.pdf> accessed 9 Feb 2009.

process for patents and trademarks operates to identify undeserving applicants and registrants. Copyright litigation presents a different problem. Because there is no substantive examination process and low requirements of copyrightability, a critical issue in most copyright infringement cases revolves around differentiating between those portions of a work that are protected by copyright and those that are not. Perhaps this issue would be more easily resolved if copyright owners were required to identify the copyrighted portions of a work when they apply to register the same. This would have the ancillary benefit of educating copyright registrants about the limits of copyright law.

5.   CONCLUSION

At their core, laws are designed for one or both of two basic purposes: to prohibit and penalize bad behavior and to encourage and incentivize good behavior. In the case of prohibitory laws, we assume that individuals will both know about the prohibitions (either instinctively or due to educational efforts) and respect them. In the case of laws that are designed to motivate good behavior, we assume that individuals will learn of the available benefits and act to take advantage of them. IP laws are designed with both purposes in mind, but in the case of patent and copyright laws, the primary purpose is to encourage greater innovation and creativity. Indeed, it is the perceived connection between innovation and creativity and economic growth that is the principal justification for more and greater IP protection worldwide. It is assumed that if a strong system for the protection of IP is built, individual actors will: (1) learn the benefits of the system; (2) be motivated to invent and create due to the incentives that are provided; and (3) contribute to the economic growth of a country. These assumptions, however, do not tell the whole story of why individuals invent and create or how they may contribute to the well-being of a society.

Long before there were any IP laws and before the scope and length of IP protection was extended to its current levels, numerous individuals such as Franklin, Salk and Berners-Lee were motivated to invent and create. Although their decisions not to seek or enforce IP protection are often characterized as being altruistic or stupid, there is more to their stories. We should not assume that because some individuals act in a manner that is inconsistent with the assumed behavior of rational IP actors that their actions are not valuable or worthy of encouragement. Instead, if we are truly interested in encouraging greater innovation and creativity, we should learn as much as possible about the multitude of factors that motivate individuals to invent and create.

It is the nature of human existence that individuals must learn, explore, create, invent, and express. One need only observe the activities of a two-year-old to know this is true. Thus, it is ironic that what sets humans apart from most other creatures on earth – a rational mind – is used as part of rational choice theory to limit our view of what is needed to encourage and support such behavior. As noted in the introduction to this chapter, there are a lot of benefits that society can derive from inventors and creators who choose to act irrationality. Ultimately it is a choice about the behaviors we want to reward. Few would argue that innovation and creativity should not be rewarded in some manner. But there are other behaviors that contribute to innovation and creativity, and to society, that policy makers may wish to promote. Ultimately, the establishment of an IP system should be about creating a culture in which innovation and creativity thrive. Policy makers should not be afraid to use their own innovative and creative powers in an effort to create such a culture.

4. Protection of cultural and biological diversity by patent law: issues to be resolved

Jerzy Koopman

1. INTRODUCTION

This chapter addresses proposals to amend patent law in view of the need for protection of cultural and biological diversity and the related interests of traditional knowledge holders and biological diversity-rich countries.[1] Primarily based on the Convention on Biological Diversity (1993) several initiatives are taken to provide new forms of protection for the resources of biotechnological R&D that come forth from such diversity.[2] Proprietary forms of protection are often deemed important. Therefore, many ini-

---

[1] The meaning and relevancy of said diversity, traditional knowledge and biotechnological research and development (R&D hereafter) is further explained in sections 2 and 3 of this chapter. For the purpose of this introduction, these terms may, however, be understood as follows. Biotechnology entails the modification and application of genetic and other biochemical compounds for, among others, medical and agricultural purposes. It combines several methods from a variety of disciplines, such as chemistry, micro-biology, and informatics. The products developed through R&D necessarily have a biological and biochemical character. See Biotechnology Industry Organization, *Guide to Biotechnology 2008* (BIO, Washington 2008) 18–31. Traditional knowledge and cultural diversity may be understood by considering that '. . .in all regions of the world are found local communities. . . Associated with many of these communities is a. . .body of knowledge. . . These. . .sets of understandings. . .are part. . .of a cultural complex that encompasses language. . .and classification systems. . .ritual, spirituality and worldview', at: <http://portal.unesco.org/en/ev.php-URL_ID=5065&URL_DO=DO_TOPIC&URL_SECTION=201.html.> Biological diversity may be defined as the 'variation of life at all levels of biological organization and its workings in ecosystems.' This variation pertains to genes and other biochemical matter, species, and ecosystems, and the interaction between these categories as well. N Campbell and J Reece, *Biology* (Benjamin Cummings, San Francisco 2002) 510 ff.
[2] Hereafter CBD, available at <http://www.cbd.int>. All websites referred to in this chapter were last accessed on 4 September 2009.

tiatives seek to further contemporary models of property, including among intellectual property law regimes. Given the fact that this chapter addresses resources for life science endeavors, which are inherently technological in kind, the focus is on the regime that applies to technological inventions – patent law. The envisaged proprietary forms of protection to be provided for traditional knowledge and biochemical material may have an offensive and a defensive character.[3] Offensive forms of protection should provide new regimes of property, such as a *sui generis* intellectual property regime for traditional knowledge, as well as a variety of national legislative regimes on access to and exploitation of biochemical materials. Defensive forms of protection seek to prevent illegitimate exploitation of knowledge and material by inventors, and should lead to alterations of existing patent law and/or its application.

An initiative for defensive protection that necessitates legislative amendment of current patent statutes envisages the expansion of the disclosure requirement. Proposals for expansive disclosure may have principal and profound implications for the make-up and workings of the patent regime. They would oblige disclosure of origin and/or prior informed consent and/or benefit-sharing as to knowledge and material used in the process of inventing. The proposed obligation to disclose should be inserted into Article 83 of the European Patent Convention (1973). This provision already requires a patent applicant to disclose the invention for which they wish to receive a patent.[4] It would so be extended to encompass both traditional knowledge and biochemical material.

The proposals at hand target contemporary patent law for primarily two reasons. On the one hand, conceptions of social justice call for the recognition of the contributions of traditional knowledge holders and biological diversity-rich countries to biotechnological R&D that emanates in patentable inventions. On the other hand, mere instrumental reasons, such as the importance of said knowledge and material for both human survival and technological endeavours, demand a critical approach to, and perhaps change in, the exclusionary workings of patent law.[5] All of these initiatives derive from a complex societal dialogue. The

---

[3]   See hereon generally WIPO, 'Draft gap analysis on the protection of traditional knowledge', WIPO/GRTKF (30 May 2008). Available at <http://www.wipo.int>.

[4]   Hereafter EPC, amended 13 December 2007, at <http://www.epo.org/patents/law/legal-texts/epc.html>.

[5]   My interpretation of the term 'social justice' is restrictive, and pertains to the manner in which whatever burdens and benefits may be distributed in a given society. In respect of patent law, it thus amounts to 'distributive justice'. The

dialogue hinges on the actual but diffuse linkages between disciplines/ perspectives such as: economics; law; science; technology; ethics; political science; anthropology and ecology. The overlapping human interests related to these realms demand an integrative dialogue among the many stakeholders. The initiatives that come forth from such dialogue, such as the envisioned offensive and defensive forms of protection, do hold promises for reconciliation of the various interests involved. As such, they should be embraced. Conversely, in my opinion, both proposed forms of protection are flawed. Among their many fierce proponents one may observe a tendency to ignore the complex realities of the subject.[6] Too often they oversimplify the characteristic and features of both traditional knowledge and the biochemical material concerned. The same happens when it comes to the manner in which R&D in the life sciences is conceived. They, furthermore, appear to conceptualize intellectual property law-related initiatives as some sort of legal 'holy grail', which should solve the many problems that are faced in this dynamic and challenging world. Particularly, in the area at hand, it is evident that law – let alone patent law – cannot solve problems that may not (solely) relate to legal deficits, are not (only) legal in kind, but exist in the substantive issues themselves.

It would fall beyond the scope of this chapter to discuss all initiatives related to intellectual property law. Therefore, only some problems in respect of only one of the aforementioned initiatives are analysed. They pertain to the defensive initiative; the one that pursues protection of

---

term 'instrumentality' pertains to the most efficient way to employ certain means to reach a certain end. In its absolute form, no attention is given to, e.g., the values or side-effects of achieving a certain goal. Theories on 'social justice' and understandings of instrumentality can be found in SM Cahn, *Classics of Political and Moral Philosophy* (Oxford University Press, Oxford 2002). Particularly in relation to notions of the narrower term 'distributive justice,' see e.g. the online Stanford Encyclopedia of Philosophy at <http://plato.stanford.edu/entries/justice-distributive/>. The reasons deriving from notions of justice and instrumentality are further explained in section 3 and section 4 of this chapter, and explicitly tied to the proposals at hand in section 7 thereafter.

[6]   See e.g. M Chouchena-Rojas et al. (eds), *Disclosure Requirements: Ensuring Mutual Supportiveness Between the WTO TRIPS Agreement and the CBD* (Union Internationale pour la Conservation de la Nature et de ses Ressources, Geneva 2005); and V Shiva, *Biopiracy: The Plunder of Nature and Knowledge* (South End Press, Cambridge, MA 1997). For non-governmental organizations, see for example the ETC Group, at <http://www.etcgroup.org/en/issues/biopiracy.html>; the Indigenous Peoples Council on Biocolonialism, at <http://www.ipcb.org/>; and GRAIN, at <http://www.grain.org/briefings/>. Other references to governmental views are provided in the course of this chapter.

interests in traditional knowledge and associated biochemical material by means of legislative amendments to the disclosure requirement contained in the EPC. This chapter ultimately shows that two major problems with regard to traditional knowledge and biochemical material need to be resolved before the defensive initiative can be implemented in patent law. Before discussing this initiative in more detail, it is worthwhile to address the relation between traditional knowledge and biochemical material in biotechnological R&D.

2.   R&D OF TRADITIONAL KNOWLEDGE AND BIOCHEMICAL MATERIAL

Some years ago, it became clear that '. . .genetic resources have assumed increasing economic. . .value to a wide range of stakeholders. . .traditional knowledge. . .associated with those resources. . .has also attracted wide-spread attention. . .'.[7] Biochemical material and associated traditional knowledge have rapidly become essential resources for biotechnological R&D. Both globalization and the enhancement of biotechnology and informatics have shifted R&D in agriculture and medicine. Most importantly, globalization accelerates access to and exchange of material and knowledge.[8] The life science industry rapidly globalizes, and generates its raw products, knowledge, financing, and so forth, on a global scale. Furthermore, it conducts R&D, and commercially exploits its outcomes, at many locations. This industry supersedes national boundaries; it is a global and dynamic conglomerate of activities, entities and persons.[9] But this does not entirely explain the accelerated exchange of biochemical material and knowledge. These exchanges are caused by mere scientific advances. The development of biotechnology has taken away some of the previous restraints to R&D on so-called 'natural products'. Biotechnology allows for effective identification, isolation, modification and application of biochemical matter – molecules, such as genes, proteins and other compounds.[10] These technologies allow for inquiry and use of materials

---

[7]   D Gervais, *The TRIPS Agreement: Drafting History and Analysis* (Sweet & Maxwell, London 1998) 57.

[8]   D Slater, 'Rethinking the geopolitics of the global. The case of north south relations' in E Kofman and G Youngs (eds), *Globalization: Theory and Practice* (Continuum, London 2003) 47–63.

[9]   See R Narula, *Globalization and Technology* (Polity Press, Cambridge 2003).

[10]   See note 1.

that are not contained in ordinary pharmacological compound libraries. Moreover, conventional pharmaceutical R&D, such as combinatorial chemistry, has not always yielded optimal results, and does not necessarily accommodate the complex materials found in nature. Hence, the advent of biotechnology, which combines both conventional and non-conventional means. In past decades, bio-industries have increasingly prospected bio-chemical material in nature (*in vivo*), and they are expected to continue along this path.[11] Given the earth's huge biological diversity, most of which is still unknown, the search for useful compounds and other materials is not a simple affair. The search can be made more effective if peoples living in the ecosystems wherein the biochemical materials can be found are willing to lend a hand. Many populations rely on traditional health care systems. Within these systems, many local doctors make use of plants and, therefore, have extensive knowledge of applications of plant-related compounds.[12] Information technologies and easier means of transportation – both imperative to the process of globalization – have enhanced exchanges and understanding of this knowledge. Moreover, traditional knowledge increasingly proves to be directly relevant to further R&D on the materials prospected – and sometimes even touches upon the ultimate invention. Although traditional medicinal applications nearly always require follow-up work, as the herbal materials used necessitate further modifications before they can be exploited in an industrial and sufficiently safe and effective manner, they may directly relate to the product finally exploited. An active compound taken from a plant may not extensively differ from the compound worked in a laboratory (for example, if the latter modifications were aimed at maintaining its functionality, whilst enhancing its potency). One of the compounds then functions as a sub-stantive template for the other.[13] The knowledge-exchanges and scientific

---

[11]　G L Patrick, *An Introduction to Medicinal Chemistry* (Oxford University Press, Oxford 2005) 178 ff.; R Verpoorte, 'Pharmacognosy in the new millennium: leadfinding and biotechnology' (2000), 52 Journal of Pharm & Pharmacol, 253–262; AM Rouhi, 'Betting on natural products for cures' (2003) 81 Chemical and engineering News available at <http://pubs.acs.org/cen/coverstory/8141/8141 pharmaceuticals3.html>.

[12]　See <http://www.who.int/topics/traditional_medicine/en/> and WHO, *Monographs on Selected Medicinal Plants Volume I* (Geneva 1999) and Volume II (Geneva 2004).

[13]　E.g. see R Gupta et al., 'Nature's medicines: traditional knowledge and intellectual property' (2005) 2 Current Drug Discovery Technologies 203–219; WH Lewis and MPF Elvin-Lewis, *Medical Botany. Plants Affecting Human Health* (Wiley, London 2003); NR Farnsworth et al. (eds), *Intellectual Property Rights, Naturally Derived Bioactive Compounds and Resource Conservation* (Elsevier

collaborations between, say, the shaman and the micro-biologist may illustrate some of the promises of globalization.

3. DOWNSIDES OF GLOBALIZATION: WHAT ABOUT PATENT LAW?

These promises do not negate the unfavorable connotations of globalization.[14] Criticism of globalization is rooted in the observation that this process progresses in an economically uneven and unsustainable manner, and negatively affects the pursuit of the common good and results in distributive injustices.[15] The process is highly determined by the global regulatory framework, administered by the World Trade Organisation (WTO). The WTO presides over more than 140 treaties in a variety of fields, including labor, finance and intellectual property.[16] The neo-liberal policies that underpin this legal framework lead to an emphasis on the economic side of things, which can have serious downsides.[17] The United Nations Educational, Scientific and Cultural Organization (UNESCO) finds that '. . .globalization, in its powerful extension of market principles, by highlighting the culture of economically powerful nations, has created new forms of inequality, thereby fostering cultural conflict rather than cultural pluralism' and concludes that this is a threat to cultural diversity.[18] The Millennium Ecosystem Assessment Synthesis Report concludes that globalization has weakened the connections between ecosystems and cultural diversity and that this contributes to the loss of biological diversity.[19] It also finds that during the past decades of globalization '. . .humans

---

Science, London 1997); MJ Balick et al. (eds), *Medicinal Resources of the Tropical Forest. Biological Diversity and its Importance to Human Health* (Columbia University Press, New York 1996); and JD Phillipson et al., 'Ethnopharmacology and western medicine'(1989) J Ethnopharmacol 25, 61–72.

[14] See N Klein, *No Logo: No Space, No Choice, No Jobs* (Picador, New York 2002).

[15] M Williams, 'Social movements and global politics' in E Kofman and G Youngs (eds), *Globalization: Theory and Practice* (Continuum, London 2003) 88.

[16] At <http://www.wto.org/english/docs_e/legal_e/legal_e.htm>.

[17] See D Held and A McGrew, *The Global Transformations Reader* (Polity Press, Cambridge 2003) 299–420.

[18] M Garzon et al., *Cultural Diversity, Common Heritage, Plural Identities* (UNESCO, Paris 2002) 3 ff. Available at <http://unesdoc.unesco.org/images/0012/001271/127161e.pdf>.

[19] Millennium Ecosystem Assessment, *Ecosystems and Human Wellbeing: Synthesis* (Island Press, Washington, DC 2005) 120 ff, available at <http://www.millenniumassessment.org>.

have changed ecosystems more rapidly and extensively than in any comparable period of time in human history, largely to meet rapidly growing demands. . . This has resulted in . . . irreversible loss in the diversity of life on Earth'.[20] Even worse: 'Human activity is putting such a strain on the natural functions of the Earth that the ability of the planet's ecosystems to sustain future generations can no longer be taken for granted'.[21]

The intellectual property law framework that is part of the WTO's regulatory umbrella is considered to add to some of the downsides of globalization. It may have negative effects on '. . .scientific and artistic progress, biological diversity, access to information, and the cultures of indigenous and tribal peoples. . .'[22] In respect of biotechnology, it is alleged that patent law (in no particular order) hampers innovation;[23] deteriorates the public domain from which all should draw for inspiration;[24] deprives the needy of affordable health care products;[25] fosters unethical scientific behavior in respect of human bodily and other biochemical materials;[26] and results in distributive injustices to traditional knowledge holders and biological diversity-rich countries, thereby hampering sustainable use of their resources (traditional knowledge and biochemical materials).[27] Hence, a host of arguments, which derive from conceptions of social justice and instrumental rationality, are set forth against the workings of contemporary patent law.

---

[20]   Ibid. at 2; 26–70.

[21]   Ibid.

[22]   Bellagio Declaration 1993. J Boyle, *Shamans, Software & Spleens: Law and the Construction of the Information Society* (Harvard University Press, Cambridge, MA 1997) 193 (Declaration in Appendix B, 192–200).

[23]   See R Castro Bernieri, 'Ex-post liability rules: A solution for the biomedical anti-commons?' (Chapter 5 in this book). For an underlying analysis see e.g. RS Eisenberg, 'Property rights and the norms of science in biotechnology research' (1987) 97 Yale Law Journal, 177–223.

[24]   E.g. Papers of Duke Public Domain Conference 2003, available at: <http://www.law.duke.edu/journals/lcp/indexpd.htm>.

[25]   E.g. WR Cornish et al., *Intellectual Property Rights and Genetics. A Study Into the Management of Intellectual Property Rights Within the Healthcare Sector* (Genetics Knowledge Park, Cambridge 2003).

[26]   E.g. Nuffield Council of Bioethics, *The Ethics of Patenting DNA* (Nuffield, London 2002).

[27]   E.g. D Posey and G Dutfield, *Beyond Intellectual Property: Toward Traditional Resource Rights for Indigenous Peoples and Local Communities* (IDRC, Canada 1996). For interfaces with human rights law see J Koopman, 'Human Rights Implications of Patenting Biotechnological Knowledge' in PLC Torremans (ed), *Intellectual Property and Human Right* (Wolters Kluwer, Alphen aan de Rijn 2008) 553–558.

This chapter particularly addresses the last assertion in respect of traditional knowledge and biochemical materials. Presently, patent law and the agents applying and making use of this system are not held to contribute positively to the protection of the domains from which these resources stem. They may thus negate the collective urge to actively conserve cultural and biological diversity when dealing directly with their inventions and rights.[28] The next section addresses one of the initiatives that should redirect this situation – the defensive one aimed at widening the disclosure requirement in patent law.

4. REDIRECTION OF THE GLOBAL LEGAL FRAMEWORK: PATENT LAW!

This initiative derives from Articles 3, 8(j), 15 and 16 of the CBD.[29] With regard to the particular interests of traditional knowledge holders, Article 15(1)(c) of the International Covenant on Economic, Social and Cultural Rights (ICESCR) may provide an additional basis.[30] It provides that '. . .States Parties to the present Covenant recognize the right of everyone: [c] [T]o benefit from the protection of the moral and material interests resulting from any scientific, literary or artistic production of which he is the author.' Preventing others from appropriating traditional knowledge (a production), by compelling them to disclose prior-informed-consent and benefit-sharing agreements in patent law, then contributes to traditional knowledge holders' (authors') ability to benefit there themselves.[31] These conventions may call for a change, perhaps

---

[28] Patent law regimes were always established to stimulate technological progress only. See P Drahos, *A Philosophy of Intellectual Property* (Ashgate, Aldershot 1996) 119–140; and KW Dam, 'The economic underpinnings of patent law' (1994) Journal of Legal Studies (13/1), 247–271. See also Section 5.

[29] Article 3 CBD provides that states have the sovereign right to exploit their resources. Article 8(j) CBD provides that states should respect knowledge of indigenous and local communities, to promote their application with their approval, and to encourage equitable sharing of benefits. Article 15(7) CBD provides that exploitation of genetic resources must be on mutually agreed terms and provide for equitable benefit-sharing. Article 16(2) and 16(5) CBD provide the nexus with patent law and obliges states to ensure that access and benefit-sharing should not negate effective protection of intellectual property, but also that intellectual property regimes are supportive of the CBD.

[30] 1966 (ICESCR), available at <http://www2.ohchr.org/english/law/cescr.htm>.

[31] The Committee on Economic, Social and Cultural Rights expansively interprets this provision and finds that claims to knowledge by traditional

diversification, of patent law. The Doha Development Agenda (2001) envisions such in a manner consistent with TRIPS and builds on previous work of WIPO and UNESCO.[32] Article 19 of the Doha Development Agenda provides:

> We instruct the Council for TRIPS. . .to examine. . .the relationship between the TRIPS Agreement and the Convention on Biological Diversity, the protection of traditional knowledge and folklore. . . In undertaking this work, the TRIPS Council shall be guided by the objectives and principles set out in Articles 7 and 8 of the TRIPS Agreement. . .[33]

Article 7 provides that:

> [t]he protection and enforcement of intellectual property rights should contribute to the promotion of technological innovation and to the transfer and dissemination of technology, to the mutual advantage of producers and users of technological knowledge and in a manner conducive to social and economic welfare, and to a balance of rights and obligations.

Article 8(1) allows for the adoption of '. . .measures necessary to. . .promote the public interest in sectors of vital importance to their socio-economic and technological development, provided that such measures are consistent with the provisions of this Agreement.' Clause (2) recognizes that '. . .measures, provided that they are consistent with the provisions of this

---

knowledge holders derive from it, and should be safeguarded by means of free-informed-consent to use by third parties. Committee on Economic, Social and Cultural Rights, 'General Comment No. 17' (12 January 2006) E/C.12/GC17 (the Comment) at 32. This interpretation may be incorrect. See J Koopman, 'Human Rights Implications of Patenting Biotechnological Knowledge' in PLC Torremans (ed), *Intellectual Property and Human Right* (Wolters Kluwer, Alphen aan de Rijn 2008) 533–582.

[32] Doha Development Agenda, available at <http://www.wto.org/english/tratop_e/dda_e/dda_e.htm>. For the work of WIPO and UNESCO as of the 1960s, see WB Wendland, 'Intellectual Property and the Protection of Cultural Expressions: The Work of the World Intellectual Property Organization (WIPO)' in FW Grosheide and JJ Brinkhof (eds), *Intellectual Property Law: Articles on Cultural Expressions and Indigenous Knowledge* (Intersentia, Antwerp 2002) 101–138. WIPO boosted current initiatives in 2001: WIPO, *Fact-finding Mission. Intellectual Property Needs and Expectations of Traditional Knowledge Holders* (WIPO, Geneva 2001).

[33] At   <http://www.wto.org/english/thewto_e/minist_e/min01_e/mindecl_e.htm>. The Agreement on Trade Related Aspects of Intellectual Property Rights (TRIPS) (1994) is available at: <http://www.wto.org/english/docs_e/legal_e/legal_e.htm#TRIPS>.

Agreement, may be needed to prevent the abuse of intellectual property rights by right holders. . .'

It has already been mentioned that the defensive means of protection addressed in this chapter hinge on prevention. This should be done by imposition of an obligation on patent applicants to disclose information with regard to the resources of their endeavours. They should so be held to hand over information on the origin, prior-informed-consent and benefit-sharing agreements with regard to used knowledge and/or materials when filing the patent application.[34] Section 5 and Section 6 in this chapter address the contemporary disclosure requirement, and the proposals to widen it to rebut the alleged social injustices and instrumental inefficiencies.

5. CONTEMPORARY REQUIREMENT: DISCLOSURE OF INVENTIONS

In addition to other requirements for patentability of an invention – such as the novelty, inventivity, and industrial applicability of inventions (Article 27(1) TRIPS) – Article 29(1) TRIPS provides that '. . .an applicant for a patent shall disclose the invention in a manner sufficiently clear and complete for the invention to be carried out by a person skilled in the art.' Article 83 EPC provides the same. One purpose of this requirement is to ascertain the extent to which an invention contributes to the prior art and does not derive therefrom in an obvious fashion (fulfils the requirements of novelty and inventivity, Articles 54 and 56 EPC). Through disclosure of the invention for which a patent application is filed, the patent office can also inquire whether it can be enabled (whether the invention can be reproduced and turned into practice).[35] Of course, disclosure – and publication of patent applications and eventually granted patents – is central to the working of the system. In return for making the invention known, and enabling others to further the state of technology, the inventor/patentee may exclusively commercialize the invention for a certain period of time.[36]

---

[34] A brief overview of these initiatives can be found in WIPO, *Intellectual Property and Traditional Knowledge* (WIPO Booklet 2, Geneva 2004) 25–30, available at <http://www.wipo.int/freepublications/en/index.jsp?cat=tk>.

[35] M Singer and D Stauder, *European Patent Convention. A Commentary. Volume I. Substantive Patent Law – Preamble, Articles 1 to 89* (Carl Heymanns Verlag, Cologne 2003) 356–357.

[36] The term is 20 years (Article 33 TRIPS). On the rights conveyed, see Article 28 TRIPS.

The European Patent Office (EPO) generally applies the disclosure requirement as follows. The invention must be disclosed in some detail. However, not every detail of, not every step in R&D, and not all knowledge relevant to the invention need be disclosed. Common general knowledge – for example, knowledge in handbooks or knowledge that may be assumed to be possessed by the average skilled person, or is readily available – does not have to be disclosed. Thus even essential information may not have to be disclosed. Nevertheless, information that requires a search by the examiner of the patent office is not considered common general knowledge. As to the enablement to be brought about, it is most important that the average skilled person understands the technical problem and the solution provided by the invention. For disclosure of nucleotides and amino acid sequences particular disclosure methods are prescribed, which should reveal the sequences and allow for comparison.[37] In respect of biological material it may be necessary to deposit a sample.[38] Deposit is required when the material is not available to the public and cannot be described in the patent application in such fashion that it can be examined in light of the requirements. If the examiner can achieve the same by acquiring alternative materials, deposit is not required.[39] The importance of the aforementioned application of the disclosure requirement by the patent office is that, according to current standards and practices, traditional knowledge and biochemical material used to attain an invention has to be communicated in the course of the patent application, if and insofar as it implicates the reproducibility and/or novelty and/or inventivity and/or industrial applicability of the invention. Biochemical material may need to be disclosed to acquire insight in the object as such (for example, its structural features, functions, and so on). However, this does generally not concern the material initially prospected and used in R&D, but the material that comprises the invention. Traditional knowledge may, of course, reflect on the novelty and/or inventivity of an invention for which a patent application is filed.[40] This hinges on the closeness of that knowledge to the central concept of the invention. Three situations can be identified that may be deemed close enough to be relevant (albeit not necessarily deter-

---

[37]   Rule 30 Implementing Regulations EPC, available at <http://www.epo. org/patents/law/legal-texts/html/epc/2000/e/ma2.html>.

[38]   Rule 31 Implementing Regulations.

[39]   M Singer and D Stauder, *European Patent Convention. A Commentary. Volume I. Substantive Patent Law – Preamble, Articles 1 to 89* (Carl Heymanns Verlag, Cologne 2003) 358–375.

[40]   See also WIPO, 'Draft gap analysis on the protection of traditional knowledge' WIPO/GRTKF (30 May 2008) 11–12 <http://www.wipo.int>.

minative) in this regard. Traditional knowledge may, first, have pointed to the invention (for example, traditional knowledge that a plant has certain medicinal properties may lead researchers to explore active compounds in such plant); second, it may have directly contributed to the invention (for example, traditional knowledge that a certain plant extract was effective in treating a certain disease); and, third, it may comprise the invention itself (for example, traditional knowledge pertained to a new and inventive use of a plant compound for a certain medical treatment, which became the invention).[41]

It may be concluded that the current disclosure requirement sees to some traditional knowledge and some biochemical material used in the attainment of a biotechnological invention only. Hence, this requirement does not implicate most of the situations in which biochemical material and traditional knowledge may be used in the course of reaching an invention. It is clear that such material and knowledge is extensively used in R&D, but often relates to the outcome thereof as, say, 'cow milk does to cheese'. Knowledge and material are relevant and sometimes even inherent to doing R&D in a certain field. However, it often shows that they ultimately relate indirectly and/or unrecognizably to the invention reached. The relation may be indirect, because the R&D was jump-started but not substantively directed by the knowledge and material concerned. The relation may conversely be direct but unrecognizable, because of the manner in which it is depicted in the patent application (which is in the jargon of molecular biology, genomics and so on), whereas the traditional knowledge used was expressed in local scientific and/or spiritual and/or artistic ways (for example, by a painting of a plant used in medicine).[42] Whereas the current disclosure requirement may provide some defensive protection against the appropriation of traditional knowledge and related

---

[41] WIPO, 'Technical Study on Disclosure Requirements in Patent Systems Related to Genetic Resources and Traditional Knowledge' (WIPO Study 3, Geneva 2004) 37, <http://www.wipo.int/tk/en/publications/technical_study.pdf>

[42] On the ways in which scientific knowledge may be represented, and the distinction between 'traditional' and 'modern' science, see e.g. International Counsel for Science, 'Report from the Study Group on Science and Traditional Knowledge' (2002) 1–16 <http://www.icsu.org>; J Koopman, 'Bumps and bends in the road to intellectual property for traditional knowledge: on knowledge models, legal orders and the anti-commons in biotechnology' in FW Grosheide and JJ Brinkhof (eds), *Intellectual Property Law. Articles on Crossing Borders: Between Traditional and Actual* (Intersentia, Antwerp 2004) 251–262, 263–265; P Sillitoe, 'What know natives? Local knowledge in development' (1998) 6/2 Social Anthropology 203–220; A Agrawal, 'Dismantling the divide between indigenous and scientific knowledge' (1995) 26 *Development and Change* 413–439.

biochemical materials, it does not refute most types of use and exploitation by inventors/patentees. Furthermore, it is clear that the contemporary disclosure requirement does not see to the manner in which the patent applicant has behaved, or will behave, towards the ones that have interests of their own in relevant knowledge or material. The views and wishes of, for example, the traditional knowledge-holding community or the bio-diverse country that provided the initial knowledge and/or material are irrelevant in the realm of the EPC and its application by the patent office.[43] Hence, it is not necessary to reveal the origin of and/or prior-informed-consent as to and/or benefit-sharing in respect of traditional knowledge and/or biochemical materials used in the attainment of an invention. The disclosure requirement does not bear upon the need to rebut the alleged distributive injustices to suppliers of material and knowledge at all. Furthermore, it is in its current make-up not set up to reach more remote societal goals, such as the conservation of cultural and biological diversity.[44] This deals with compliance of the patentee with obligations that fall beyond the scope of contemporary patent law, but derive from other sources, such as the CBD or ethics. Proposals are made to incorporate these obligations in Article 83 EPC. These proposals are discussed in Section 6.

6.   PROPOSALS FOR ADDITIONAL DISCLOSURE BY PATENT APPLICANTS

Several proposals are set forth to amend the contemporary disclosure requirement. Whereas all of them pursue to widen the current obligation to disclose information in the course of the patent procedure by the applicant, they vary in terms of their scope and contents. In respect of their contents, the envisaged obligations: may entail mere disclosure of the origin of the knowledge and material used in the course of reaching an invention; may comprise the obligation to disclose their origin and prior-informed-consent by the supplier or facilitator; or may entail disclosure of information pertaining to these topics and on the prior conclusion of benefit-sharing agreements too. In respect of the scope of the envisaged

---

[43] J Koopman, 'Human Rights Implications of Patenting Biotechnological Knowledge' in PLC Torremans (ed), *Intellectual Property and Human Right* (Wolters Kluwer, Alphen aan de Rijn, 2008) 562–564.

[44] NP de Carvalho, 'Requiring disclosure of origin of genetic resources and prior informed consent in patent applications without infringing the TRIPs agreement: the problem and the solution' (2000) 2 Wash U Journal of Law and Policy, 380.

amended requirement, the following may be noted. 'Weak' proposals favor amendment of the disclosure requirement, as to only impose a voluntary obligation on the application in respect of traditional knowledge and biochemical material. Non-fulfilment would not result in the rejection of patent applications or non-enforceability of patent granted. It may result in no sanction whatsoever or, alternatively, in non-examination of the patent application, until reparatory measures are taken by the patent applicant. 'Medium' proposals envisage a disclosure requirement that has less friendly effects. Such requirement would be triggered within, but sanctioned outside of, patent law – for example by criminal penalties. Last, 'strong' proposals seek to impose disclosure obligations that are imposed both within and outside of patent law. This implies that non-fulfilment would result in rejection of applications and/or non-enforceability of patents and lead to sanctions in, for example, criminal law.[45]

7. CONCRETE JUSTIFICATIONS AND BASES FOR ADDITIONAL DISCLOSURE

As to the legal basis, it has already been mentioned that Articles 7 and 8 of TRIPS allow for flexibility in respect of the implementation of intellectual property regimes and for the purpose of balancing their primary economic means and goals with other interests. They have been specified

---

[45] Countries that are biological diversity-rich, and in which traditional knowledge may be found, generally favor strong and medium-strong disclosure requirements: African countries (e.g. Tanzania, Kenya, and South Africa), Latin-American countries (e.g. Brazil, Ecuador, and Peru), Middle-American countries (e.g. Mexico, El Salvador), South-East Asian countries (e.g. China, Thailand, and Indonesia), South-Asian countries (e.g. India, Pakistan, and Bhutan) and Middle Eastern countries (e.g. Egypt). Weak disclosure obligations are favored by Western European countries (such as Norway, Denmark, Sweden, Portugal, and The Netherlands) and also by the European Community. The use of weak obligations may, of course, principally be doubted. Japan and the United States oppose any additional obligation. See WIPO, 'Draft Gap Analysis on the Protection of Traditional Knowledge' WIPO/GRTKF (30 May 2008) 26; Queen Mary, University of London Intellectual Property Research Institute, 'Report on Disclosure of Origin in Patent Applications (prepared for the European Commission, D-G Trade) (London, 2004) 30–56; WIPO, 'Technical study on disclosure requirements in patent systems related to genetic resources and traditional knowledge' (WIPO Study 3, Geneva 2004) 34–39; NP de Carvalho, 'Requiring disclosure of origin of genetic resources and prior informed consent in patent applications without infringing the TRIPs agreement: the problem and the solution' (2000) Wash U Journal of Law and Policy 2, 374–379.

in, among others, Article 27 (3)b TRIPS, which allows for exceptions from patentability in respect of, among other things, plant and animal varieties. The TRIPS Council discusses the initiatives at hand in the context of this provision.[46] The European Biotechnology Directive, which has been implemented in the EPC, contains explicit references to the CBD – as well as topics and interests discussed here – too.[47] These provisions may arguably provide some legal bases in intellectual property law for the effectuation of the proposals to widen the contemporary disclosure requirement. As to its non-positivist socio-legal justification, it may be noted that amendment of the disclosure requirement may derive from the recognition of some of the flaws of contemporary patent law – that is, of the distributive injustices that may be caused by the manner in which traditional knowledge and biochemical materials are exploited and patented by the bio-industry.[48] That which may be drawn upon and used is extensively determined by the borders – the scope – of contemporary property systems and rights and, conversely, the domains, things, and so on, not subjected to any such system and right. However, these borders have not

---

[46]   Article XX of the WTO's GATT provides general exceptions, in view of which said provisions may be read too. They pertain to the protection of national treasures of artistic, historic or archaeological value; and the conservation of exhaustible natural resources. Article XX (f) and (g) at <http://www.wto.org/english/docs_e/legal_e/gatt47_02_e.htm#articleXX>.

[47]   European Parliament and Council Directive 98/44/EC of 6 July 1998 on the legal protection of biotechnological inventions [1998] OJ L213, 13–21. The considerations provide: '(27). . .if an invention is based on biological material. . .the patent application should. . .include information on the. . .origin of such material, if known; whereas this is without prejudice to the processing of patent applications or the validity of rights arising from granted patents. . .'; '(55). . .whereas. . .States must give particular weight to Article 3 and Article 8(j), the second sentence of Article 16(2) and Article 16(5) of the [CBD] when bringing into force the laws. . .necessary to comply with this Directive.' Last, consideration 56 generally refers to the Third Conference of the Parties to the CBD, at which it was decided that the relation between the CBD and TRIPS must be addressed. The main body – not these considerations! – of the directive was implemented in the EPC through inclusion in the Implementing Regulations. See Decision of the Administrative Council of the EPO 16 June 1999. See (1999) 8/9 OJ EPO, 545–87 and Rules 26 to 29 of the Regulations. Because considerations 27, 55 and 56 were not incorporated in the body of the directive, they are not binding per se. European Court of Justice, 9 October 1998, Case C-377/98 *(The Netherlands v Parliament and Council)* (at 63–7). Because this chapter addresses European patent law (EPC), other regional legislation is ignored. See, e.g., The Andean Community of Nations' Common Regime on Access to Genetic Resources, Decision 391 (1996) <http://www.comunidadandina.org/ingles/normativa/d391e.htm>.

[48]   See NP de Carvalho (note 44) 375.

been carved in stone: every place and every time renders its own needs, means and goals, and so requires a continuously dynamic and adaptive approach, particularly in respect of property laws. Property is a powerful tool of policy, and conveys powerful rights. The acknowledgement hereof necessitates a critical and flexible approach to this tool and those rights. The initiatives to widen the disclosure requirement in patent law may correspond with our

> . . .ongoing commitment to redefine property rights over time to prevent the re-emergence of pockets of illegitimately concentrated power. To maintain the requisite amount of both dispersal of access and de-concentration of power, the property system must be dynamic, with the definition and allocation of property rights changing over time.[49]

The workings of patent law are clearly part of the problem of the purported distributive injustices. In themselves, these workings cannot cause deprivation of cultural and biological diversity though. Simply put: a patent does neither lead to global warming nor to marginalization of a local culture. This is not to say that patent law and patentees should not add to the search for solutions. Looked at from a perspective of instrumentality, it may appear awkward that inventors of biotechnological inventions that make use of biochemical materials deriving from the earth's biological diversity are not compelled to actively contribute to its conservation.[50] The same may be said in respect of cultural diversity, which generates knowledge that is paramount to R&D. Inventors/patentees are not held to do so by the patent system and in the manner in which they may exploit their rights. This may appear awkward if one accedes that mankind is not a mere economic community. Perhaps mankind is first and above all a moral community; we relate to one another and depend on each other for our survival. This calls for recognition and protection of the interests of traditional knowledge holders and biological diversity-rich countries, which primarily develop and guard local knowledge and *in vivo* biochemical material that are central to the maintenance of cultural and biological diversity. But also our practical interest in survival as a species – an instrumental argument – calls for relentless attempts to change the tides, among others by using mechanisms that were previously considered to be

---

[49] J Singer and JM Beerman, 'The social origins of property' (1993) 24 The Canadian Journal of Law and Jurisprudence 242.

[50] The same may of course be said of other industries that dwell upon nature, such as those engaged in (eco)tourism, petrochemical, steel, timber and solar industries.

unrelated to the topic(s) concerned – such as patent law.[51] Patent law may be employed to achieve goals that should be set pursuant to the challenges and needs of this era, may complement its mere economic and instrumental set-up, and thus may entail restoration of (perceptions of) justice and protection of cultural and biological diversity too.[52] This aligns with overall efforts to redirect the global regulative framework, and attempts to reconcile our economic goals (such as the dispersion of wealth through opening of markets and enhancement of trade) with social and ecological goals (such as the conservation and sustainable exploitation of cultural and biological resources such as traditional knowledge and biochemical material).[53] Patent law is part of that global framework, and there is no reason why it should be secluded from those efforts and attempts. It may well be asserted that these considerations justify the proposed amendment of the disclosure requirement indeed.[54]

There are also practical advantages to such an approach. If one looks at the proposals from within the cultural and ecological perspective – starting with the respective interests of traditional knowledge holders and biological diversity-rich countries – they appear attractively logical. A disclosure requirement in this respect allows for, first, a single-stop moment in time at which, second, all relevant information is revealed (who has used what kind of knowledge and/or material in what way), whereby, third, scientific and commercial transparency and tracking capabilities are enhanced, but

---

[51] Mankind as a 'moral community'; see BVA Röling, *Volkenrecht en Vrede* (Kluwer, Deventer 1985) 137. Some plead for the conclusion of a 'contract' between mankind and nature. M Serres, *Le Contrat Naturel* (Bourin Julliard, France 1990). Others want to extend this idea to culture too. See F Mayor and J Bindé, *The World Ahead: Our Future in the Making* (Zed Books, London 2001).

[52] See GB Ramello, 'Intellectual property, social justice and economic efficiency: insights from law and economics' (Chapter 1 of this book), in which the interface between social justice and economic instrumentality is explored. For overriding studies see: Commission on Intellectual Property Rights, *Integrating Intellectual Property Rights and Development Policy* (CIPR, London 2002); C May, *A Global Political Economy of Intellectual Property Rights* (Routledge, London 2000); P Drahos, *A Philosophy of Intellectual Property* (Ashgate, Aldershot 1996).

[53] For attempts to reformulate these interrelations see A Ong and SJ Collier, *Global Assemblages: Technology, Politics, and Ethics as Anthropological Problems* (Blackwell, New York 2004); F Mayor and J Bindé, *The World Ahead: Our Future in the Making* (Zed Books, London 2001); J Dunning, *Making Globalization Good: The Moral Challenges of Global Capitalism* (Oxford University Press, Oxford 2001).

[54] WIPO acknowledges this: WIPO, 'Draft Gap Analysis on the Protection of Traditional Knowledge' WIPO/GRTKF (30 May 2008) 31.

only insofar as the knowledge and material have already led to potentially valuable products or processes – a presumably patentable invention. Additional advantages of using the patent system in this respect are, fourth, that the administrative infrastructure is already in place and that, fifth, the market participant's behavior is adapted thereto (patent applicants already disclose some information before the EPO).

However, justifications and bases for a certain course of action do not necessarily reflect upon the feasibility thereof. Whereas the aforementioned justifications and bases have already led to the legislative implementation of the disclosure proposals in some countries, two issues continue to stand in the way of their practical application, or even lead to adverse side-effects.[55] These issues are discussed in Section 8.[56] The two issues essentially arise out of remaining ambiguities about, on the one hand, biological diversity and the material it sets forth and, on the other hand, cultural diversity and the knowledge that derives therefrom.

8.   WIDENING THE DISCLOSURE REQUIREMENT IN PATENT LAW: TWO ISSUES

8.1   Ambiguity About Biological Diversity and Biochemical Material

Despite the overwhelming attention given to environmental issues and to conservation of biological diversity, we are still ignorant. The lack of understanding affects the feasibility of certain initiatives with regard to the disclosure requirement in patent law. It is difficult to compel patent

---

[55] Widened disclosure requirements have already been implemented in the patent regimes of countries like India, South Africa, Denmark, Norway, and Peru. See <http://www.wipo.int/tk/en/laws/genetic.html#special> and <http://www.cbd.int/abs/measures.shtml>. These measures may have adverse effects: '. . .the CBD resulted in a sharp decline of the exchange of genetic resources worldwide.' NP Louwaars, 'International plant genetic resources treaty – in the interest of the seed industry', (2006), Seed Info (30), 6. Simultaneously, few cases may be found in which wide disclosure requirements were applied and sanctioned, which may relate to their feasibility.

[56] Formal issues are left aside. A formal issue with respect to the disclosure proposals pertains, e.g., to the outer boundaries of TRIPS. When patent applicants are held to disclose more information than stipulated by TRIPS, this imposes additional conditions to patentability, and may violate TRIPS. On the formal issues see NP de Carvalho, *supra* note 44, 371–401 (suggesting that formal issues may be rebutted, if compliance with the CBD becomes a condition for enforcement rather than for conveyance of patents, ibid, 394).

applicants to disclose what is unknown. Major efforts are made to research and classify biological diversity. Questions pertain to what is out there (what kind of plants, animals, micro-organisms, and constituent elements such as genes): what are their characteristics and activities; what is changing (for eco-evolutionary and other causes); and what of the whole lot may be relevant for scientific and industrial activities at the local or global level.[57] However, nature's make-up and productivity surpass our observational capabilities. Estimations about numbers of species vary between one to three hundred million. From this utterly large range on the larger units (species), we should derive the even larger number of the smaller units (genes and other molecules). It shows that we cannot comprehend the sheer scope of life existing on our planet.[58] And even if we could catalogue this planet's biological diversity, it may be doubted whether its sheer abundance allows for a tracking regime – paramount to the envisioned disclosure in patent law – that is workable:

> . . .imagine for a moment that all the diversity of the world were finally revealed and then described, say one name to a species. The description would contain the scientific name, a photograph or drawing, a brief diagnosis, and information on where the species is found. If published in conventional book form, with pages bound into ordinary thousand-page volumes 17 centimetres wide inside cloth covers, this Great Encyclopaedia of Life would occupy 60 meters of library shelf per million species. . .they would extend through 6 kilometres of shelving. . .[59]

Then again, think about the number of certificates needed for the constituent elements of those species, (genes, compounds, and so on) which outnumber the amount of species expected to exist. The bureaucracy that would need to be created for the tracking and certification of origin, uses and involvements of this diversity would be breathtaking. The dynamic nature and workings of any ecosystem, and anything contained therein, further complicates this task, and may make the outcome of any

---

[57]   See reports of Millennium Ecosystem Assessment at <http://www.millenniumassessment.org> and the International Program on Biological Diversity Science at <http://www.diversitas-international.org/>.

[58]   Called the 'question of central interest' by E Wilson in his book *The Diversity of Life* (Penguin Group, UK 2001) (repr) 35. Methods that could be applied include measuring species richness, evenness, disparity, rarity or genetic variability. See ibid. 123–52. See also the biological diversity world map at <http://www.nhm.ac.uk/research-curation/research/projects/worldmap/>.

[59]   Wilson, *supra* note 58 at 143. Of course, information technologies will reduce the physical space needed.

classification and documentation effort less certain, thus less useful, for legal purposes.[60]

Another problematic element in respect of the attempts to widen the contemporary disclosure requirement in patent law derives from notions of distributive justice. So many organisms (e.g. plants) and their biochemical parts (e.g. extracts containing compounds) have been dispersed across regions and countries over time.[61] It may both ethically and factually be incorrect to attribute them to the one or other country.[62] It may, furthermore, be practically impossible as well.[63] How could distributive justice be restored, without having first reconstructed the origins and exchanges of, for example, plant material over time?[64]

These ambiguities also affect the legal initiatives that were already taken, such as those reflected in the CBD. They become, for example, apparent in the definitions used for the terms 'biological diversity', 'biological resources' and 'genetic resources'. Pursuant to Article 2 of the CBD, 'biological diversity means the variability among living organisms

---

[60] On systems for certificates of origin, see e.g. C Richerzaghen, *Certificates of Origin: Economic Impacts and Implications* (UNU/IAS, Tokyo 2005), 1–36; B Tobin et al, *The Feasibility, Practicality and Cost of a Certificate of Origin System for Genetic Resources: Preliminary Results of Comparative Analysis of Tracking Material in Biological Resource Centres and of Proposals for a Certification Scheme* (UNU/IAS, Tokyo 2003), 1–71.

[61] See e.g. L Packer et al. (eds), *Herbal and Traditional Medicine: Molecular Aspects of Health* (CRC, UK 2004) and WH Lewis and MPF Elvin-Lewis, *Medical Botany: Plants Affecting Human Health* (Wiley, London 2003). See also <http://www.plantcultures.org>.

[62] As envisaged by Article 3 CBD: 'States have. . .the sovereign right to exploit their own resources. . .'

[63] It may be impossible to track and interlink all materials along the chain of R&D too. Materials may have undergone numerous modifications, performed by many in several countries, and over long periods of time. See Queen Mary, University of London Intellectual Property Research Institute, 'Report on disclosure of origin in patent applications' (prepared for the European Commission, D-G Trade) (London, 2004) 62–67; International Federation of Pharmaceutical Manufacturers Organization, *Biological Diversity Resources, Traditional Knowledge, Innovation and Health* (IFPMA, Geneva 2003) 15; K ten Kate and S Laird, *The Commercial Use of Biological Diversity: Access to Genetic Resources and Benefit-sharing* (Earthscan, London 1999) 58, 314. Relevant initiatives in this respect may be the Earth System Science Partnership (at http://www.essp.org/) and the BGCI online resource (at <http://www.bgci.org/resources/abs/>).

[64] An alternative approach to the CBD may be the establishment of a bio-collecting society, which would collect and distribute proceeds. G Dutfield, *Intellectual Property: Biogenetic Resources and Traditional Knowledge* (Earthscan, London 2004) 121.

from all sources including ... terrestrial, marine and other aquatic ecosystems and the ecological complexes of which they are part; this includes diversity within species, between species and of ecosystems.' Furthermore, 'biological resources include genetic resources, organisms or parts thereof, populations, or any other biotic component of ecosystems with actual or potential use or value for humanity.' 'Genetic resources' refers to the term 'genetic material' that, in the same article, is defined as 'any material of plant, animal, microbial or other origin containing functional units of heredity.' Ambiguities appear when it comes to the information that should be disclosed during patent examination procedures. Whereas Article 8(j) CBD addresses the relation between traditional knowledge with 'biological diversity' (including e.g. simple compounds) Articles 15 and 16 require prior-informed-consent and benefit sharing in respect of 'genetic resources' only. Given the narrow term used in the latter provisions, it may legally be asserted that non-genetic compounds are not subjected to the consent and benefit-sharing requirements, central to the envisaged widened disclosure in patent law. These compounds are surely most important in traditional medicine. Articles 8(j) and 15 and 16 CBD are inconsistent. One may wonder how the many public and private entities, groups and individuals involved will be able to distinguish among the different legal objects so defined, and as may perhaps be implicated in a concrete patent application. A further complication derives from the distinction made between *in vivo* and *in vitro* material and between plant, animal, human and other types of biochemical material. As to the former distinction, it is noted that pursuant to the CBD, the ultimate obligation by the user of resources persists *vis-à-vis* the country of origin (where the material can be found *in situ* so *in vivo*), but which is not necessarily the providing country (where the material may solely be found *in vitro*). Whereas it was already addressed that there may in fact be several countries of origin, there may also be several subsequently involved providing countries. This may particularly be the case if material is kept in collections and/or worked over time in different countries. These distinctions complicate affairs. The aim for transparency of the relations may so be hampered from the outset, rendering the disclosure requirement that relies thereon unfeasible. The overlap between plant, animal and human materials, which often occurs in the practise of biotechnological R&D, is ignored as well. The CBD surely does not apply to human materials. The result may be that two consent and benefit-sharing mechanisms should be implemented in the future. One mechanism with respect to non-human and one mechanism for human material, whereas the invention related to these materials most likely consists in one product, which bears upon some of their elements.[65] These mechanisms must then converge in disclosure at the patenting stage. Another legal issue arises because the CBD provisions are formulated in an open-ended fashion in respect of both contents and timing. Hence, they appear to provide ever lasting, all-inclusive rights with regard to the knowledge and material concerned. One may wonder where the substantive or timely delineation of these property-like rights may be found and, therefore, where the limitations of the envisaged disclosure requirement should be put. The aforementioned ambiguities, which may be perceived as issues themselves, render the initiative pertaining to the disclosure requirement, and the related initiative to devise a system for conveyance and tracking of (certificates of) origin, unfeasible at this time.

8.2 Ambiguity About Cultural Diversity and Traditional Knowledge

Similar ambiguities persist in respect of traditional knowledge and the cultural diversity it derives from. Estimations indicate that at least 5000 cultures are vibrant to date. Describing and delineating these cultures is a tricky task.[66] The same necessarily applies to the knowledge set forth from within those cultures. Most knowledge developed in this world is a combination of different types of knowledge, with different origins and characteristics.[67] It is cyclonically developed, and dwells upon uncountable

---

[65] With regard to human bodily material, see a.o. Article 22 of the Convention on Human Rights and Biomedicine (1997) at <http://conventions.coe.int/treaty/EN/Treaties/Html/164.htm>. Hereon J Koopman, 'Human donors' right to consent to patenting biochemical inventions: Is it real?' (2008) 5(3) *Personalized Medicine* 199–203. It may in fact concern three mechanisms, because also a.o. Articles 10 and 13 of the International Treaty on Plant Genetic Resources for Food and Agriculture (2001) envision such mechanism. At: <http://www.plant-treaty.org>. See generally NP de Carvalho, see note 44 at 373; de Carvalho favours an expansive approach to the CBD's definitions, which would take away some of the ambiguities mentioned. The legal bases therefore may be ambivalent.

[66] See the *Encyclopaedia of World Religions* (Merriam Webster, Springfield, MA 1999). Also UNDP, *The Human Development Report: Cultural Liberty in Today's Diverse World* (UNDP, New York 2004); M Garzon et al., *Cultural Diversity, Common Heritage, Plural Identities* (UNESCO, Paris 2002). Some 300 million people in the world may be indigenous, making up 90% of the world's cultural diversity, dispersed over 70 countries.

[67] Traditional knowledge is usually called 'traditional' as to distinguish it from types of knowledge that are considered 'modern.' Perhaps what is meant is that one type of knowledge is developed pursuant to local methods, whereas the other type of knowledge entails globally used methods, as well. The 'traditionality' so refers to the locality of its means, not to the moment in time in which it is created,

sources that surpass national and cultural boundaries – which can also be said of the associated biochemical materials. An example is knowledge about the Neem Tree, which received attention in this context for the European patent that was granted on some of its extracts.[68] Its origin is often attributed to India. The plant, its extracts and compounds have been used for agricultural and medical purposes by communities in India for thousands of years. However, it may be hard to conclusively attribute the related knowledge to one or the other community or peoples. And these communities and peoples may have now dispersed throughout India, as well as to surrounding countries such as Pakistan and Sri Lanka. This plant has even been used by many peoples around the world, including in the Middle East.[69] Hence, our knowledge on the dispersion of knowledge and the peoples involved may be grossly inadequate to rebut the appropriation in concrete cases.

Attempts are made to map the world's cultural diversity. Some of these studies are especially aimed at descriptions of traditional knowledge in respect of the enhanced commercial and industrial exploitation of such knowledge.[70] Databases of traditional knowledge have been created.[71] However, like biological diversity, cultural diversity is a complex phenomenon, comprising multiple evolving puzzles whereof bits and pieces are exchanged over time. It may be beyond our means to describe it accurately.[72]

---

let alone its effectiveness. Of course, this distinction is utterly artificial, since all forms of knowledge are essentially cultural and local in origin and kind. Cultural bias is inevitable. See *supra* note 1.

[68] Patent EP 436 257 B1. This patent was revoked because the requirement of inventivity (Article 56 EPC) was not fulfilled. This decision was sustained on 8 March 2005 by the Technical Boards of Appeal of the EPO in Case T 416/01 (*Method for controlling fungi on plants by the aid of a hydrophobic extracted neem oil*). The purified concentrations of the Neem oil used by the patent applicant differed slightly from the concentrations used for the same purpose in the prior art, and were thus novel (rendering the entire method novel, see Article 54 EPC). At 4.3 of the Decision. However, such was not deemed inventive pursuant to Article 56 EPC. At 4.4 of the Decision.

[69] See on the Neem tree, its origin(s), international and multicultural uses, HS Puri, *Neem: The Divine Tree Azadirachta Indica* (Harwood Academic Publishers, Amsterdam 1999).

[70] E.g. D Posey (ed), *Cultural and Spiritual Values of Biological Diversity* (IT/UNEP, Nairobi 2000).

[71] See WIPO's listings on: <http://www.wipo.int/tk/en/databases/tkportal/index.html>. See also the Indian database at: <http://www.sristi.org/wsa/>. B Tobin et al., *The Role of Registers and Databases in the Protection of Traditional Knowledge. A Comparative Analysis* (UNU-IAS, Tokyo 2003).

[72] This applies to knowledge passed along the chain of biotechnological R&D as well, alike with regard to biochemical materials. See *supra* note 63.

Moreover, it may be very unjust to attribute some knowledge to one or the other community. Whereas this may serve its interest, it may further deprive other groups of means to hang on to their knowledge and its inherent benefit. However, the envisioned widened disclosure requirement would force inventors to seek prior-informed-consent, and to conclude benefit-sharing agreements with one or the other community. No matter how many other traditional knowledge holders will thereby be ignored and left empty-handed. Instead of rebutting the alleged distributive injustices caused by contemporary patenting practises, it would foster them.

Many of the aforementioned ambiguities appear in the legal approaches taken towards the topics at hand. Hence, WIPO states that:

> . . .the term traditional knowledge refers to the content or substance of knowledge resulting from intellectual activity in a traditional context, and includes the know how, skills, innovations, practices and learning that form part of traditional knowledge systems, and knowledge embodying traditional lifestyles of indigenous and local communities, or contained in codified knowledge systems passed between generations. It is not limited to any specific technical field, and may include agricultural, environmental and medicinal knowledge, and knowledge associated with genetic resources.[73]

This definition is too broad. It does not provide a delineable legal object that may be subjected to a regime and/or rights in a legally meaningful and certain fashion. The definition contains awkward terminology: isn't the 'content' or 'substance' of knowledge the knowledge itself? More important, perhaps, is the scope of the definition. Taken on face value, the definition may include *all* knowledge. Doesn't all 'intellectual activity' occur in a 'traditional context'? Likewise, isn't all knowledge somehow 'passed between generations' and doesn't it all somehow originate locally? Moreover, the proposed association with genetic resources appears meaningless in this context. So much knowledge is 'associated with genetic resources'. One may wonder whether cooking is subjected to this definition; beer brewing; mixing herbs in a brass pot; isolating a protein, and so on? Is the ordinary ethno-botanist's knowledge, developed at university *and* in the rainforest, included? What about the knowledge of a biologist who obtained his or her knowledge at school, through visits to the zoo, in the laboratory *and* villages in a biological diversity-rich country? What about the knowledge of the indigenous shaman, who became a pharmacist selling both herbal and chemical medicines? And what about knowledge

---

[73] WIPO, 'Draft gap analysis on the protection of traditional knowledge' WIPO/GRTKF (30 May 2008) 6.

of my wife, Rachel, who heals me with her simple yet effective 'traditional' and 'local' means without resorting to pills and syringes?

The terms 'traditional', 'local' and 'association' are much too relative. If the proposed disclosure requirement were to be implemented anyhow, patent applicants will undoubtedly be confronted with startling questions, such as: should *all* knowledge related to the biochemical material(s) used in the course of reaching the invention be disclosed during patent examination, and – for that matter – proof of prior-informed-consent and benefit-sharing be provided? If not, which knowledge particularly? Which people or individual should one contractually turn to? How should one check its conclusive legal competency? Clearly, the proposed disclosure mechanism in respect of traditional knowledge should not be implemented, absent further resolution of these issues.

9.   CONCLUSION: LET'S TRY AND GET IT RIGHT!

The enhancement of both globalization and biotechnology allows for and necessitates utilization of an unprecedented variety of different types of knowledge and biochemical materials. The manner in which patent law stimulates global R&D in the life sciences may, however, require alterations such as those reflected in the proposed disclosure requirement. This requirement may condition the conveyance of patents on disclosure of information on the origin of and/or prior-informed-consent and/or benefit-sharing as to traditional knowledge and biochemical materials used in the attainment of inventions. Sanctions may also be provided outside of patent law. This should prevent uses of resources that would amount to distributive injustices towards the ones that develop and facilitate them – such as traditional knowledge holders and biological diversity-rich countries. It may prevent conflicts between the latter and the ones engaged in R&D. Hence, it may qualitatively and quantitatively contribute to their collaborations. This would benefit society, because biotechnological R&D would be enhanced, for example in the field of medicine. The proposed requirement may, furthermore, incite sustainable R&D: inventors would be held to actively contribute to efforts to conserve the cultural and biological diversity on which they rely for their endeavours. This myriad of social and instrumental justifications for the proposed disclosure requirement may be given a concrete effect by means of the legal bases already available, such as in TRIPS. Nevertheless, it is concluded that implementation of the proposed requirement in Article 83 of the EPC – but perhaps even worldwide – is not feasible at this time. Our lack of insight in biological and cultural diversity – including their tangible and intangible manifestations in materials and knowledge – complicate the establishment of an effective tracking and certification scheme, necessary for a widened disclosure requirement. Preliminarily, implementation of the envisioned requirement in patent law will impose obligations on inventors/patent applicants that cannot be fulfilled. Moreover, the fact that both traditional knowledge and biochemical materials are dispersed over countries and among communities may prevent just and concise attribution of rights and distribution of benefits. Compelling inventors to arrange benefit-sharing, and to disclose such in the course of the patent application procedure, will surely lead to new distributive injustices and thus frictions. This may hamper the emergence of these new collaborations in the life sciences instead. The impractical obligations that would be imposed on inventors could even have a negative effect on the overall pace and direction of biotechnological R&D. Inventors could turn away from certain endeavors to prevent legal complexities. This would not serve the interests of traditional knowledge holders and biological diversity-rich countries. It would also not serve the interests of mankind as a whole, which needs realization of the promises of the life sciences, and conservation of cultural and biological diversity at the same time.

Nevertheless, the justifications and bases that may be identified with regard to the proposed widened disclosure requirement in patent law may easily incline legislators to move forward and seek its implementation regardless. Some countries have already done so. They act upon the saying '*ich bin lieber ein Optimist und ein Trottel als ein Pessimist, der recht hat*'.[74] Issues of social justice and the need for instrumental efficiency in respect of the exploitation of traditional knowledge and biochemical material may *want* us to be optimistic. The dwindling of cultural and biological diversity, and its excepted consequences for mankind, may even *urge* us to be overly optimistic in respect of *any* attempt to change the tides. Hence, this may lead to excessive activism. It may be best, however, to be an optimist that is right at the same time. Any solution that may be justified and based in law, but is ultimately unfeasible and cannot be given practical effect is wrong. No matter how preferable an optimistic approach may be, such a solution amounts to a 'trottelism'. The analysis of aforementioned issues – the lack of relevant knowledge about traditional knowledge and biochemical material – suggests that this is the case with the proposed disclosure requirement at this time. The lack of substantive knowledge about the resources concerned primarily necessitates attention by more

---

[74] 'I would rather be an optimist and an idiot, than a pessimist and right'. Commonly attributed to Albert Einstein.

than just lawyers. Hence, those working with the knowledge and material concerned, such as traditional knowledge holders, (ethno)botanists, pharmacologists, ecologists, etc. They must fill in the substantive gaps and subsequently find ways to appropriately represent the knowledge and materials. Rights and interests of, broadly formulated, participants in biotechnological R&D and pertaining to one or the other legal object may then be distinguished, recognized and attributed. The same applies to the distribution of benefits deriving from the exploitation of those objects. The imposition of new obligations as to the protection of cultural and biological diversity by means of patent law can then be considered too. Of course, (patent) lawyers may be facilitative beforehand. But they cannot themselves provide the essential information that is lacking at this time.

I remain optimistic about our search for solutions, which should ultimately result in biotechnological R&D that is both just and instrumental in all respects. Information deficits are meant to be filled, and we may know tomorrow what we don't know today. Thereafter, we could act upon the insights gained and pursue to use (patent) law to steer the actions of those involved in biotechnological R&D. This may include employment of additional disclosure mechanisms; they certainly deserve to be explored. In the mean time, the important underlying interests call upon us to try and get it right!

5. *Ex post* liability rules: a solution for the biomedical anti-commons?*

Rosa Castro Bernieri

1. INTRODUCTION

While patents are mainly justified in the law and economics literature as temporary exclusive rights that foster innovation incentives, the guiding principle of efficiency requires that exclusive rights over technological and scientific knowledge do not preclude their further advancement. Thus, efficiency suggests that patent rights should not extend beyond social optimalization in a similar way to social justice calls for limitations on the exclusive nature of rights, in order to avoid patents encroaching upon other public interest goals such as access to knowledge.[1] In the biomedical arena, patents are considered as a vital source for innovation incentives, while undue limitations on access are perceived as a growing concern. In particular, the increasing number of patents issued for biomedical research tools has been singled out as a potential catalyst for the emergence of anti-commons.[2]

Most proposals to deal with the emergence of anti-commons in

* An earlier version of this chapter was presented as a paper at the 3rd Annual Workshop on the Law and Economics of Intellectual Property and Information Technology, Centre for Commercial Law Studies, Queen Mary, University of London. I thank discussants and participants in the Workshop for their useful comments. My special thanks to Maria Lillà Montagnani for her comments on the earlier draft. All errors remain my own.

[1] Giovanni B. Ramello, 'Intellectual property, social justice and economic efficiency: insights from law and economics' (2007) in this book, Chapter 1.

[2] In the tragedy of anti-commons, a resource is prone to underuse because multiple owners on upstream technologies have a right to exclude the use by others and none has a privilege to use the resources. For the general theory see Michael Heller, 'The tragedy of the anticommons: property in the transition from Marx to markets' (1998) *Harvard Law Rev.* 111(3), 621–88; and for the application to the biomedical sector see Michael A. Heller and Rebecca S. Eisenberg, 'Can patents deter innovation? The anticommons in biomedical research' (1998) *Science* 280 (5364), 698–701.

biomedical research either attempt to diminish the number and lower the quality of patents, or target the consequences of the increasing fragmentation of rights through market arrangements, such as patent pools, or through such institutional arrangements as compulsory licensing. The latter is an established yet controversial mechanism that permits the unauthorized use of patent rights by third parties under certain conditions now established by the TRIPS Agreement.[3] Compulsory licenses may respond to the necessity of maintaining a healthy competition in the market or to public interest reasons, especially those related with public health.

One consequence of issuing a compulsory license is to transform the right to exclude, granted to patent holders, into a right to receive remuneration. As a corollary, a special type of compulsory license is put in place when courts deny permanent injunctive relief for valid and infringed patents, since in those cases the patent holder only receives monetary remedies. Such possibility exists – although rarely used – in common law countries, where injunctive relief is considered an equitable remedy subject to the court's discretion.[4] Furthermore, in a path-breaking decision, the US Supreme Court recently stated that district courts should exercise their discretion by applying a balancing test that considers four factors in order to decide whether to grant or deny permanent injunctive relief for patents, as is done in other legal areas.[5] Following this decision taken in the context of the *eBay* case, district courts have applied the above-mentioned test and reviewed the four factors with dissimilar results in an important number of decisions, including some related to biotechnologies and pharmaceuticals that we will discuss below.

The possibility that courts deny a permanent injunction after a patent has been found to be valid and infringed during trial can be categorized as a 'liability rule', following the Calabresi and Melamed[6] distinction

---

[3]   See Article 31 of the Agreement on Trade Related Aspects of Intellectual Property Rights (TRIPS Agreement), Annex 1C of the Marrakesh Agreement Establishing the World Trade <http://docsonline.wto.org>.

[4]   This possibility is allowed by the terms of Article 44 of the TRIPS Agreement, which mandates member countries to ensure that its judiciary has 'the authority to order a party to desist from an infringement' but leaves the grounds and regulations of injunctive orders to member states.

[5]   *Ebay Inc. v. MercExchange, L.L.C.*, 126 S. Ct. 1837 (2006).

[6]   Guido Calabresi and Douglas A. Melamed, 'Property rules, liability rules and inalienability: one view of the cathedral' (1972) *Harvard Law Rev.* 85(6), 1089–128. The authors noticed how legal entitlements can be protected either through a property rule when third parties cannot take an entitlement without prior permission of the owner, or under a liability rule that allows the use of another's right as long as the owner is compensated. Comparing both rules, they

between property and liability rules. This special type of 'ex post liability rule' – here named '*ex post*' to differentiate it from liability rules regulated '*ex ante*' by statutes[7] – may be justified, under particular circumstances, to allow judges to balance innovation incentives with access to knowledge in light of public interest. Under such rule judges may additionally take into account the potential blocking effect of patents granted on certain difficult areas such as biomedical research. Whereas the automatic grant of injunctions favors legal certainty in enforcement, the standard adopted by the *eBay* case might facilitate the adaptation of patent laws to the particularities and needs of different industries[8] – a need commonly highlighted by efficiency analysis – and to the interest of the public (that is, the motivation of social justice approaches to patent law).[9]

This chapter examines if and how the availability of injunctive relief for biomedical innovations could be a positive development for the biomedical industry, an area of growing economic importance and challenges. One such challenge is the risk of the emergence of a biomedical anti-commons. Section 2 presents the basic features and challenges, including the problem of anti-commons in biomedical research. Section 3 illustrates *ex post* solutions to the risk mentioned in the previous section. Section 4 discusses the case for and against injunctive relief in the context of the *eBay* case and under the lens of the property rules versus liability rules' discussion in the patent system. Section 5 presents some cases applying the four-factor case of *eBay* to a biomedical patent and compares them with some landmark cases in the UK. We conclude by discussing the implication of these decisions in the context of efficiency and social justice and whether the above mentioned trend has opened, or could open, a more social-justice oriented approach to intellectual property (hereinafter IP) law when superior interests – such as those involved in biomedical research tools – are involved.

---

argued a property rule would be superior to a liability rule whenever transaction costs are low and information imperfect, whereas liability rules would be superior when transaction costs are high, for instance: when there are many parties, risks of holdouts, high likelihood of strategic bargaining or high transaction costs.

[7] Examples of compulsory licenses established by the law are those allowed by some jurisdictions for the case of dependent patents, in case of lack of working patents or on the grounds of public interest reasons.

[8] Antonio Nicita, Giovanni Ramello and Frederic Scherer, 'Intellectual property rights and the organization of industries: new perspectives in law and economics' (2005) *International Journal of the Economics of Business* 12 (3), 289–96.

[9] See Ramello (note 1).

2.   BIOMEDICAL ANTI-COMMONS

Modern biotechnologies are defined as 'the application of science and technology to living organisms as well as parts, products and models thereof, to alter living or non-living materials for the production of knowledge, goods and services'.[10] The biotech sector has generated great expectations in terms of demand for innovative diagnostic and therapeutic processes and opening new avenues for research. Its importance is accentuated by an ever-growing demand for new diagnostic and therapeutic tools and subject to the influence of the patent system, but also to a complex web of other regulations.[11]

This industry has interestingly developed along with an increasing scope for patentability that often induces some scholars to argue for even stronger rights and others to be wary of excesses. The landmark decision in *Diamond* v. *Chakrabarty*[12] initiated an expanding trend to protect DNA sequences, proteins and similar substances barely qualifying for protection within older standards of patentability.[13] Patent protection has been justified – especially by economic scholars – as critical for the development of the biotech industry, given that research is costly and uncertain and that strong rights are deemed necessary in order to encourage innovation.[14]

However, while patents are deemed to be fundamental in encouraging innovation in the biotech sector, the interaction or interference of such exclusive rights with health and other public interest needs is highly debated. According to some scholars, innovation incentives could also be

---

[10]   OECD, Statistical Definition of Biotechnology (2005) available at <http://www.oecd.org/document/42/0,2340,en_2649_37437_1933994_1_1_1_37437,00.html> accessed 28 January 2009.

[11]   Given the complex set of regulatory hurdles associated with marketing approval and the fact that pharmaceuticals tend to be more of the one-patent-one-product case, we subsequently focus more on genetic diagnostic tools. See Rebecca S. Eisenberg, 'Will pharmacogenomics alter the role of patents in drug development?' (2002) *Pharmacogenomics* 3(5), 571, 572–3.

[12]   *Diamond* v. *Chakrabarty*, 447 U.S. 303 (1980).

[13]   See Dan Burk and Mark A. Lemley 'Policy Levers in Patent Law' (2003) UC Berkeley Public Law Research Paper No. 135, available at <http://ssrn.com/abstract=431360> accessed 28 January 2009.

[14]   See Wesley M. Cohen, Richard R. Nelson and John P. Walsh, 'Protecting their intellectual assets: appropriability conditions and why US manufacturing firms patent or not' (2000) NBER Working Paper 7552, available at <http://www.nber.org/papers/w7552> accessed 28 January 2009. The authors show that patents are secondary in importance with respect to other mechanisms such as first-mover advantages and trade secrets in other industries, while they remain significant for pharmaceuticals and biotechnology.

served if patents are transformed, at least in some cases, in rights to receive monetary compensation by means of compulsory licenses.[15] Conversely, the emergence of anti-commons property[16] follows from the increasing number of patents, considered in the traditional conception as rights to exclude all others from the use of a technical solution.[17]

The above-mentioned risk derives from the fact that the vast upsurge in biotech patents particularly has involved products known as research tools,[18] in this way departing from an era when basic research was widely left in the public domain. Although it is difficult to separate biotech products into categories such as research tools and end-products, especially in the area of genomics, research tools are by definition the inputs of future research, which makes it imperative that patent laws do not preclude their efficient use.[19] Nevertheless, many products of biomedical research such as diagnostic tests may derive directly from and be mixed with basic research.

Furthermore, many research tools are patented as end-products, on the basis of one specific function. This is the case of patents over the DNA or sequences of a virus, which allow the development of diagnostic tests and vaccines, but which could also be needed to develop further therapeutic

---

[15]   See Mark A. Lemley and Phil Weiser, 'Should property or liability rules govern information?' (2007) *Texas Law Review* 85(4), 783–841, available at <http://ssrn.com/abstract=977778> accessed 28 January 2009.

[16]   See Ramello (note 1).

[17]   Empirical findings about the emergence of anti-commons and patent thickets within biotechnologies are ambiguous. See F. Murray and S. Stern, 'Do formal Intellectual Property rights hinder the free flow of scientific knowledge? An empirical test of the anti-commons hypothesis' (2007) *Journal of Economic Behavior and Organization* 63(4), 648–87 (finding an anti-commons effect in citation rates after a patent is granted). Contra John P. Walsh, Ashish Aurora and Wesley M. Cohen, 'Working through the patent problem' (2003) *Science* 299 (5609), 1021 (finding that the IP system does not preclude sequential innovation but nevertheless mentioning some important problems related to patentability of research tools).

[18]   Biotech products have traditionally been classified in two main categories: research tools and end products. For definition, see World Health Organization Commission of Intellectual Property Rights, Innovation and Public Health, 'Innovation and Public Health', Final Report (2006), available at: <http://www.who.int/intellectualproperty/documents/thereport/ENPublicHealthReport.pdf> accessed 28 January 2009.

[19]   The study of genes and their functions (genomics), proteins and their functions (proteomics) and the application of computer databases and algorithms to manage biological information (bioinformatics) constitute important areas for current and future biomedical R&D, with the suffix 'omics' implying the activity of assembling different parts.

targets or different tests. Blocking could also arise when network effects de facto preclude the emergence of such products by 'artificially' imposing lock-ins for certain protected products, usually linked with standards.[20]

Providing optimal incentives for basic and applied research under these circumstances is more difficult than balancing incentives between innovators and access to innovation. It also necessitates keeping enough incentives for first and second innovators. Moreover, the line between basic and applied research is not obvious in 'unique' products, and the holder of a patent over a gene and, for instance, an immunodiagnostic kit, would not have any clear incentive to provide 'access' for others to develop new immunodiagnostic kits, and could presumably claim any royalty from researchers developing therapeutic inventions using the same gene.

Nonetheless, the problem of anti-commons is not only confined to the increasing number of patents and their blocking potential, but also involves the emergence of patent thickets[21] and the stacking of royalties that could preclude downstream research, thus making it too costly to develop further technologies.

An important research area especially inclined towards anti-commons and patent thickets is the use of genetic information, including genes, sequences and fragments which could permit therapeutic, diagnostic and drug discovery.[22] The fact that many patented technologies are 'unique' in the sense of having both end-product and research tool features appears to be even more severe in relation with diagnostic arrays, including those for genetic diseases. In this field, patents on research tools are deemed to be the main cause of complexity, transaction costs and delays in research. Moreover, the concept of research tools is vague and many products can qualify as such, for instance the CCR5 receptor and the NF-KB messenger

---

[20]   See R. Dreyfuss, 'Works/unique challenges at the intellectual property/ competition law interface', in Claus-Dieter Ehlermann and Isabela Atanasiu (eds), *European Competition Law Annual, The Interaction Between Competition Law and Intellectual Property Law* (Hart Publishing, Oxford 2005), available at: <http:// papers.ssrn.com/sol3/papers.cfm?abstract_id=763688> accessed 28 January 2009 (arguing that products can be intrinsically unique, like DNA sequences or become so through network effects that lock-in a certain technology and that the impossibility to substitute for these technologies poses new issues for IP laws and antitrust).
[21]   See OECD, 'Genetic Inventions, Intellectual Property Rights and Licensing Practices: Evidence and Policies' (2002) 61, where 'patent thicket' has been defined as the term '. . . coined to characterize a technological field where multiple rights owned by multiple actors may impede R&D because of the difficulty or cost of assembling the necessary rights.'
[22]   See T.J. Ebersole, M.C. Guthrie and J.A. Goldstein, 'Patent pools and standard setting in diagnostic genetics' (2005) *Nature Biotechnology* 23(8), 937–8.

protein, also accused of being patented technologies for which there was too limited access.[23]

In Europe a landmark case involved a patent owned by Myriad Genetics on a method for genetic diagnosis of breast and ovarian cancer, which was revoked and subsequently maintained on a modified version.[24] This controversy was highly motivated by public health concerns, the broadness of the patent claims and its potential blocking effect over improvements.[25] The decision of the European Board of Appeals followed a patent opposition procedure initiated by several medical institutions for research that at the same time triggered processes of legal reform to expand compulsory licenses to *in vitro* diagnostic methods for public health purposes in Belgium, France and the Netherlands. In Canada the same patent was refused and a reform to Canadian law was also suggested to allow opposition of patents and to restrict broad patents. Potential exclusivity and stacking problems in the diagnostic genetics area may continue to grow, due to the increasing ability to test several mutations at the same time through mass spectrometry or panels of antibody arrays for proteins and oligo-nucleotide arrays.[26]

As mentioned above, the anti-commons literature has identified how licensing problems and royalty stacking could preclude further research. Such problems are critically present in the biomedical area where research tools are often licensed non-exclusively, whereas genetic tests licenses tend to be subject to restrictions. Although the royalty-stacking problem in diagnostic tests is an important ongoing concern, there is not a clear threshold as to which percentage royalty would preclude research and

---

[23] See OECD (2002), at 69–70 referring to two studies within the US: one in patents over genetic tests, where 65% of clinical laboratories were contacted by patent holders, while among laboratories that were offered the test, 25% said that patent owner's prevented them from continuing its testing service and 53% did not develop or offer tests because of patent reasons; and a second study on a diagnostic test on a gene associated with hereditary haemochromatosis that showed how license fees impeded a great number of laboratories from offering the test.

[24] See Maurice Cassier, 'Patents and public health: European opposition to the myriad breast cancer patent', (2004), 4th EPIP Conference, Paris, 1–2 October 2004, available at <http://www.epip.eu/papers/20041001/paris/papers/MCassier.pdf> accessed 28 January 2008.

[25] Ibid, at 7.

[26] See John H. Barton, 'Emerging patent issues in genomics diagnostic' (2006) *Nature Biotechnology* 24(8), 939–41, describing the problem as follows: 'This is a version of the problem of royalty stacking, because each holder of a patent on a diagnostic sequence or marker used in the array could, under traditional law, legally block marketing or use of the array. There is a particular hold-up risk when licensing rights from many different entities must be assembled.'

how relevant the problem is in reality.[27] However, the higher the number of research tools needed, the more problematic royalty stacking will be in the future. Thus, in spite of controversy about the existence and extension of anti-commons in biomedical research, a growing concern seems to be palpable within different organizations, including the OECD.[28]

3. PATENT LAW DESIGN AND BIOMEDICAL PATENTS

Proposals dealing with the aforementioned problems can either adopt an *ex ante* or an *ex post* approach. Proponents of *ex ante* approaches maintain that solutions to the increasing number and lower quality of patents should lie in the reform of substantive patent law, including the grant of fewer patents and limits to patents for upstream products, such as research tools or DNA sequences, as highlighted in many studies.[29]

Proponents of *ex post* approaches attempt to address the consequences of anti-commons, patent thickets and their accompanying effects by ways of market or institutional arrangements, that is, working within the current patent setting.[30] Market solutions comprise the formation of patent pools and clearing houses. Institutional arrangements refer to the use of compulsory licensing and other mechanisms already incorporated in the current legal system.[31] A patent pool or clearing house

---

[27] Some data indicates that royalties might be around 1–4% of net sales for non-exclusive licenses, and could reach even 10%, while being 6–10% for exclusive licenses and sometimes approaching 20%. See OECD (note 21) at 71.

[28] See OECD, 'Guidelines for the licensing of Genetic Inventions' (2006) <http://www.oecd.org/dataoecd/39/38/36198812.pdf> accessed 28 January 2009.

[29] A. Rai, 'Fostering cumulative innovation in the biopharmaceutical industry: the role of patent and antitrust' (2001) *Berkeley Tech. L.J.* 16 (Spring 2001) 813, 838–48 (arguing in favor of using patent doctrine to limit the patentability of upstream research, while reserving a secondary role for antitrust as an *ex post* approach that might allow precompetitive arrangements such as patent pools and restrict conduct that blocks innovation).

[30] See for instance Ebersole et al. (note 22), and B. Verbeure, E. van Zimmeren, E. Matthijs and G. Van Overwalle, 'Patent pools and diagnostic testing' (2006) *Trends in Biotechnology* (TIB) 24(3), 115–20.

[31] See OECD, 2002 (note 21), 82, presenting the results of a workshop where participants concluded that changes in patent examination procedures, codes of conducts and compulsory licenses were more acceptable than legal reforms 'because they can be better targeted to meet an identified licensing dysfunction'.

model could mainly facilitate the processes of identifying the parties and negotiating licenses for the patented technologies; however this solution is practically absent from the biotechnology sector, in spite of reiterated proposals.[32] Moreover, contractually negotiated solutions in the form of patent pools have faced problems of opportunistic behavior of patentees that participate in Standard Setting Organizations in other areas of technology.[33]

Among the available *ex post* solutions, which establish compulsory licenses for patents, is that adopted in the *eBay* case that will be analysed in the following section.

4.   *EX POST* LIABILITY RULES FOR INFRINGED PATENTS

4.1   The eBay Case

In *eBay* v. *MercExchange* the US Supreme Court evaluated the conditions under which courts should grant injunctions against infringers.[34] MercExchange held a patent on the 'Buy it Now' feature incorporated in the eBay website. Having failed in its attempts to negotiate a license with eBay, MercExchange sued for patent infringement. The jury found the patent to be valid and infringed, but the District Court denied an injunction on the basis that MercExchange was willing to license and did not practice its patents, concluding that it was not likely to suffer an irreparable harm. The US Court of Appeals for the Federal Circuit (CAFC) overturned this decision on the basis that 'courts will issue permanent injunctions against patent infringement absent exceptional circumstances',[35] which usually involve public health or environmental concerns.

The US Supreme Court decided that according to principles of equity, in the US, a plaintiff seeking a permanent injunction must satisfy a

---

[32]   For an account of initiatives on the use of patent pools and similar arrangements see J. Clark, 'Patent Pools: A Solution to the Problem of Access in Biotechnology Patents?' (2000) White Paper commissioned by the Under Secretary of Commerce for Intellectual Property and Director of the U.S.P.T.O. available at <http://www.uspto.gov/web/offices/pac/dapp/opla/patentpool.pdf> accessed 28 January 2009; OECD, 2002 (note 21); Verbeure et al. (note 30) and Ebersole et al. (note 22).
[33]   See J. Farrell, J. Hayes, C. Shapiro and T. Sullivan, 'Standard setting, patents, and hold-up' (2007) *Antitrust Law Journal* 74(3), 603–70.
[34]   *Ebay Inc.* v. *MercExchange, L.L.C.,* 126 S. Ct. 1837 (2006).
[35]   *MercExchange, L.L.C.* v. *eBay, Inc.*, 401 F.3d (2005), 1323,1339.

four-factor test demonstrating: (1) that she has suffered an irreparable injury; (2) that remedies available at law, such as monetary damages, are inadequate to compensate for that injury; (3) that, considering the balance of hardships between the plaintiff and defendant, a remedy in equity is warranted; and (4) that the public interest would not be disserved by a permanent injunction. The Court decided that whether to grant or deny permanent injunctive relief is an act of equitable discretion by district courts, as the Patent Act provides that courts 'may' issue injunctions.[36]

This decision departed from a precedent[37] rejecting the contention that courts could not grant injunctive relief to a patent holder who has unreasonably declined to use the patent. Since then, most courts had followed an automatic grant of injunctive relief upon a finding of validity and infringement of a patent.[38]

In *eBay* the Supreme Court disagreed that lack of use by the right holder would necessarily preclude an injunction, especially because patent holders, such as universities or self-made inventors, frequently opt for licensing their patents instead of commercializing their inventions by themselves. For such patent holders that may be able to satisfy the traditional four-factor test, the court expressed that there was no reason for denying them the opportunity of asserting an irreparable injury and the other requirements of the four-factor test and eventually obtain an injunction. However, the Supreme Court sustained that an injunction will not necessarily follow the finding of patent infringement and held that both the District Court and the Court of Appeals erred in formulating categorical rules with respect to the decision about whether to grant or deny injunctive relief.

In two concurring opinions by seven of the Court's nine members to the short but unanimous decision, there were expressly divided and contradictory justifications for granting or denying injunctive relief. Justice Roberts (with Justices Scalia and Ginsburg) highlighted that injunctive relief was the remedy in the majority of patent cases 'from at least the early

---

[36] Section 283 provides that '[t]he several courts having jurisdiction of cases under this title may grant injunctions in accordance with the principles of equity to prevent the violation of any right secured by patent, on such terms as the court deems reasonable'.

[37] *Continental Paper Bag Co.* v. *Eastern Paper Bag Co.*, 210 U.S. 405, 422–430 (1908).

[38] See for instance *Richardson* v. *Suzuki Motor Co.*, 868 F.2d 1226, 1246–47 (Fed. Cir. 1989), stating that injunctions could not be denied for valid and infringed patents because patent rights are a right to exclude.

nineteenth century', and found this choice correct given the 'difficulty of protecting a right to exclude through monetary remedies that allow an infringer to use an invention against the patentee's wishes'.[39]

In contrast, Justice Kennedy (with Justices Stevens, Souter and Breyer) opined that courts usually favored injunctions not because of valuation problems but because the application of the four-factor test depended on the type of inventions, which has radically changed during the last years, both with regard to the nature of patents and the economic function of the patent holder. A recent emergence of firms devoted to using patents to obtain licensing fees and not to produce and use its inventions was viewed as an opportunity to engage in strategic behavior, whereby injunctions are used 'as a bargaining tool to charge exorbitant fees'.[40]

This opinion highlighted that hold-ups may occur when a patent covers only a small component of a product and the threat of injunctive relief is used for 'undue leverage in negotiations',[41] in which case it was argued that damages would be sufficient to compensate, whereas injunctions would not serve the public interest. In addition, the judges considered the harmful effect that injunctions could have over patents, especially those on business methods, which in a similar way to some biomedical patents, often face important problems of vagueness and validity. The view of this concurrent opinion was that 'equitable discretion over injunctions, granted by the Patent Act, is well suited to allow courts to adapt to the rapid technological and legal developments in the patent system'.[42]

In its decision, the US Supreme Court opened the door for the application of *ex-post* liability rules, contradicting the opinions that had opposed the use of compulsory licenses, including those awarded by courts:

> A rule distinguishing patents by whether the patent holder 'uses' the invention is directly contrary to Congress's command. Not only would such a rule diminish the value of the patent, it will inexorably result in court-imposed compulsory licensing.[43]

---

[39] See *Ebay Inc.* v. *MercExchange, L.L.C.*, 126 S. Ct. 1837, 1841 (2006) (Roberts, C.J., concurring).

[40] *Ebay Inc.* v. *MercExchange, L.L.C.*, 126 S. Ct. 1837, 1842 (2006) (Kennedy, J., concurring).

[41] Ibid.

[42] Ibid.

[43] Brief of Biotechnology Industry Organization as Amicus Curiae in support of Respondent, N° 05–130, available at <http://bio.org/ip/amicus/20060310.pdf> accessed 28 January 2009.

4.2   *Ex Post* Liability Rules: Economic Consequences

An injunction is an order to stop infringement activity that gives the patent owner relief under a 'property rule' and is considered to be a key deterrent remedy for future infringement. Damage compensation is usually given to patentees as a complementary remedy to injunctions that aim at compensating for past losses.[44] However, when injunctive relief is denied and damages are considered as a substitute for injunctions, the patentees' right to exclude is transformed in a right to get compensation, as is now the case in decisions applying the rule stated by the US Supreme Court in *eBay*.

The exclusive nature of IP rights is usually viewed as the heart of innovation incentives given to right holders. However, exclusiveness could lead to less than socially desirable use of technologies. Under-use of technologies is justified under patent law as the consequence of exclusivity and a price to pay for fostering innovation incentives. Nonetheless, exclusiveness can pose several problems on static efficiency grounds and also affect the same innovation incentives that it is intended to advance. Under sequential or incremental innovation, patented products are the building inputs for follow-on research and this problem is compounded in the presence of unique products, which become 'captured' either by nature or market forces.

Both 'property rules' and 'liability rules' are imperfect protection mechanisms, which exist in patent law as well as other legal fields. Liability rules are often criticized because of the higher costs that courts and regulators have to face in order to determine the amount of compensation, which may also induce errors, presumably because courts would avoid calculating subjective values and may thus under-compensate right holders. As a consequence, the use of liability rules for intellectual property rights, including patents, has also been criticized for undermining incentives for parties to bargain.[45] However, the prevention of strategic behavior cannot

---

[44]   While both compensation and remuneration are compatible with the notion of liability rules, enhanced damages that seek to punish behavior and thus, to deter it, will likely amount to a property rule. Under a property rule, the user price is settled by the consensual approval of the right owner and though in punitive damages such price is determined by a court, it amounts in fact to the prohibition of non-consensual takings, at least in the long-run. See Henry Smith, 'Property and property rules' (2004) *New York University Law Review* 79, 1719–98, available at <http://ssrn.com/abstract=638723> accessed 28 January 2009.

[45]   See, for instance, Robert Merges, 'Contracting into liability rules: intellectual property rights and collective rights organizations' (1996) *California Law*

only be entrusted to market-driven responses. The emphasis on assessment costs and errors of courts or regulatory agencies as reasons to prefer strong property rules assumes that market players can usually come up with a better-negotiated price and overlooks the harmful effects of strategic behavior, especially in the form of hold-ups.

Some arguments against the use of strong property rules are, on the one hand, that market players can more easily find solutions that minimize the transaction costs related to finding the parties relevant to the negotiation and, with developing mechanisms to enforce or monitor their rights, by contracting into different types of liability rules.[46] But such market solutions would rarely solve the problems arising out of strategic behavior and difficult negotiations. In these cases, the insights of economic analysis of law suggest that a liability rule may be preferable. While critics of liability rules focus on assessment and error costs, the recognition of costs and errors in tailoring injunctive relief has, in comparison, received much less attention.[47] On the contrary, scholars have discussed at length whether property rule protection enhances innovation incentives and efficient bargaining,[48] and to what extent expansive control over innovation can curtail further improvements so that policy makers have to turn to liability rules in patent law.

Whereas most scholars argue that the baseline patent protection should remain a property rule because of the difficulty of asserting the economic value of patents, some have increasingly warned about patent cases where anticompetitive conduct and hold-ups are preferably dealt by liability rules. This view underlines the importance of compulsory licenses in

---

Review 84(5) available at <http://ssrn.com/abstract=11497> accessed 28 January 2009 (arguing that patent pools, collective organizations and other type of pooling agreements have developed because IP rights are 'strong', e.g. they are protected by a property rule).

[46]   Ibid.

[47]   For an exception see M. Lemley and P. Weiser (note 15).

[48]   See for instance Lemley and Weiser (note 15), 784, 786–8, referring to the view of Robert Merges who finds that IP protection is justified on a transactional view that enhances efficiency by decreasing transaction costs; and the view of Richard Epstein who reiteratively sustains that, due to assessment and error costs, there would be systematical under-compensation. Critics of this view highlight the differences that should prevail between rival entitlements as real property and non-rival entitlements, as knowledge and information for which the law should attempt to maintain a balance between protection of innovations and access. Lemley and Weiser themselves sustain that: '[t]he founding vision of intellectual property (IP) viewed owners of governmentally conferred rights – in patent and copyright – as the beneficiaries of a government license and as entitled only to remedies sufficient to encourage innovation.' Ibid, 783.

industries characterized by anti-commons, where patentees may hold out for a disproportionately high royalty and obstruct downstream production, and also for patents covering important products for society, such as pharmaceuticals and agricultural products that should be available at lower prices under compulsory licenses.[49] Other authors argue that patent systems like those in the US systematically over-reward the owners of patents who license rather than practice their patents, especially in the information technology sector, or whenever patents are weak and cover minor features of complex products precisely because of the ability of right holders to obtain injunctions.[50]

Therefore, although the cases in which courts deny permanent injunctions for valid and infringed patents remain confined to specific circumstances, even after *eBay*, it is undeniable that the range of circumstances has expanded to embrace the cases of dubious patents, both in terms of validity and ambiguous boundaries; of patents on a small component of a product and of patentees who may be compensated fully through monetary awards. Provisions for compulsory licenses are scarce in the US and had a limited impact before the *eBay* case. Whereas other legislation provides for compulsory licensing, these rules are seldom used in practice. However, law and economics insights point towards the potential effect that the presence of such statutes could have in the process of negotiating licenses. Such potential effects may also take place 'under the shadow of the eBay rule', in the sense of discouraging certain types of strategic behavior and abuses of the patent system.

In addition to the consequences of the *eBay* decision in terms of efficiency, also important from a social justice viewpoint is the fact that district courts in the US are now in practice considering a broader range of circumstances in their decisions over whether to grant or deny injunctions. In Section 5 we examine some cases in the biomedical sector, in which courts have given consideration to different circumstances related to the use of such patented technologies. Although the decisions mentioned below were not taken upon public interest reasons, the possibility remains that courts could in the future give greater weight to such considerations. Meanwhile, courts that deny injunctions in order to avoid unduly blocking of competition and anti-commons effects are also indirectly favoring the public interest in a healthy patent system.

---

[49]   See D. Burk and M. Lemley (note 13), 168–74.
[50]   See Mark Lemley and Carl Shapiro, 'Patent holdup and royalty stacking' (2007) *Texas Law Review* 85, 1991–2049, available at <http://ssrn.com/abstract=923468> accessed 28 January 2009.

5.   THE CASE FOR *EX POST* LIABILITY RULES IN THE BIOTECH INDUSTRY

The case of *Innogenetics, N.V,* v. *Abbott Laboratories*[51] concerned a patent claiming a method for genotyping the Hepatitis C virus (HCV), which permits not only isolating but also classifying the virus. The District Court gave consideration to the fact that Innogenetics manufactures but does not commercialize the tests. Nonetheless, the court concluded that Innogenetic's reputation and market share were at stake, even if Bayer was the actual producer, and decided to grant permanent injunctive relief. The court considered it improper that a plaintiff's willingness to license its patents could be seen as sufficient to establish that the patent holder would not suffer irreparable harm if an injunction did not issue. Moreover, it ruled that 'it would denigrate the value of plaintiff's patent rights to allow defendant to continue to sell plaintiff's invention as its own in exchange for the same fee it would have paid without a lawsuit'.[52]

The District Court also decided that public interest was sufficiently protected because the plaintiff had enough capacity to supply HCV diagnostic products and complied with manufacturing practices and FDA requirements, therefore being able to supply the needed diagnostic services for patients with HCV. When analysing potential risks to public health from under-provision of the diagnostic tests, the court dismissed such concerns because other diagnostic kits exist, which would be enough to cover the demand for such tests, even if they were less effective than Abbott's. The court also deemed that Hepatitis C was a chronic disease in which genotyping was not required instantaneously: '[a] delay in obtaining a test would not have any perceptible adverse effect on a person suffering from the disease'.[53] These latter arguments are debatable, since the fact that diagnostic tests are less effective may in fact pose several health problems including the increase of diagnostic errors. Furthermore, even if Hepatitis C is a chronic disease, genotyping is fundamental for doctors to decide the appropriate treatment and its duration, and to evaluate the progress of treatment.

On appeal, the CAFC reversed the decision by the District Court for abuse of discretion and denied the permanent injunction while granting a

---

[51]   *Innogenetics N.V.* v. *Abbott Laboratories*, U.S.D.C.W.D.W.05-C-0575-C, January 3rd, 2007.

[52]   *Innogenetics N.V.* v. *Abbott Laboratories*, U.S.D.C.W.D.W.05-C-0575-C, January 3rd, 2007.

[53]   *Innogenetics N.V.* v. *Abbott Laboratories*, U.S. D.C. W.D.W. 05-C-0575-C, January 12th, 2007, available at <http://patentdocs.typepad.com/patent_docs/files/innogenetics_pi.pdf> accessed 28 January 2009.

compulsory license.[54] Some commentators have considered this case as an outlier, given that courts have generally granted injunctions when patentees compete with infringers – either directly or through licensors – even after the *eBay* decision.[55]

However the CAFC in *Innogenetics* explicitly denied that irreparable harm could occur when a patentee receives reasonable royalties that include an upfront fee based upon future sales in a long-term market.

Likewise, the court said that injunctive relief should not be held as a form of 'extra damages' that compensate litigation costs because otherwise injunctions would be granted automatically and it added that Innogenetics was entirely compensated for past infringement and possible future sales by Abbott. An important factor in this case was that Innogenetics had already licensed the same patent to Roche, which made the calculation of royalties easier for the court, and also that infringement was found to be non-willful. Importantly, the CAFC reversed the decision on permanent injunctive relief and agreed on a compulsory license, even in the absence of a compelling public interest justification.

This decision is in evident contrast with the view that patents can only be protected through property rules, which was the prevailing view in the case of *Amgen* v. *Hoffmann-La Roche*.[56] In this case the controversy centered on the infringement by Hoffmann-La Roche of six patents protecting Amgen's recombinant erythropoietin (EPO), a naturally occurring protein that stimulates the production of red blood cells, which Amgen managed to produce through the introduction of exogenous DNA into host cells (Chinese hamster ovary CHO cells) that then express the human rEPO, which only differs from naturally occurring human EPO by its glycosilation. Amgen's patents were accused of being obvious, but the District Court finally ruled its validity and granted permanent injunctive relief based on the following arguments:

> Here, were the court were to deny Amgen's request for a permanent injunction, Roche would enter the ESA market as Amgen's competitor. The vast majority of Roche sales would be to the exclusion of Amgen sales, resulting in lost profits, market share, and good will.[57]

---

[54]   *Innogenetics N.V.* v. *Abbott Laboratories*, 512 F.3d 1363–8 (2008).
[55]   See D. Ellis et al., 'The economic implications (and uncertainties) of obtaining permanent injunctive relief after *eBay* v. *MercExchange*' (2008) FED. CIR. B.J. 17(4), 437, 442–3.
[56]   *Amgen, Inc.* v. *F. Hoffmann-La Roche Ltd.*, 581 F.Supp.2d 160, 210, n. 12, WL 4452454 at *45, n. 12 (D.Mass. Oct. 2, 2008).
[57]   Ibid, 32–45.

As regards the interaction of an injunction with the public interest, the court ruled that allowing Roche to introduce its product MIRCERA into the market would probably benefit some patients and help in reducing costs for Medicare, but if such arguments prevailed – the court considered – almost any pharmaceutical patent would have to be subject to the same limitation to obtain injunctive relief. The consequence, according to the court, would be that denying injunctions for pharmaceutical patents based upon a speculative estimation of benefits would undermine the right to exclude and innovation incentives for patent owners.

In a similar way, UK courts may award damages as a substitute for an injunction,[58] but in practice they have only denied injunctions under unusual circumstances. Such circumstances have been precisely found in cases regarding biomedical and pharmaceutical patents. In *Roussel-Uclaf* v. *G D Searle & Co Ltd.*,[59] it was held that in the case of a life saving drug 'it is at the least very doubtful if the court in its discretion even ought to grant an injunction'. However, in a different case, even though the defendant argued that an injunction would be contrary to the public interest and the patent in question could prevent the public having access to the kits and hinder research and development, an injunction was granted. Nonetheless, the judge highlighted how discretion could entail either balancing the parties and public interest stakes:

> I conclude that in most cases the approach suggested in the Shelfer case should be sufficient to decide whether damages should be granted instead of an injunction. However the Court's discretion under the section is not limited. Therefore the court should in appropriate circumstances take into account the interests of persons who would be affected by the grant of the injunction. That may involve considering the interests of the public.[60]

A possible answer to why cases denying injunctions are nevertheless confined to a few examples was provided in the same decision of *Chiron* v. *Organon*, when the judge referred to the exceptions and limitations established in the Patent statutes, including license of rights, and highlighted how public interest may be better served by such other ways:

> It is also necessary to bear in mind that the legislature envisaged that in certain situations the public interest required a fetter upon patent rights and took

---

[58]   Section 50, UK Supreme Court Act of 1981.
[59]   *Roussel-Uclaf* v. *G D Searle & Co Ltd.* [1977] FSR 125, 6.
[60]   *Chiron Corp* v. *Organon Teknika Ltd.* (No. 10) [1995] FSR 325, 7.

appropriate steps to safeguard the interests of the public. For instance, the Crown can authorize the use of the patent in certain circumstances. That suggests that the interests of the public will normally be protected by the provisions of the Patents Act 1977 and an injunction should normally be granted restraining infringement unless the contrary is indicated in the Act. Thus it is a good working rule that an injunction will be granted to prevent continued infringement of a patent, even though that would have the effect of enforcing a monopoly, thereby restricting competition and maintaining prices. Something more should be established before the Court will depart from the good working rule suggested in the Shelfer case.[61]

Other similar patent cases in the UK highlight the importance of liability rules for patent protection. Compulsory licensing provisions are, as described in the above-mentioned decisions, present in the UK patent statutes where, independently of their use in practice, they shape the incentives of patent owners to license and litigate their patents. Conversely, general provisions for compulsory licensing are widely absent in the US, at least with regard to blocking patents or lack of use by patentees with few exceptions that regard governmental uses and antitrust cases. Now, under the *eBay* four-factor test the use of compulsory licensing by district courts could be extended to difficult patent cases, including biomedical patents that could block improvements or affect the interest of the public.

6. CONCLUSIONS

Although economic arguments are ambiguous about whether a discretional rule that permits judges to deny injunctive relief when the costs of enjoining uses surpass the costs of errors due to the assessment of compensation, the case for a discretionary *ex post* liability rule for patent cases is supported when anti-commons and broad or ambiguous patents threaten to block further innovation:

> In short, where injunctions cannot be well tailored to the scope of the property right at issue but necessarily restrain the use of property not owned by the plaintiff, those consequences can overwhelm the benefits of property rules in enforcing legal rights.[62]

The case is even more compelling with regard to technologies that are needed to solve cases in which the interest of the public is involved, as often happens with health-related technologies in the biomedical area.

---

[61] Ibid, 9.
[62] See Lemley and Weiser (note 15), 784.

The implications of the *eBay* rule and any similar standard to decide about the appropriateness of patent remedies are manifold. The uncertainty that now surrounds the grant of injunctive relief in the US has effects on the incentives to infringe, to negotiate licenses and to follow a specific line of research. It is often argued that such uncertainty may diminish innovation incentives. However, the factual test laid down by the US Supreme Court allows judges to incorporate a broader set of arguments in order to decide whether an injunction is the most appropriate means of protecting a patent. This is an important opportunity to incorporate both efficiency and social justice considerations into patent law, especially as it relates to industries with particular vested concerns such as the biomedical sector.

6. The search for EU boundaries: IPR exercise and enforcement as 'misuse'

Anne Flanagan, Federico Ghezzi and Maria Lillà Montagnani

1. INTRODUCTION

In 2006, the EU Commission fined pharmaceutical company AstraZeneca (AZ) €60 million, finding that AZ had violated Article 82 of the EC Treaty via its misuse of pharmaceutical marketing authorization procedures and patent systems in seven Member States, in order to prevent or delay entry by generic drug manufacturers.[1] Specifically, AZ misled certain national patent offices about the inception of its product marketing in order to obtain longer supplementary protection certificates (SPCs). This SPC strategy was intended to stretch AZ's patent duration for its leading medicinal product far beyond the term provided under patent law. At the same time, AZ, as part of a post-patent-strategy, changed its product formulation in countries where the patent/SCP was close to expiring, thereby preventing generic manufacturers that were ready to produce and market the original formulation and parallel importers from entering the market until they could manufacture and produce the new formulation.

These behaviors, sometimes called the 'evergreening' of patents, permitted AZ to control the market access for both generic producers and for parallel traders by exploiting its patent far beyond its term of duration and, to a certain extent, beyond its scope. The full implication of AZ's

---

[1] *AstraZeneca* [2006] OJ L 332/24, appealed on 25 August 2005 AstraZeneca/Commission (Case T-321/05) (2005/C 271/47), OJ of the European Union 29 October 2005. The Lisbon Treaty, 2007 OJ C 306/01 (17 December 2007) amended the EC Treaty to rename it the Treaty on the Functioning of the European Union (TFEU); its provisions were also numbered. Relevant references to the EC Treaty here should be understood to refer to the TFEU, the article numbers to be changed as follows: 28, now Article 34, TFEU; 29, now Article 35, TFEU; 30, now Article 36, TFEU; 49, now Article 56, TFEU; 81, now Article 101, TFEU; and 82, now Article 102, TFEU.

conduct, however, needs to be analysed in the context of its overall strategy which encompassed not only the above-mentioned abusive behaviors, but also its litigation strategy adopted against generic producers when the SPC was revoked,[2] and its defensive posture adopted in response to the generic producers' accusations.[3]

The *AZ* decision caused a buzz in the EU intellectual property community. Some criticized the legal basis of the decision[4] or noted a new kind of abuse of dominance under Article 82.[5] Others questioned whether a European response to the US IP 'misuse' doctrine could be envisaged in this decision.[6] Answering this question requires at least a brief exploration of the parameters of intellectual property 'misuse' in the USA. However, misuse is not a doctrine easily ring-fenced as there are conflicting cases and views, which have led some to call it 'amorphous'[7] or 'hopelessly entangled'[8] with other doctrines, especially antitrust. The following section of this chapter will attempt, in turn, an overview of each of the two primary distinct avenues of misuse doctrine: that violating the public policy underlying the grant of intellectual property and that amounting to a violation of antitrust law.[9] Also considered is whether or how IP enforcement via

---

[2]   Ibid. § 231.

[3]   Ibid. §§ 736–738.

[4]   See, e.g., M Manley and A Wray, 'New pitfall for the pharmaceutical industry' (2006) Journal of Intellectual Property Law & Practice 266 (arguing an inconsistency with the EU legal framework and prior ECJ jurisprudence).

[5]   S Lawrence and P Treacy, 'The commission's Astra Zeneca decision: delaying generic entry is abuse of a dominant position' (2005) Journal of Intellectual Property Law & Practice 7.

[6]   M Negrinotti, 'Abuse of Regulatory Procedures in the Intellectual Property Context: the AstraZeneca Case' (2008) 29 ECLR 446.

[7]   JM Mueller, 'Patent misuse through the capture of industry standards' (2002) 17 Berkeley Technology L Rev 623, 671.

[8]   Robin C Feldman, 'The insufficiency of antitrust analysis for patent misuse' (2003) 55 Hastings LJ 399, 399.

[9]   Some consider that these are distinct doctrines and should not be conflated, see, e.g., ibid. 400 et seq; Mueller (note 7) 654. Others would include within misuse those cases such as in *Astra Zeneca* that involve fraudulent IP formalities or otherwise wrongful conduct in obtaining of an IP grant, see, e.g., JB Kobak (ed), *Intellectual Property Misuse: Licensing and Litigation* (American Bar Assoc Section of Antitrust 2000) 68 (positing the confusion of misuse with a distinct doctrine of inequitable conduct). Agreement with the analysis that there is antitrust and misuse distinctly does not obviate the reality that there is a considerable body of case law which considers 'misuse' under each of those heads. Further, arguably all of three avenues involve conduct that seeks to extend the grant of IP in scope or duration since with the third category if no true grant has been made, any attempted exercise comprises an extension. The limits of this chapter, however, do

recourse to legal action can comprise such misuse. This is relevant in the context of whether a doctrine of misuse is emerging in the EU, since large and well-financed undertakings like AZ seek to protect their valuable inventions or trademarks and works throughout the world pursuant to proactive plans. They prosecute aggressively and tenaciously claims of infringement, including where the use is not infringing as claimed, or outside the scope of the right that is ultimately questioned. These facts, however, might never be determined to raise a misuse defense if the targeted defendant does not have the ability to fight the claim. A lack of defense resources thus enables misuse comprising overbroad enforcement or litigation (that is, the bringing of a legal action or petition objectively unjustified but privileged as relying on an IPR). This concern is one which the EU itself has raised in the context of European small and medium enterprises and their lack of recourse to patent protection.[10]

Clearly there are some likely differences between the American misuse doctrine and the principles developed in the *AZ* decision. The US doctrine of misuse under intellectual property law is an affirmative defense in a private law action that under antitrust is also usually raised as a claim or counterclaim in a private lawsuit seeking damages under the US antitrust statutes, which allows for such.[11] In contrast, *AZ* is a regulatory competition law enforcement action by the Commission. The recent devolution of full EU competition law enforcement to the Member States under Regulation 2003/1,[12] however, will likely result in growing numbers of private competition law claims or counterclaims asserted in the context of IP-related matters, possibly including assertions of IP misuse.

In light of this eventuality, Section 3 of this chapter explores the existence, if any, of EU doctrinal equivalents to the US misuse doctrine as it has developed under both IP law and antitrust. European Union-level legal doctrines that could comprise equivalents must have their basis in EU treaties or general principles of law. Misuse under US antitrust law is

---

not permit a detailed examination of inequitable conduct or the fraud doctrines in obtaining the grant outside a brief analysis of the scope of sham enforcement.

[10] See generally, e.g., 'Enforcing Small Firms' Patent Rights: Key Findings' (EU SME/Innovation Policy Studies 2001), <http://cordis.europa.eu/innovation-policy/studies/IM_study3.htm> accessed 24 March 2010.

[11] Section 4 of the Clayton Act permits treble damages and costs including attorney's fees to anyone injured by anything forbidden under the antitrust laws.

[12] Council Regulation (EC) No 1/2003 of 16 December 2002 on the implementation of the rules on competition laid down in Articles 81 and 82 of the Treaty [2003] OJ L1, 1–25.

the best avenue to begin analysis, with its seeming parallels to EU competition law premised on EC Treaty Articles 81 and 82 (hereafter Articles 101 and 102). The second avenue of misuse inquiry – based on violations of policy underlying the grant of intellectual property – is likely to pose more difficulties for coherence with EU law, as IPRs are national rights in origin and that can stem from different underlying policies. Here, however, there are several potential sources of equivalence. The first of these arises under the EC Treaty provisions regarding Freedom of Movement, Articles 28–30 (hereafter Articles 34–36), whereunder the EU courts have recognized that national IP rights can damage the Single Market when exercised beyond their scope.[13] Despite the distinct theoretical foundation, the practical reality is that the cases are usually so intertwined with competition law findings as not to be amenable to distinct application. Thus, this is considered solely within the competition law analysis. Other theories, however, offer interesting possibilities for parallels with US misuse under IP law: the emergent EU doctrine of abuse of rights within the community process of IP law harmonization. Claims and counterclaims on IP-related matters will also be considered.

Finally, the chapter asks whether the EU should adopt such a doctrine, even if it could do so. Here it considers whether there is a likely economic or other benefit, including social justice that would justify this restriction on the exercise of intellectual property rights.

2. THE US IP MISUSE DOCTRINE

US courts have recognized an affirmative defense arising from the misuse of IP rights and pursuant to legal theories distinct from antitrust violation for more than 90 years. There is not however a single, cohesive, consistent and fully developed 'doctrine' of 'IP misuse'. In addition to the variations in its application by the courts, IP misuse beyond patent can still be labeled 'emergent'. Its applicability to copyright is fairly recent[14] and

---

[13]   Text to notes 80–82.

[14]   While early cases based solely on 'unclean hands' applied the affirmative defense in copyright and trademark cases, see *Morton Salt* v *Suppiger*, 314 US 488, 494 (1942) (and cases cited therein), IP misuse has seemed to become somewhat detached from pure equity. Although the Supreme Court had clearly recognized patent misuse in numerous cases, the first modern case applying the misuse doctrine in copyright was *Lasercomb America* v *Reynolds*, 911 F 2d 970 (4th Cir 1990). However, some significant US courts continue to apply 'unclean hands' in an IP context without distinction, as the cases referenced in note 16 indicate.

still not fully agreed[15] and there are only very recent suggestions that it could apply to trademark.[16] Since the mentioned variations stem partly from its roots in another doctrine, the principles of equity and, specifically, 'unclean hands', a brief exploration of the history of IP misuse is needed here, as well as an attempt to define its parameters.

2.1   The Emergence and Foundations of IP Misuse as Violation of IP Public Policy

The affirmative defense of IP misuse to a claim of IP infringement or breach of IP contract[17] is directly founded on the equitable principle that one cannot seek equity with 'unclean hands'. Thus, where a claimant seeking equitable relief 'has violated conscience, or good faith, or other equitable principle, in his prior conduct . . . the court will refuse to interfere on his behalf, to acknowledge his right, or to award him any remedy'.[18] As one scholar notes, 'any and all misfeasance that smacks of injustice may constitute unclean hands'.[19] While unclean hands is not limited to intellectual property law, as the Supreme Court noted in its 1942 decision in *Morton Salt*,[20] courts at equity have refused to condone attempts to extend the privileged grant of IP exclusivity and upheld the unclean hands defense in the context of patent, trademark and copyright.[21] Because unclean hands'

---

[15]   See *Video Pipeline Inc* v *Buena Vista Home Entertainment, Inc* 342 F 3d 191 (3rd Cir 2003) (noting its lack of a decision on the issue to date). The Second Circuit appears not to have adopted copyright misuse either, with its decisions continuing under antitrust analysis or 'unclean hands'. At least one commentary has suggested that some courts may be awaiting Supreme Court approval of the doctrine. See MA Glick, LA Reymann, and R Hoffman, *Intellectual Property Damages: Guidelines and Analysis* (John Wiley & Sons, 2002) 300.

[16]   See e.g., *Google Inc* v *American Blind & Wallpaper Factory, Inc* (ND Cal CV 03-5340 JF 4/18/07) (Google had failed to establish 'unclean hands' as a bar to trademark infringement claim); *Estee Lauder* v *The Fragrance Counter* 189 FRD 269 (SDNY 1999) (denying motion to strike as legally insufficient a defense of 'unclean hands' in trademark infringement claim).

[17]   See JM Jacobson, 'C. Patent Copyright Misuse' in ABA Section of Antitrust Law, *Antitrust Law and Developments* (6th edn vol I ABA, 2007) 1140.

[18]   *Keystone Driller Co* v *General Excavator Co* 290 US 240, 245 (1933) (claimant which failed to disclose possible prior use of invention and obtained agreement from possible inventor to conceal such prior use in connection with related patents was sufficient to establish misuse).

[19]   TL Anenson, 'Treating equity like law: a post-merger justification of unclean hands' (2008) 45 Am Bus LJ 3, 455, 460.

[20]   *Morton Salt Co* v *GS Suppiger*, 314 US 488, 494 (1942).

[21]   See ibid. 494 (and cases cited therein).

public policy underpinnings include the courts not wishing to 'lend their power' to a wrongful act,[22] the defense can serve as a bar to enforcement of the intellectual property while the misuse continues and even where the other party was not harmed by the misuse, or is not blameless himself.[23] The courts have full 'free and just' discretion whether to allow the defense, since it is not intended as a punishment but rather to advance 'right and justice' in those circumstances.[24]

Although some courts continue to apply equity and unclean hands in cases involving the overbroad use and enforcement of IP rights,[25] misuse was untied from purely equitable foundations in *Morton Salt Co* v *GS Suppiger*.[26] In *Morton Salt* the claimant alleged that Morton Salt had infringed its patent in a machine for adding salt in commercial canning by Morton Salt's manufacture and sale of salt tablets, specially configured for the machine to licensees/lessees of the machine, whose licenses were conditioned on the use of Suppiger's own salt tablets. Below, the Court of Appeals for the 7th Circuit had overturned the trial court's dismissal of the complaint, granted on the basis that the patent was being used to restrain competition in the sale of unpatented salt tablets. The 7th Circuit concluded that it had not been shown that the tying had violated §3 of the Clayton Act either by the creation of a monopoly, or a substantial lessening of competition.[27] On appeal, the Supreme Court reversed and held that it need not reach the question of whether an antitrust violation had been established.[28] Rather, it found that Suppiger had used its monopoly, in the machine to restrain competition in the market for the unpatented salt tablets. In doing so, it had aided in the creation of a limited monopoly in the salt tablets that was not within the grant of the patent. The Court, in refusing to enforce the patent, considered patent law itself and the public

---

[22] *Johnson* v *Yellow Cab Transit Co* 321 US 383, 387 (1944).

[23] See, e.g., *Morton Salt* (note 20) 492; *Management Information Corp* v *American Medical Association* 121 F 3d 516 (9th Cir 1997) (misuse in AMA's licensing of its medical coding system to US government under condition that it not use any competing system despite that AMA did not enforce provision).

[24] *Keystone Driller* (note 18) 245; accord, *Johnson* v *Yellow Cab Transit Co* (note 22) 387.

[25] See e.g., *Google Inc* v *American Blind & Wallpaper Factory, Inc* (ND Cal CV 03–5340 JF 4/18/07) (Google had failed to establish 'unclean hands' as a bar to trademark infringement claim); *Estee Lauder* v *The Fragrance Counter*, 189 FRD 269 (SDNY 1999) (denying motion to strike as legally insufficient a defense of 'unclean hands' in trademark infringement claim).

[26] 314 US 488 (1942).

[27] Ibid. 489–91.

[28] Ibid.

policy underlying it. It held that patent law grants the patentee only the exclusive right to use or license a new and useful invention and to enforce those rights for the limited statutory period of exclusivity, a special privilege the grant of which effects a public policy to promote progress in useful arts and science.[29] The public policy, however, excludes everything that is not within the invention and 'equally forbids the use of the patent to secure an exclusive right or limited monopoly not granted by the Patent Office and which it is contrary to public policy to grant'.[30] This adverse effect on the public interest underlying the grant of the intellectual property right, together with the nature of the intellectual property right holder's conduct, prevented it from seeking the aid of the courts to enforce the grant where it is being used to subvert that public policy.[31]

The great discretion of courts at equity, noted by the *Morton Salt* Court, in applying this 'doctrine' of misuse that the Court appears to have premised simultaneously on possible harm to IP public policy, the conduct that subverts it, here anticompetitive,[32] and the principles of equitable justice, further appears to have contributed significantly to the lack of a cohesive body of law. Thus, as with the purely equitable application of 'unclean hands' every seeming 'rule' for IP misuse, including to whom it applies, how it is applied and whether it should be applied at all as described above has found variation in the courts. For example, even in the threshold issue of when the defense can be raised considerable differences exist: some courts require that the misuse be limited to the specific IP exercise at issue in the lawsuit; others, in contrast, permit a misuse defense, even where it involved a third party and not the defendant.[33] Sometimes the defendant's

---

[29]   Ibid. 492.

[30]   Ibid. 492.

[31]   Ibid. 494.

[32]   The nature of the conduct subverting the public policy underlying the particular IP grant need not always be anticompetitive. See, e.g., *Rosemont Enters, Inc v Random House, Inc* 366 F 2d 303 (2d Cir 1966) (Lumbard CJ and Hays J) (concurring opinion) (injunctive relief, an equitable remedy, should have been denied Howard Hughes company created to purchase copyright in three articles briefly quoted in a biography about Howard Hughes in order to try and restrain publication of a biography about him where substantial similarity to prior works inevitably due to the need to treat major events in a life and purpose was merely to restrain publication, thereby subvert that public policy underlying copyright to promote creative expression and disseminate information) (under 'unclean hands' doctrine since copyright misuse not doctrine in the 2d Circuit). See *Video Pipeline, Inc v Buena Vista Home Entertainment, Inc* 342 F 3d 191 (3rd Cir 2003).

[33]   See, e.g., *Morton Salt Co v GS Suppinger* 314 US 488, 492 (1942), *Management Information Corp v American Medical Association* 121 F 3d 516 (9th Cir 1997) (misuse in AMA's licensing of its medical coding system to US govern-

lack of 'clean hands' has precluded misuse from being asserted; other courts have held otherwise. Adding to the confusion, as previously noted, is the continued application of 'unclean hands' in the IP context.[34]

In terms of the conduct constituting misuse, some courts have upheld the defense based solely on the overbroad exercise of IP attempting to expand the subject matter of the protection (or the substantive scope of the right) and applied the distinct IP policy considerations under *Morton Salt*.[35] Other courts, including the Federal Circuit Court of Appeals with its nearly exclusive patent jurisdiction, have set virtually the same requirements for establishing both misuse under IP public policy and misuse that gives rise to antitrust violation.[36] Other courts fail to make a distinction between the two bodies of law[37] requiring market power and harm to competition,[38] as described below.

2.2   IP Misuse and The Interface With Antitrust

The overlapping of the affirmative misuse defense under IP law and equity, with a claimed misuse of IPRs comprising a violation of antitrust law – the former a shield, the latter a sword – has caused some confusion. However, an attempt to exercise IPRs overbroadly, such as, beyond their scope or term, is not likely to infringe antitrust law unless it involves a per se violation like minimum post-sale price restrictions[39] or post-patent royalties[40] or the rights owner has market power and the exercise causes competitive harm to the market, as with other antitrust violations.[41] Some view the requirement to show market power of itself as possibly

---

ment under condition that it not use any competing system despite that AMA did not enforce provision).

[34]   See, e.g., cases cited in note 16.

[35]   See *Assessment Technologies of WI, LLC* v *WIREdata, Inc* 350 F 3d 640 (7th Cir 2003) (Posner J); *Lasercomb America* v *Reynolds*, 911 F 2d 970 (4th Cir 1990).

[36]   See H Hovenkamp, MD Janis and MA Lemley, 'Principles of Patent Misuse' in *IP and Antitrust* (Aspen Publishers 2005 Supplement) § 3.2; Feldman (note 8) (questioning the validity of such approach).

[37]   Ibid. § 3.1.

[38]   See, e.g., *Windsurfing Int'l, Inc* v *AMF, Inc* 782 F 2d 995 (Fed Cir), *cert denied*, 477 US 905 (1986). The Federal Circuit has however also indicated that misuse is broader than antitrust.

[39]   *Mallinckrodt* v *Medipart*, 976 F 2d 700 (Fed Cir 1992).

[40]   *Brulotte* v *Thys* 379 US 29 (1964) (patent misuse claim under patent law, but since the focus of this much criticized decision was the harm to competition and monopoly, it is arguable that a per se antitrust violation could exist as well).

[41]   See Feldman (note 8) 400.

excluding much patent-related behavior from the reach of antitrust.[42] However, since patent is no longer presumed to confer market power, this showing becomes somewhat less likely.[43] While conduct that amounts to an infringement of antitrust is likely to establish IP misuse therefore,[44] the reverse is not necessarily true.[45]

In further contrast to the affirmative IP law defense, under antitrust the conduct of the claimant is largely irrelevant unless it is sufficient to comprise an independent antitrust violation that can be pursued by the government or private parties in appropriate proceedings, which can include a counterclaim by the defendant.[46] Otherwise, the Supreme Court has held that neither unclean hands in the context of unrelated illegal conduct,[47] nor another analogous common law defense, *in pari delicto* ('equal guilt') in the conduct in issue, can be raised as a defense in the context of a private antitrust suit, as it would undermine the public policy that private suits should serve as an ever-present threat to anticompetitive behavior.[48]

In one instance, however, the intellectual property law itself creates

---

[42]   See, e.g., JM Mueller (note 7) 654.

[43]   *Illinois Tool Works* v *Independent Ink* 547 US 28 (2006) (holding that plaintiff alleging antitrust violation in the tying of patented and unpatented product must prove market power and can no longer benefit from presumption that patent confers same).

[44]   The DOJ/FTC recent report 'Antitrust Enforcement and Intellectual Property Rights: Promoting Innovation and Competition' opines that, as far as the agencies are concerned in the context of their antitrust enforcement activity, while the Patent Law at 35 USC § 271(d)(4) removes from patent misuse the refusal to license, it does not create an exemption from antitrust. See ibid. at Ch 1, s IV (A) <http://www.ftc. gov/reports/innovation/P040101PromotingInnovationandCompetitionrpt0704. pdf> last accessed 24 March 2010.

[45]   See e.g., *Transitron Electronic Corp* v *Hughes Aircraft Co* 487 F Supp 885, 892–93 (D Mass 1980), *aff'd*, 649 F 2d 871 (1st Cir 1981).

[46]   See *Bubis* v *Blanton* 885 F 2d 317, 321(6th Cir 1989).

[47]   *Kiefer-Stewart Co* v *Joseph E Seagram & Sons, Inc* 340 US 211, 214 (1951), overruled on other grounds, *Copperweld Corp* v *Independence Tube Corp* 467 US 752 (1984).

[48]   *Perma Life Mufflers* v *Int'l Parts Corp* 392 US 134 (1968), overruled on other grounds, *Copperweld Corp* v *Independence Tube Corp* 467 US 752 (1984). Other courts have limited *Perma Life* to analogous situations and have allowed an *in pari delicto* defense where the plaintiff is equally culpable and its application would not contravene antitrust enforcement. This distinction in the context of antitrust is not at first glance logical since private copyright enforcement is also statutory and also based on public policy that could be undermined by unclean hands defense. However, unlike antitrust, an IP misuse is not premised on the deterrent effect but on the court's participation in the undermining of the limited grant of the IP right.

a requirement parallel to antitrust. An amendment to the Patent Act requires that market power be established to assert an affirmative defense of patent misuse for tying, a change made by Congress to bring it in conformity with antitrust.[49]

No such limitation exists in the Copyright Act, however.[50] This may partly be due to the fact that the misuse doctrine under copyright public policy was largely dormant until the 1990 decision in *Lasercomb America* v *Reynolds*,[51] which affirmed its viability.[52] This case also, however, upheld the affirmative defense in a situation not arising to the level of an antitrust violation. *Lasercomb* has led some to conclude that it makes clear that misuse, both patent and copyright, is premised on different policy considerations from antitrust and is, therefore, not tied to antitrust. Indeed, this was suggested by Judge Posner in *Assessment Technologies* v *WireData* stating that *Lasercomb* and other cases 'cut misuse free from antitrust, pointing out that the cognate doctrine of patent misuse is not so limited'.[53] This would seem the better reasoned analysis, although some contend that *Lasercomb*'s analysis is limited to copyright, pointing to the greater conflation of patent misuse with antitrust and ascribing this to inherent differences in the policy underpinnings of patent and copyright[54] or contend that *Lasercomb* is wrongly decided, even in the context of copyright, in light of the recent trend to apply an economic analysis and rule of reason to intellectual property.[55] The practical difference in terms of misuse or antitrust may be limited since, as Judge Posner further notes, patent will more often and more likely confer market power than will copyright.[56]

---

[49]   See Rudolph Peritz, 'Competition Policy and its Implications for Intellectual Property Rights in the USA' in S Anderman (ed), *The Interface between Intellectual Property Rights and Competition Policy* (Cambridge University Press, Cambridge 2007) 152. Indeed, as Hovenkamp notes (note 34, §22.3c), the proof of tying product market power proceeds under the ordinary antitrust analysis.

[50]   35 USC § 271(d)(5). While some claimed this suggested a requirement of market power for other misuse claims, courts applying the doctrine beyond the patent tying context have not found themselves so constrained. The act also defines conduct which cannot be considered misuse such as conduct that would otherwise amount to contributory infringement by a patent owner and the refusal to license.

[51]   911 F 2d 970 (4th Cir 1990).

[52]   Congress has had occasion to amend the Copyright Act since then but has not made this change.

[53]   350 F 3d 640, 647 (7th Cir 2003).

[54]   See, e.g., Peritz (note 49).

[55]   Ibid.

[56]   350 F 3d at 647.

These and other developments[57] signal a continuing viability of an IP misuse defense distinct from antitrust. Arguments that the IP misuse defense is nearly defunct are largely based on the Federal Circuit's previously noted conflation of the requirements for both doctrines, as this Court has exclusive statutory appellate jurisdiction in patent cases.[58] This has had a significant impact on the doctrine of patent misuse; the 2002 Supreme Court decision in *Holmes Group, Inc v Vornado*[59] could change that somewhat. Here the Supreme Court limited the Federal Circuit's patent appeal jurisdiction to only those civil actions where 'the right to relief necessarily depends on resolution of a substantial question of federal patent law', stated in a well pleaded complaint but not other civil law claims.[60] As IP misuse is an affirmative defense and primarily judge-made law, other circuit courts of appeal under *Holmes* may therefore have the opportunity to decide patent misuse defense issues in cases raising patent-related contract claims, counterclaims or declaratory judgments where they could still have subject-matter jurisdiction premised on the parties' diversity of domicile. Unless and until Congress reverses the effects of *Holmes* in subsequent legislation, the other Circuits under their equitable discretion are free to apply other requirements for patent misuse[61] subject to the statutory or per se limitations previously discussed.[62] Also, unless the Supreme Court does rule otherwise

---

[57] For other cases following *Lasercomb*, see, e.g., *Alcatel USA, Inc v DGI Techs, Inc* 166 F 3d 772 (5th Cir 1999) (copyright misuse in restriction of software license to claimant's operating system); *Practice Management Info Corp v American Medical Association* 121 F 3d 516, 520 (9th Cir 1997) (copyright misuse in restriction on licensee to buy competing product); *PRC Realty Sys, Inc v Nat'l Ass'n. of Realtors, Inc* 972 F 2d 341 (4th Cir 1992).

[58] 28 USC § 1295 (1983) created the Federal Circuit granting it exclusive jurisdiction over appeals from federal district courts in all IP related claims in which they have original jurisdiction under 28 USC § 1338 except copyright: patents, plant variety protection, mask works, designs, trademarks, and unfair competition.

[59] 535 US 826 (2002).

[60] Ibid. 830 (quoting *Christianson v Colt Industries Operating Corp.*, 486 US 800, 809 (1988).

[61] This does not mean that they will necessarily do so. A 7th Circuit decision, *Country Materials v Allan Block*, while deciding that it had *Holmes* jurisdiction in a declaratory judgment action seeking a declaration that a patent license for a concrete block manufacturing process was unenforceable due to patent misuse in the 18 month non-compete clause beyond the contract's termination, applied followed the Federal Circuit. It applied the test of *Virginia Panel Corp v MAC Panel Co* 133 F 3d 860 (1997) and required a showing of anticompetitive effect on the broader market for concrete blocks.

[62] Text to notes 38–39.

on copyright and other IP misuse, the Circuits are free to continue to exercise their equitable discretion and refuse to enforce IP rights where their owners seek to broaden them beyond the bounds of the right as granted.

2.3   IPR Enforcement as Misuse

Litigation brought to enforce an IPR can in limited instances[63] comprise either of the common law torts of malicious filing of civil proceedings or abuse of process, as well as an antitrust violation, irrespective of the action having been 'privileged' as relying on that IPR. Malicious filing of civil suit requires that an action be filed or continued without probable cause to believe it will succeed, with an improper motivation and be concluded in favor of the defendant with resulting damage suffered.[64] Abuse of process is a bit broader in that it extends to the process beyond the original filing of the suit. The Restatement Second of Torts at section 682 provides that '[o]ne who uses a legal process . . . against another primarily to accomplish a purpose for which it is not designed, is subject to liability to the other for harm caused by the abuse of process.' Effectively an abuse of process is using a lawsuit to accomplish a purpose collateral to the lawsuit. In the context of IP misuse it has been noted that this could include where a party brings an:

> . . . infringement suit to obtain property protection, that the . . . law clearly does not confer, hoping to force a settlement or even achieve an outright victory over an opponent that may lack the resources or the legal sophistication to resist effectively.[65]

Although a prevailing claim or the filing of the suit itself could have an anticompetitive effect, for litigation, including IP enforcement, to rise to the level of an antitrust violation, it must fall within the 'sham' litigation

---

[63]   Concerns that claimants would be unduly deterred from recourse to the courts to protect valid interests have resulted in these being fairly limited in scope and application.

[64]   Restatement Second of Torts, §§ 677–9. With malicious prosecution as it is sometimes called (which can apply to criminal actions as well), some jurisdictions require a showing of ill will or malice in the filing of the lawsuit.

[65]   *Assessment Technologies of WI, LLC* v *WIREdata, Inc* 350 F 3d 640, 647 (7th Cir 2003)(Posner J) (speaking of a lawsuit to obtain copyright in pure data). For an economic analysis of why a defendant would yield to the threat of such likely weak claims, see MJ Meurer, 'Controlling Opportunistic and Anticompetitive Intellectual Property Litigation' (February 2007) 44 BC Law Rev 510.

exception to what is called the 'Noerr-Pennington' doctrine.[66] This US doctrine protects the exercise of First Amendment rights to petition government bodies including courts via the filing of lawsuits by generally precluding antitrust liability therefore.[67] The Supreme Court in *Professional Real Estate Investors, Inc, v Columbia Pictures Industries, Inc*[68] articulated a two-part test for when litigation falls within this 'sham' exception and, notably, in the context of a copyright claim that the appellant contended was a sham. The test requires both a showing that the action is objectively baseless in that 'no reasonable litigant could realistically expect success on the merits' and, only where this is established, that the litigant's subjective motivation in filing the suit was 'an attempt to interfere directly' with a competitor's business relationships. A lawsuit has been held not to be objectively baseless 'simply because a litigant lost'[69] or 'had a reasonable belief' that there was a chance its claim would be upheld.[70] Because subjective intent alone cannot be the basis for a finding of sham litigation, the second part of the 'sham test', focusing on the existence of an anticompetitive animus in bringing the suit, cannot even be considered unless the essential legal meritlessness is objectively established.[71] With regard to Section 2 of the Sherman Act, the second prong considers whether the conduct may be deemed as aiming at monopolization of markets through the unlawful elimination or weakening of competitors.[72] If both prongs are

[66] The Noerr-Pennington doctrine balances First Amendment rights with antitrust law, holding that it is not a violation of antitrust to petition government such as to influence laws or their enforcement even to eliminate competition. This doctrine stems from two earlier cases, *Eastern Railroad Presidents Conference* v *Noerr Motor Freight, Inc* 365 US 127 (1961) (holding that while Sherman Act does not prohibit private parties from together lobbying the government to take action that would 'produce a restraint or a monopoly' if those efforts 'directed toward influencing governmental action, is a mere sham to cover what is actually nothing more than an attempt to interfere directly with the business relationships of a competitor. . . the application of the Sherman Act would be justified.') and *United Mine Workers* v *Pennington* 381 US 657 (1965) (holding that the party's intent is irrelevant to antitrust immunity). Since a lawsuit is merely another form of petitioning government, i.e., the courts, the doctrine applies to lawsuits.

[67] CJ Renk, ES Maurer and ML Krashin, 'Practical Antitrust at the Antitrust-Patent Interface: Sham Litigation, Fraudulent Procurement, Bad Faith Enforcement, and Illinois Tool Works' (May 2006) IP Litigator.

[68] 508 US 49 (1993).

[69] *Baltimore Scrap Corp* v *David J Joseph Co* 237 F 3d 394, 399 (4th Cir 2001).

[70] *Prof Real Estate Investors*, 508 US 49, 63 (1993).

[71] Ibid. at 60.

[72] This is a much-applied principle. See, most recently, *Applera Corp* v *MJ Research Inc* 303 F Supp 2d 130 (D Conn 2004); *Organon Inc* v *Mylan*

satisfied, the filing of a proceeding will be considered 'sham' and outside of the Noerr-Pennington immunity, thereby bringing the provisions of antitrust law into play.

However, one cannot disregard how difficult it is in practice to satisfy the test, given that courts must not take into account the outcome of the proceedings, but instead must consider matters as they stood *ex ante*.[73] In other words, the assessment is centered on whether, at the time the undertaking brought the suit, it was in good faith and could 'reasonably' have believed its action was well-founded in law, based on relevant precedent. The Second and Ninth Circuit Courts of Appeal have limited, however, the *Professional Real Estate Investors* two-part test to the filing of a single action and have held that a 'pattern' of vexatious litigation or other government administrative processes can give rise to the 'sham' exception to Noerr-Pennington where, prospectively, it can be shown that the legal filings were made, not out of a genuine interest in redressing grievances, but as part of a pattern or practice of successive filings undertaken essentially for purposes of harassment.[74] In these cases the fact that some of the claims might, 'as a matter of chance' have merit is immaterial to the claim. Rather, the relevant issue is whether the legal challenges are file pursuant to a policy of starting legal proceedings without regard to the merits and for the purpose of injuring a market rival.[75]

Although some courts merge it with the 'sham' litigation exception, a distinct and further exception to the Noerr-Pennington doctrine is the '*Walker Process*' exception after the Supreme Court holding in *Walker Process Equipment, Inc* v *Food Machinery & Chemical Corporation*[76] that

---

Pharmaceuticals, Inc 293 F Supp 2d 453 (DNJ 2003); *Fedders Corporation* v *Elite Classics* 279 F Supp 2d 965 (SD Ill 2003); *Mariana* v *Fischer* 338 F 3d 189 (3rd Cir 2003).

[73] The test has been widely criticized as overly restrictive. See e.g. the statement of Judge Posner in *Grip-Pak, Inc* v *Illinois Tool Works, Inc* 694 F 2d 566 (7th Cir 1982): 'litigation could be used for improper purposes even when there is probable cause for the litigation: and if the improper purpose is to use litigation as a tool for suppressing competition in its antitrust sense, it becomes a "matter of antitrust course".' Cf. L Wood, 'In praise of the Noerr-Pennington doctrine' (18-Fall) Antitrust 2003, 72; M Lad, 'Reforming immunity doctrine' (2003) 55 Rutgers LR, 965.

[74] See *Primetime 24 Joint Venture* v *Nat'l Broad Corporation*, 219 F.3d 92, 101 (2d Cir 2000) (quoting *USS-POSCO Indus* v *Contra Costa County Building & Construction Trades Council*, 31 F 3d 800, 810–11 (9th Cir 1994)); see also *Amarel* v *Connell*, 102 F 3d 1494, 1519 (9th Cir 1996) (while adopting the USS-POSCO test, finding it inapplicable to the two lawsuits alleged to meet it).

[75] Ibid.

[76] 382 US 172 (1965).

enforcing a patent procured by fraud on the Patent Office can be the basis of an antitrust violation where the other elements of an infringement are present.[77] The tests for this vary among different courts with some imposing greater evidentiary burdens than others, including requiring proof of common law fraud and a threshold level of enforcement of the allegedly fraudulently procured patent (which likely gives rise to categorization of it as a 'sham' litigation exception).[78]

3.   DOES EU LAW PROVIDE A MISUSE DOCTRINE EQUIVALENT?

Whether the EU has in *AZ* recognized, or opened the door for, a doctrine of IP misuse requires exploring doctrinal equivalents to the US IP misuse doctrine within Community Law. European Union-level legal doctrines that could comprise such equivalents must have their basis in EU treaties or general principles of law.

TFEU Articles 101 and 102, the competition law articles, are the more likely avenues to begin analysis. An IP misuse amounting to a breach of competition law within the EU system and similar to the US IP misuse violating antitrust law arguably exists. A Community-based doctrine of misuse grounded on IP law policy violations (not caught under competition law) poses more difficulties since IPRs are national in origin and scope. Even where Community harmonization of IP law exists, it varies among the IPRs and in how Member States implement it. However, several potential sources of this misuse equivalence are theoretically available. The first of these arises from early EU court decisions holding the exercise beyond the substantive scope of the IPR in question, that is, beyond the 'specific subject matter' of the protection, as not justifiable under Article 36 of the EC Treaty, governing exceptions to freedom of

---

[77]   Ibid. 174. See, e.g., *Bristol-Myers Squibb Corporation* v *Ben Venue Laboratories*, 90 F Supp 2d 540, 542 (DNJ 2000) (fraudulent procurement of a patent or enforcement of a patent knowingly obtained by fraud as a basis of Sherman Act violation, under *Walker Process*); *CR Bard, Inc* v *M3Systems, Inc*, 157 F 3d 1340, 1340, 1367 (Fed Cir 1998) (holding that antitrust liability under section 2 of the Sherman Act may arise when a patent has been procured by knowing and willful fraud).

[78]   See BD Daniel, '*Walker Process* proof: the proper prescription' (Draft) (5 January 2010), Rutgers Law Journal, Forthcoming; Lawyers, Drugs & Money Symposium, *Lawyers, Drugs & Money: A Prescription for Antitrust Enforcement in the Pharmaceutical Industry*, available at SSRN: <http://ssrn.com/abstract=1531854>.

movement principle.[79] The conduct in these cases was also typically found to breach competition law.[80] As the ECJ has noted, the application or exercise of an IPR can serve equally as an arbitrary discrimination or a disguised restriction on trade between the Member States, as well as give effect to an agreement, decision or concerted practice which may have as its object or effect the prevention, restriction or distortion of competition within the common market. [81]

Because the conduct exercising IPR beyond its geographical, substantive or temporal scope that has been analyzed under the freedom of movement provision was in most cases also infringing competition law, and because there are some textual similarity in the language of these distinct treaty provisions,[82] the holdings of these two lines of cases are not always amenable to distinct analysis. This well-established EU case law related to IPR exercise beyond its scope needs therefore to be considered also in the context of the competition law breaches.

The second avenue of IP misuse enquiry which, in principle, such cases could also fall is one that offers interesting possibilities for doctrinal parallels with US misuse under IP law: the emergent Community abuse of rights doctrine. This would address conduct violative of the policy underlying the grant of IPRs, yet not amounting to breach of competition law or harm to the Single Market. Both avenues are addressed below.

3.1 IP Misuse, Competition Law and Harm to the Single Market

Both the physical, or substantive, scope and the temporal scope of IP protection can be exercised in a way that comprises a violation of EU competition law. This can arise from either multilateral or unilateral conduct, the former caught under the prohibition of anti-competitive agreements

---

[79] *Consten and Grundig* v *Commission* Joined Cases 56 & 58/64 [1966] ECR 299; [1966] CMLR 418; *Deutsche Grammophon* v *Metro* (78/70) [1971] ECR 487; Case C-15/74 *Centrafarm* v *Sterling Drug* [1974] ECR 1147; [1974] 2 CMLR 480.

[80] *Consten and Grundig* v *Commission* Joined Cases 56 & 58/64 [1966] ECR 299; [1966] CMLR 418; *Deutsche Grammophon* v *Metro* (78/70) [1971] ECR 487; Case C-15/74 *Centrafarm* v *Sterling Drug* [1974] ECR 1147; [1974] 2 CMLR 480.

[81] See, *Coditel* v *Cine Vog*, [1982] ECR 3381, 13–14; *Coditel Cine Vog*, [1980] ECR 881, 15.

[82] The language of the treaty provisions themselves can also be seen as contributing to the lack of precision in the decisions between the two doctrines: restrictions on trade under Article 36 vs. agreements restricting competition where they affect trade under 101, abuse of dominant position affecting trade under Article 102, between Member States. However, each doctrine has a distinct purpose as discussed further. See text accompanying notes 87–102, *infra*.

of Article 101 – the latter under the Article 102 abuse of dominant position prohibition. In both cases, competition law principles are applied
notwithstanding the existence of an IPR. The holding in *AZ* confirms this.
At a basic level the EU Commission finds that AZ breached EU competition law in abusing its dominance by fraudulently extending the temporal
and substantive scope of its patent monopoly (Article 102 Treaty).[83] As
expressly stated by the Commission:

> . . . AZ conduct can hardly be described as belonging to the subject-matter of
> the rights in question. . . . [T]he making of misleading representation is not
> included in the bundle of rights forming part of the subject-matter of a SPC.
> Moreover, the acquisition of a right may amount to an abuse and there is there-
> fore no reason why the conduct in the procedure relating to the acquisition of
> the right cannot be considered as an abuse.[84]

AZ's conduct, however, not only constitutes abuse of dominant position according to Article 102, but would also fall within the case law that
forbids the exercise of nationally-based IPRs beyond their proper scope,
under freedom of movement Articles 34–36 EC Treaty.[85] A few considerations are necessary here regarding the relation between Articles 101
and 102 on the one hand and Articles 34–36[86] on the other, as both sets of
provisions have been used to prevent IPR exercise beyond their scope.

Articles 101 and 102 prohibit anti-competitive agreements having as their
object or effect the prevention, restriction or distortion of competition and

---

[83]   AZ (note 1) § 773.

[84]   Ibid. § 742. Moreover the Commission affirms that '. . . although the IPR
laws are national and it is for national legislature to determine the conditions and
rules regarding the protection conferred by intellectual property rights'; however,
Member States' laws '. . . are not affected by qualifying as abusive the misleading
representations made in the context of the applications for intellectual property
rights, in the absence of which the right or rights in question would not normally
have been granted.' (§ 741)

[85]   See *Consten and Grundig* v *Commission* and other cases cited in note 80.

[86]   There are four EU treaty 'freedoms' which are considered the cornerstones
of this economic union or the 'single market'. These are the freedom of movement of goods, services, capital and people that are enshrined in various treaty
articles. While the discussion here concerns the freedom of goods under Treaty
articles 34–36, when IP issues involved non-corporeal exercises such as downloads
or broadcasts, considered services, the ECJ accorded analogous treatment under
now Article 56 which precludes restrictions on freedom of movement of services,
see *Coditel SA* v *Ciné-Vog Films SA*, ECJ Reports 1982, p. 3381, ¶ 13, despite no
equivalent derogation for services to now Article 36 for industrial property protection which the Court has construed to include copyright, patent, trademark,
design, etc.

abuse of dominance respectively, where such activities have an effect on interstate trade within the Single Market; Articles 34–36 prohibit restrictions on the free movement of goods between Member States. Specifically, Articles 34 and 35 prohibit restrictions on imports and exports – and equivalent measures – between Member States. Article 36 specifies limited derogations from this ban, as well as any equivalent measure, on the grounds including, *inter alia*, the 'protection of industrial and commercial property', under which the ECJ has construed IPRs to fall. Therefore, the existence of state-based IPRs, per se, does not run afoul of the treaty. When a conflict arises between free movement of goods and IPRs a 'qualified priority' should be given to the latter. [87] However, the Treaty requires that such restrictions 'shall not constitute a means of arbitrary discrimination or a disguised restriction on trade between Member States' (Article 36). Community law, therefore does not affect the *existence* of IPRs,[88] but can limit their *exercise* when this comprises a restriction on trade between Member States violating Article 34.[89]

The same *exercise* of IPRs beyond their scope can infringe competition law where it consists of right holders' behaviors that are not consistent with the exclusive right which they have been granted, as was the case with AZ's use of IPRs beyond their temporal scope.[90] Although two distinct areas of Community law,[91] the continued intertwining of principles between Articles 101 and 102 on the one hand and 34–36 on the other by the EU bodies has been noted.[92] Both sets of rules can limit IPR exercise beyond the scope and both aim at preventing trade between Member

---

[87] DT Keeling, *Intellectual Property Rights in EU Law* (Oxford University Press, Oxford 2003) 28.

[88] This is not fully accurate although stated sweepingly by the court in the cases mentioned in note 79.

[89] *Deutsche Grammophon* v *Metro* (note 80) 487. *Coditel* v *Ciné-Vog* (note 81), ¶

[90] Indeed, such restrictions should not impede right holders from commercially exploiting and morally protecting their works, rather, they should prevent them from expanding the boundaries of their rights outside their traditional scope through the adoption of behavior falling outside the specific subject matter of the exclusive right. For a survey of 'existence versus exercise', 'exhaustion of rights', and the 'specific subject matter' doctrine, see P Craig and G De Burca, *EU Law* (3rd edn Oxford University Press, Oxford 2003) 1108.

[91] R O'Loughlin, 'EC Competition Rules and Free Movement Rules: an Examination of the Parallels and their Furtherance by the ECJ Wouters Decision' (2003) ECLR 62, 62.

[92] A Martinazzi, 'The Effect of *Wouters* on Professional Regulation Intertwining Public Policy, Proportionality and the Rule of Reason' (Cahiers Europeen), http://www.cahiers.org/new/htm/articoli/martinazzi_wouters.htm.

States from being restricted, thereby both have been applied to the same situation to curtail the abuse of IPRs.[93] The dual application of both set of rules is most frequent when situations involving IPR exercise beyond their scope are at stake. Such factors make it difficult to draw a neat line in practice between cases traceable back to Articles 101 and 102 and cases traceable back to Articles 34–36, especially where the conduct involves dominant players in any event, although not required for either Articles 101 or 34. Theoretically, though, the distinction is very clear and needs to be pointed out, as it enriches the avenue of misuse enquiry – IPR misuse amounting to a violation of EU competition law – as a parallel means and possibly 'shortcut' to the other avenue.

Both sets of the Treaty provisions share the same goal: establishing and fostering the Single Market, yet they pursue their goal through different paths.[94] Articles 101 and 102 achieve this aim by protecting competition among market players, Articles 34–36 by protecting freedom of movement of goods.[95] In cases involving Articles 34–36, the Single Market is directly impaired by the overbroad exercise of a national IPR amounting to a disguised restriction on trade, with no need to assess further the actual harm to competition. IPR exercise beyond its scope comprising such restriction therefore enables courts to consider the free movement Treaty provisions impaired. The EU jurisdictional threshold is met as the restraint on the freedom of movement affects trade between Member States. In cases involving Articles 101 and 102 the harm to the Single Market is indirect, as it is not the sole effect or object of the agreement or concerned practice, nor the sole result of an abuse of dominant position. This is the case with both those IPR licensing agreements that do not deal with territorial restric-

---

[93]   Ibid. 64–65 (noting that '[t]he duality of the operation of free movement principles with competition rules is very much apparent in the ECJ's treatment of the issue of parallel imports. . . . The synthesis with Arts 81 and 82 is that where an undertaking attempts unilaterally, or as part of an arrangement with another undertaking, to cause such a market partitioning, it is in breach of Arts 81(1) and/or 82. The uniformity of operation of Arts 81 and 82, on the one hand, and Art 28, on the other, is very apparent here as both operate to recognise the existence of intellectual property rights and to curtail the abuse of their exercise.').

[94]   P Craig and G De Burca, *EU Law* (note 90).

[95]   Or, as pointed out by I Govaere, *The Use and Abuse of Intellectual Property Rights in E.C. Law* (Sweet & Maxwell, London 1996), 42, '[t]he first are aimed at curtailing anti-competitive behaviour of economic actors which may affect intra-Community trade whereas the latter are mainly aimed at removing obstacles posed by national law to intra-Community trade.'

tions, yet are still caught under the Article 101 prohibition,[96] or those abuses of dominant position where the dominant undertaking uses its IPR in a way to breach Article 102 but does not partition the Single Market. In such cases, when requirements under Articles 101 and 102 are met,[97] the conduct can be straightforwardly assessed as violative of competition law, even though harm to the Single Market is not established. While concerns about the Single Market still tend to be mentioned, this dicta seems more to strengthen the courts' position than to serve as a real weapon to prevent IPR holders, using their exclusive rights beyond their scope.

Thus, there exists in the EU a multilayered system that theoretically can reach misuse in the IPR exercise beyond the scope of the right. That which harms competition can be caught under Articles 101 and 102 when the respective requirements therein set are met; that which directly hampers the Single Market can be caught under Articles 34–36. IPR exercise beyond the scope that hampers both competition and the Single Market can be caught under both sets of provisions,[98] a scenario most likely to occur as confirmed by the *AZ* case, where both the Single Market and competition were harmed. AZ's behavior is specifically deemed to harm the Single Market.[99] It seems, however, that the Single Market harm is raised merely to reinforce the anti-competitiveness of AZ's overall behavior; it does not serve as an independent basis of liability. Its deregistration of the capsule formulation and shift to a new formulation in order to avoid parallel imports were deemed to impede the Single Market,[100] yet being part of the overall anticompetitive strategy of AZ, these have been absorbed within the abuse of dominant position. When dominance can be readily assessed, as in the case of *AZ*,[101] competition law is the easiest and most efficient way to prevent the dominant undertaking's behaviors, and no specific challenge under any other body of provisions is needed.

The EU avenue of misuse amounting to breach of competition law appears somewhat broader than the US misuse amounting to violation of antitrust. IPR exercise beyond its scope can be considered to be the doctrinal equivalent of IP misuse amounting to violation of antitrust law when typically the IPR holder abuses its dominant position. However, within

---

[96]   R Whish, *Competition Law* (5th edn Reed Elsevier, Suffolk 2003) 743.
[97]   See generally ibid., chapters 3, 4 and 5.
[98]   A thorough discussion of the different situations that trigger the application of one set of provisions or the other as well as the remedies is outside the scope of this work and is available in O'Loughlin (note 91) 62.
[99]   AZ (n 1) §§ 794–5.
[100]   Ibid. §§ 818–20.
[101]   Ibid. § 601.

this avenue there falls also the case of IPR exercise beyond its scope that harms the Single Market, infringing Articles 34–36 on freedom of movement, unique to the EU system.[102]

3.2   IP Misuse and the 'Abuse of Rights' Doctrine

Having established that US IP misuse doctrine amounting to violation of antitrust law finds analogy within EU law, the assessment of conduct violating the public policy underlying the grant of IPRs but not violative of competition law remains to be explored. In the US this conduct would be assessed according to the standards of the IPR misuse doctrine. In the EU there is no equivalent to IPR misuse per se; however, there is a recent jurisprudential development within which IPR misuse may fall: the emerging Community 'abuse of rights' doctrine.[103] Although IPR cases have not yet been evaluated in light of these principles, a closer analysis of this doctrine is warranted for possible application to IP.

There is not an established definition of 'abuse of rights', but there is a growing number of Community cases identifying the circumstances in which an abuse of right may be deemed to have occurred.[104] The EU abuse of rights is rooted in the analogous concept encompassed in many Member States' legal systems of continental Europe.[105] At the national level, a basic form of abuse of rights can be defined as 'the exercise of a person's rights in a manner which is unreasonable, with consequent harm to another, whether there was an intent to harm or mere carelessness or indifference as to harm resulting.'[106] At the Community level, EU courts have recognized an abuse of rights doctrine in various areas of Community law.

---

[102]   In the early decisions mentioned in note 80, the emphasis on Articles 34–36 is to trace back to the early phases of the EU's establishment and to the need establishing firmly the Single Market. This pushed the Commission and the ECJ to consider additional and more direct means to limit the use of national IPRs to repartition the Single Market. The Treaty provisions on free movement provided those means even in the absence of the dominance required under Article 102, or of an agreement or concerned practice required under Article 101. Whether parallels with this doctrine might be found with the intersect of state granted IPRs and the interstate commerce clause of the US Constitution would need to be explored further.

[103]   KE Sorensen, 'Abuse of rights in community law: a principle of substance or merely rethoric?' (2006) 43 CML Rev 423.

[104]   A Kjellgren, 'On the border of abuse' (2000) European Business Law Review 179.

[105]   P Schammo, 'Arbitrage and abuse of rights in the EC legal system' (2008) 14 European Law Review 351, 355–7.

[106]   R Cordara QC, 'Abuse of Law—Origins & History in EU Law' (26 May 2006) Essex Court Chambers.

Several cases have concerned the attempt by economic actors to circumvent national rules by recourse to the European law of fundamental freedoms, such as the free movement of goods, services, capital and persons and the freedom of establishment.[107] In the *TV10* decision on broadcasting services, for example, the ECJ held that:

> ... the Treaty provisions on freedom to provide services are to be interpreted as not precluding a Member State from treating as a domestic broadcaster a broadcasting body constituted under the law of another Member State and established in that State but whose activities are wholly or principally directed towards the territory of the first Member State, if that broadcasting body was established there in order to enable it to avoid the rules which would be applicable to it if it were established within the first State.[108]

The principle emerging from these decisions is that *Community law cannot be used to circumvent national legislation* and national courts can prevent such conduct by showing artificial arrangements solely aiming at avoiding national provisions.[109]

Similarly, the EU courts have also addressed cases where the attempt was not to avoid the national provisions but rather *to benefit unduly from national laws*.[110] Here the concern is a person trying to bring himself within the law of a Member State to take advantage of, for example, social or other benefits. Even in this instance, Member States can take measures to prevent such conduct, provided that objective evidence of the intent is achieved and that an undue benefit is actually sought.[111]

Another line of EU cases with doctrinal equivalence to the US Supreme Court decision in *Morton Salt*,[112] although here applied to date mainly in the field of company and tax law,[113] addresses the use of Community law

---

[107]   Case C-23/93 *TV10* [1994] ECR I-4795; Opinion of 7 April 2005, Joined Cases C-255/02 and C-419/02. See Joined Cases C-255/02 *Halifax plc and Others* v *Customs*, C-419/02 *BUPA Hospitals Ltd.* and C-223/03 *University of Huddersfield*, [2006] ECR I-1609. Further cases cited in Sorenson (note 103). The principle of abuse in connection with human rights is embedded in EU law with Article 54, 'Prohibition of abuse of rights', Chapter of Fundamental Rights of the European Union, [2000] OJ C364/1 (18 December 2000).

[108]   *TV10 supra*, § 2b.

[109]   Sorensen (note 103) 446.

[110]   Case 39/86, *Lair* v *Universität Hannnover*, [1998] ECR 3161; Case C-200/02, *Zhu and Chen*, [2004] ECR I–9925. Further cases cited in Sorenson (note 103) 448.

[111]   Sorensen (note 103) 449.

[112]   See text and accompanying notes 26–31, *supra*.

[113]   Case C-367/96 *Kefalas* [1998] ECR I-2843; Case C-373/97 *Diamantis* [2000] ECR I-1705; *Emsland –Stärke* [2000] ECR I-11569. Comments to these cases in HL McCarthy, 'Abuse of rights: the effect of the doctrine on VAT planning'

provisions in order to *obtain improper advantages manifestly contrary to the objectives pursued by the provisions at stake.* That is, the objective pursued by the exercise of a right is contrary to the objective of a Community provision. In *Diamantis* the ECJ held that 'Community law cannot be relied on for abusive or fraudulent ends' as would occur if 'a shareholder, in reliance on Article 25(1) of the Second Directive, brought an action for the purpose of deriving, to the detriment of the company, an improper advantage, manifestly contrary to the objective of that provision.'[114] Here the abuse of rights' scope is much broader than under the above cases and is likely to apply to all areas of Community law, IP law included, provided that the conditions laid down in *Emsland-Stärke* are met. These first require 'a combination of *objective circumstances* in which, despite formal observance of the conditions laid down by the Community rules, the purpose of those rules has not been achieved' and, second, 'a subjective element consisting in the intention to obtain an advantage from the Community rules by creating artificially the conditions laid down for obtaining it.'[115]

These situations were all included in the abuse of rights doctrine articulated by the ECJ in *Centros*[116] where it identified abuse of rights as falling within two different contexts. The first comprised those attempts under the cover of the rights created by the Treaty to improperly circumvent national provisions[117] which also seemingly includes obtaining excessive benefits.[118] The second and somewhat less explored context, is where Community law is relied on for abusive or fraudulent ends, that is, where Community law provisions are abusively relied upon to gain advantages in a way that conflicts with the purposes and objectives of

---

(2007) BTR 160–174; S Douma and F Engelen, '*Halifax Plc* v *Customs And Excise Commissioners*: the ECJ applies the abuse of rights doctrine in VAT cases' (2006) BTR 429–40.

[114]   *Diamantis* (note 113) §§ 33–4.

[115]   *Emsland–Stärke* (note 113) §§ 52–3.

[116]   Case C-212/97 *Centros Ltd* v *Erhervsog Selskabsstyrelsen*, [1999] ECR 1459. Here the ECJ held that the refusal of Denmark to register a branch of a UK registered company established there to circumvent the Danish minimum capitalization requirements impinged the freedom of movement provisions. The right to form a company according to the law of a Member State and to set up branches in other Member States was inherent in exercising this freedom. That a company had been set up with the sole purpose of carrying on business in another Member State did not amount to an abuse of rights.

[117]   Ibid., §24. Accord, Opinion of Advocate General Maduro of 7 April 2005, C-255/02 *Halifax plc*, [2006] ECR I–1609, § 62. See also, for example, notes 99–104 and accompanying text.

[118]   See text and accompanying notes 105–106.

those very provisions.[119] The ECJ confirmed this in *Halifax*[120] where Advocate General Maduro set a two-pronged test for a Community abuse of rights under this second context: namely, where 1) 'the aims and results pursued by the legal provisions formally giving rise to the right would be frustrated if the right claimed were actually conferred'; and 2) 'the right invoked derives from activities for which there is no other explanation than the creation of the right claimed'.[121] In this line of abuse of rights cases, a shift has occurred from a subjective to a more objective interpretation[122] – as noted in Maduro's opinion – with the subjective element tending to refer more to the *purpose* than to the *intention* first mentioned in *Emsland-Stärke*.[123] Indeed, where this second context is concerned, 'the Court takes the view that an abuse exists whenever the activity at issue cannot possibly have any other purpose or justification than to trigger the application of Community law provisions in a manner contrary to their purpose.[124] 'The AG also affirmed that:

> . . . the notion of abuse operates as a *principle governing the interpretation of Community law*, as stated by the Commission in its written observations. What appears to be a decisive factor in affirming the existence of an abuse is the *teleological scope of the Community rules invoked*, which must be defined in order to establish whether the right claimed is, in effect, conferred by such provisions, to the extent to which it does not manifestly fall outside their scope.[125] (emphasis added)

Although this second context of the abuse of rights doctrine would not apply to IPR misuse cases where the IPR does not derive from a Community law provision, *AZ* is a case that could have been evaluated under such principles. IPRs are largely rights under national law; they reach the level of Community law where the EU has harmonized them, such as in the case of the Community trademark, or of certain areas of copyright, such as computer programs and databases. This would also be the case with the SPCs in *AZ* since in 1992 the European Council adopted

---

[119] See Case C-212/97 *Centros* [1999] ECR I-2357, § 24, Opinion of AG Maduro, *supra* §§ 62–63. See also, e.g., notes 107–110 and accompanying text.

[120] See C-255/02, *Halifax plc* (note 107), § 68. See also Opinion of AG Maduro, § 72 (note 117).

[121] Ibid., § 91. See also S Douma and F Engelen (note 113) 433. Criticism of the ECJ test has been raised by R De La Feria, 'Giving themselves extra VAT? The ECJ ruling in Halifax' (2006) BTR 429, 433.

[122] HL McCarthy, 'Abuse of rights: the effect of the doctrine on VAT planning' (2007) BTR 160.

[123] *Emsland-Stärke* (note 113) §§ 52–3.

[124] See, Opinion of AG Maduro, §70 (note 117).

[125] Ibid.§ 69.

Regulation 1768, requiring 'the creation of a supplementary protection certificate granted, under the same conditions, by each of the Member States at the request of the holder of a national or European patent relating to a medicinal product for which marketing authorization has been granted', as deemed necessary for Community goals.[126] The granting of SPCs is then a harmonized area of IP law; AZ's conduct concerning the misleading information granted to the national patent offices so to unlawfully extend the SPC terms could be construed as seeking to gain a financial or other advantage by an abusive use of Community law. Some may object that Article 15(1) of Regulation 1769/92 already provides for a SPC being held invalid if it was granted contrary to the regulation provisions (Article 3). While the only sanction of SPC invalidity is its nullity, under an abuse of rights doctrine, other remedies could be available beyond this and those under competition law.[127] This was not necessary in *AZ*, as dominance was the element that triggered the Article 82 challenge. There may be cases though in which the EU jurisprudence may comprise an IPR misuse under the abuse of rights doctrine where competition law will not reach. These cases need nevertheless to rely on Community IP law provisions.

3.3   IP-Related Litigation as Misuse

IPR holders not only adopt behaviors that are abusive in terms of expansion of scope and duration of their exclusive rights, but they also adopt specific litigation strategies against their competitors in order to jeopardize their presence in the market, lead them out of the market or prevent their entry. Under the US misuse doctrine IPR enforcement can be unlawful when amounting to malicious filing or abuse of process.[128] Moreover, IPR enforcement can also be violative of antitrust law, as the Noerr-Pennington doctrine does not provide a shield to legal actions which are objectively baseless and aiming at distorting competition. In the US, specific litigation strategies related to the enforcement of IPRs are likely to be unlawful if either they constitute antitrust violation or they constitute IPR misuse,[129] regardless of the legal actions being 'privileged' as relying on an IPR. Whether the EU's emerging abuse of rights doctrine, on the one hand, and EU rules on IPR uses violative of competition

---

[126]   Council Regulation (EEC) No 1768/92 of 18 June 1992 concerning the creation of a supplementary protection certificate for medicinal products, OJ L182, 02/07/1992 P. 0001–0005, Recital 7.
[127]   Negrinotti (note 6) 454.
[128]   See section § 2.3.
[129]   Ibid.

law, on the other, also address such otherwise 'IPR privileged' litigation strategies must here be considered as well. For example, in the *AZ* case, which constitutes the starting point of this analysis, the pharmaceutical enterprise adopted an overall strategy, encompassing both abusive behaviors in terms of expansion of scope and duration of patents and a specific litigation strategy against generic producers, aimed at impeding their entry into the market at the expiration of the SCPs. Would the bringing of a legal action 'privileged' as it relies on *AZ*'s IPR similarly be unlawful in the EU under these two main avenues: competition law and abuse of rights doctrine?

Two further points require consideration: the shield that jurisdictions tend to offer to petitioning in the EU system akin to the Noerr-Pennington doctrine in the USA and, in case such an equivalent can be envisaged, the existence of exceptions similar to the sham or the *Walker Process* ones; and the fact that usually IPR misuse is invoked as a defense to a claim of infringement.

Both points are dealt with by the EU courts in the *Promedia*[130] decisions wherein they elaborate criteria that are similar to those addressing US antitrust law claims brought with anti-competitive purposes (though not yet so articulated since a real distinction between the sham and *Walker Process* exceptions has not been identified in EU Law).[131] The CFI's *Promedia* judgment upheld the Commission's principle that the right of access to a judge cannot be characterised as an abuse unless an undertaking in a dominant position brings an action (1) which cannot be reasonably considered as an attempt to establish its right and can therefore only serve to harass the opposite party; and (2) which is conceived in the framework of a plan to eliminate competition.[132] Among the differences existing between the US sham exception test and the test formulated in the *Promedia* judgment, the EU's second prong, 'plan to eliminate

---

[130] IIT *Promedia NV* v *Commission of the European Communities* (T-111/96) [1998] ECR II-2937.

[131] However, the *AZ* decision does present principles similar to those developed in *Walker Process* as far as actions to enforce invalid IPR are concerned. The Commission, though, seems to introduce a lower standard to assess this conduct since misleading information suffices to constitute abuse, while in the US case evidence of fraud in obtaining the patent was proved. See K Czapracka, *Intellectual Property and the Limits of Antitrust* (Edward Elgar, Cheltenham, UK; Northampton, MA, USA 2009) x1.

[132] Ibid. § 1: The CFI (§ 56) described the position of the EU Commission in the following way:

The fact that unmeritorious litigation is instituted does not in itself constitute infringement of Art 86 [*now* 102] of the Treaty unless it has an anticompetitive

competition', needs further analysis as it relates to the defensive use of IPR misuse. In *Promedia* the CFI premised the existence of a plan to eliminate competition on whether the prosecution of the IPR was in the form of a claim or counterclaim. According to the Court, while a proactive act such as filing a claim could comprise part of a plan to eliminate competition, the essentially reactive nature of a counterclaim rather suggests, in the absence of other evidence, that there is not a purposive anticompetitive strategy.[133] In *Promedia* two out of the three court proceedings had been brought by Promedia, while Belgacom was perceived merely to be defending its rights by bringing counterclaims. Therefore, a violation of competition law on Belgacom's part was not considered by the CFI to have occurred. Had Belgacom set up a plan, it would have brought direct action.[134]

The *AZ* decision not only confirms such position but also specifies that the Commission never ruled, in relation to the opinion set out in *Promedia*, that defensive conduct could never constitute an abuse, rather that 'by itself, such conduct could not be conceived as forming part of a plan to eliminate competition.'[135] There emerges in the European courts' opinion a principle by which defensive forms of conduct may rarely be considered abusive unless the disputed conduct is precisely the unlawful means to achieve the abuse, as was the case in *AZ*. There it was the (deviously inaccurate) information provided to domestic patent offices in order to obtain, or extend the scope of, certain SPCs. In this sense, the conduct of the defense in the proceedings can be considered as part of a wider abusive strategy of an exclusionary kind, intended to impede the entry of generics into the market for the patent-protected pharmaceutical. In a few countries, for example, Germany, Norway, and Finland, generic manufacturers were fully aware of AZ's strategy and promptly proceeded to challenge it.

4.   CONCLUSION

The above analysis shows that there are at least the colorable outlines of analogous IP misuse doctrines in the EU under competition law, freedom

---

object. Equally, litigation which may reasonably be regarded as an attempt to assert rights vis-a-vis competitors is not abusive, irrespective of the fact that it may be part of a plan to eliminate competition.

[133]   One could of course always wait to be sued as part of one's strategy, a factor not considered by the CFI.

[134]   Promedia CFI (note 130) §§ 18, 33, 34 and § 42.

[135]   *AZ* (note 1) § 737.

of movement provisions and the abuse of rights doctrine with their equity-like application to prevent instances of abuse or injustice. Whether the EU should consider actively pursuing such IP misuse doctrines, even if it could do so, remains to be considered.

There are, however, a few preliminary considerations. Firstly, there is currently a process of convergence at the level of competition law as enacted and enforced in both the US and EU jurisdictions.[136] As the many recent agreements show,[137] a similar process is taking place at international levels for IP law, although the degree of internationalization achieved is not more than basic. Where the US and EU diverge, however, is the way in which they deal with the competition/IP interface and, more generally, the way they address the relationship between competition and regulation in regulated markets, among which one may include IP.

Indeed, both IP and antitrust laws are considered to have the objective of increasing efficiency within the market by incentivizing innovation and creativity – the former – and fostering competition – the latter. In other words, both bodies of law are deemed means to achieve the same goal, the difference being that IP laws are *ex ante* means to address the balance, and competition laws are *ex post* tools. However, in pursuing the objective, IP law may also jeopardize competition and chill innovation and creativity by offering overprotection to right holders, the point at which the two bodies of law no longer appear aligned. When such clash occurs, IP law present flaws that can either be corrected within the IP system itself or via external remedies (such as competition law). While in the US certain flaws in the IP system can firstly be treated within the IP system, the misuse doctrine being an example of this approach,[138] presently in the EU competition law tends to be the only remedy in practice to address the consequences of imperfect community and national IP laws. The *AZ* decision confirms that

---

[136]   See, eg, CA Varney, Prepared Remarks, 36th Annual Fordham Competition Law Institute Annual Conference on Int'l Antitrust Law and Policy: 'Our Progress Towards International Convergence' (Antitrust Division, DOJ 2009).

[137]   Agreement on Trade-Related Aspects of Intellectual Property Rights (TRIPs), 15 April 1994, available at http://www.wto.org/english/tratop_e/trips_e/t_agm0_e.htm; WIPO Copyright Treaty (WCT), 20 December 1996, available at http://www.wipo.int/export/sites/www/treaties/en/ip/wct/pdf/trtdocs_wo033.pdf; WIPO Performances and Phonograms Treaty (WPPT), 1996, http://www.wipo.int/export/sites/www/treaties/en/ip/wppt/pdf/trtdocs_wo034.pdf.

[138]   To the extent that the misuse doctrine looks to the principles and policies underlying the grant of the intellectual property right in question it can be said to be an internal remedy within IP even where the specific law does not mention it, such as copyright. In another sense, as an application of the law of equity following its principles it can be considered an external.

the present European overall approach is to remedy IP imbalances using competition law. Here limitations to the enterprise conduct were applied according to Article 102 of the Treaty, while the conduct may also amount to an IP violation itself.[139]

There are some significant reasons for preferring a competition law approach to advocating recourse to other tools, such as the abuse of rights, to address the overbroad exercise of IPRs. The first of these are the recent efforts to ensure the feasibility of private enforcement throughout the EU of competition law, making it a tool that is much more within the reach of smaller businesses. Also included is that competition law exercise is theoretically harmonized in all Member States so that case law may have a persuasive effect. The reach of competition law is broader and can apply even where the conduct in question is not premised on rights governed by Community laws, as would be required to fall within the second prong of the abuse of rights doctrine examined here.[140] So, for example, in *AZ*, if the conduct did not amount to a competition law violation, it would need to comprise an abuse of rights within the reach of Community courts. While here that would have been possible, since Regulation 1768/92[141] governing the SPCs confers a community right that AZ clearly abused, that would not always be the case with IPRs, for example patent enforcement outside this context has yet to be harmonized by the EU.

The consequences remain that despite the ongoing EU harmonization process in the field of intellectual property, the community acquis is limited. The EU lacks competence in legislating and ruling on IP matters unless there is an issue that must be resolved in favor of the internal market development. This somewhat undermines the desirability or even the ability to pursue an IP-based abuse of rights doctrine as another way to address their overbroad, or other abusive exercise, in a situation where EU jurisdictional limits or substantive competition law competencies might not be met. It also risks a lack of cohesive application, such as that in the US misuse doctrine, and precludes a normative effect. The possible effectiveness in this context is also undermined by the present limited view of EU bodies that abuse cannot derive from defensive strategies to IP

---

[139]   Negrinotti (note 6) 453, noting that in *AZ* 'the question of the delicate balance between innovation and competition is not at stake. It is in fact evident that AZ was seeking a protection it was not entitled to, since the legislator had established that only if the first market authorisation had been obtained after the cut-off dates indicated in the directive, the SPC protection could be granted.'

[140]   An examination of IP based conduct that could fall within the first prong is beyond the scope of this analysis but is not beyond imagination.

[141]   (note 126).

litigation, for example forcing your injured licensees and competitors to sue you.

This may suggest that such an approach could be pointless. However, continuing developments signal that it is likely that EU IP harmonization will continue. For example, the Commission's recent final report on its inquiry into the pharmaceutical sector calls for a Community patent, as well as a unified European patent litigation system to address delay, cost, duplicate and needless litigation in addition to disparate outcomes from Member State courts.[142] In addition, the WIPO broadcast treaty is not as dead as might be assumed from the lack of results to date.[143] As with the Copyright and Related Rights Treaties, it is likely that the EU would as a direct signing jurisdiction seek to meet its treaty obligations via harmonized legislation, especially as long as webcasting is concerned.[144] It is likely that the areas of EU-based IP law wherein the doctrine of abuse of rights could be applied will continue to expand and nearly all of the major rights will have a significant harmonized element.

Another concern in this evaluation is whether it is better to address imbalances in IPRs solely within the IP law itself, or whether other external tools such as competition law of misuse/abuse are appropriate; this is an ongoing debate in economic and intellectual property theory.[145] One will not resolve that debate here, if ever, but some observations may be helpful. To the extent that the US misuse doctrine looks to policies that underlie the IPR grant to determine whether a misuse exists, it arguably comprises an internal tool. Indeed, the Patent Act makes direct reference to it.[146] The abuse of rights doctrine at the Member State level may indeed have this equivalence, as it will be the IPRs, yet at the EU level the principles considered will have to be within the remit of the Treaty and so it is likely that they may comprise such things as harmonization, internal

---

[142] Commission Communication on the Pharmeceutical Sector Inquiry Report, Executive Summary (July 8, 2009), http://ec.europa.eu/competition/sectors/pharmaceuticals/inquiry/communication_en.pdf.

[143] See G Hinze, 'The WIPO Broadcasting Treaty: Back from the Dead?'(07/11/08 EFF Deeplinks Blog), http://www.eff.org/deeplinks/2008/11/wipo-broadcasting-treaty-back-dead.

[144] Ibid.

[145] See, eg, KE Rockett and P Regibeau, Economic Discussion Paper 581 'The Relationship Between Intellectual Property Law and Competition Law: An Economic Approach' (2004 U. of Essex, Economics Disscussion Paper Series), http://www.essex.ac.uk/economics/discussion-papers/papers-text/dp581.pdf.

[146] See 35 U.S.C. § 271(d). To some extent it is derived from and applies an external set of rules which can be applied in many contexts where fairness or justice, that is, the 'equities' of a situation, are in issue.

market imbalances or other treaty derived analyses rather than the grant of IPRs, over which the EU has no direct power. Therefore in the EU, the abuse of rights doctrine is likely to be considered an external tool.

However, the role of additional legal frameworks as tools in promoting social justice may be critical. For example, the lack of competition law frameworks and expertise in developing countries has been noted to undermine their ability to ensure anti-competitive overreaching via licensing, and so on.[147] Moreover, frameworks such as competition law can be implemented with social policy or development goals.[148] The EU competition law application is an example of that with policies such as single market or information society development intertwined with competition principles.[149]

While the EU has not sought to expand its arsenal to include the abuse of rights doctrine in the IP context, notable is its own assessment in the recent Commission report that competition law powers provide only the ability to address specific concerns and other approaches are necessary to ensure the timely entrance of generics, in order to ensure greater, less costly access to health care for consumers and assist public budget priority conflicts across the EU, arguably social justice concerns.[150]

Abuse of rights could therefore prove to be both a meaningful and helpful avenue to address IP overreaching that can be raised where other customary EU competencies cannot fully or readily address such issues.

One further framework must be readdressed before concluding. The freedom of movement powers analysed above in connection with the parallel exercise of competition law are recently rather unused in the IP context. These, however, are distinct EU powers that could address key cross-border issues where others cannot such as, for example, the barriers to parallel import of generic drugs not encompassed within the competition law-based analysis of the recent Commission report[151] or the scope of broadcasters' and webcasters' digital rights with important access to knowledge implications remaining still to be addressed at the international and EU level and which might serve as disguised restraints on the freedom

---

[147]   See C. Correa, 'Intellectual Property and Competition Law: Exploring Some Issues of Relevance to Developing Countries' 1–4 (2007 Int' Center for Trade and Sustainable Development) (noting that competition law can be applied to support balance and development).

[148]   Ibid.

[149]   See, eg, Case 2001/696/EC, *Identrus* (2001) (highlighting the information society potential)

[150]   Commission Communication (note 142).

[151]   See ibid. 15.

of movement of services. There is an additional, if emergent, need for the EU to consider the continued and broader use of freedom of movement powers to address the overreaching of IP owners by exercise beyond their geographic, temporal and substantive scope: the proposed fifth EU freedom of movement of knowledge and creativity.[152] Although the scope of this has yet to be fully addressed, the stated bases on which this would rest, include: inter alia 'facilitating and promoting the optimal use of intellectual property created in public research organisations so as to increase knowledge transfer to industry, in particular through an "IP Charter" to be adopted . . .'; and 'encouraging open access to knowledge and open innovation'.[153] While the first speaks to commercialization of publicly funded research, the latter has distributive justice overtones. Moreover, the stated objective of such a fifth freedom is future EU growth premised on 'the full development of the potential for innovation and creativity of European citizens built on European culture and excellence in science'.[154]

As the outline of an apparent developed economy's vision of social and distributive justice, and one that is noted to have a long-term horizon, it would be short sighted to rule out the use of freedom of movement principles that were used to forge a single market in the creation of an open information society.

In conclusion, while not every aspect of the US misuse doctrine could be, or should be, pursued, there exist EU legal doctrines which can be addressed to the exercise of IPRs beyond their scope. Their significance should not be dismissed.

---

[152] See Press Release, EU Slovenian Presidency (14/03/08) (noting European Council call for introduction of this fifth EU freedom of movement), http://www. eu2008.si/en/News_and_Documents/Press_Releases/March/0314EC_Lizbona. html. Accord, Press Release, Speech 07/257, J Potocnik, EU Commissioner for Science and Research, 'The EU's Fifth Freedom: creating free movement of knowledge' (26 April 2007).
[153] Council of Europe, Slovenia Presidency Conclusions 7652/08, pp. 5–6 (13–14/03/08), http://www.eu2008.si/en/News_and_Documents/Council_Conclusions/March/0314ECpresidency_conclusions.pdf.
[154] Ibid. 5.

7. The changing market for music licenses: a redefinition of collective interests and competitive dynamics

Maria Mercedes Frabboni

1. INTRODUCTION

Collective administration of copyright and related rights is of particular significance to their enforcement. Collecting societies have emerged as the solution to the impracticality for authors to administer their rights directly. In the face of a large number of potential users, it makes economic sense to appoint intermediaries entrusted with the duty of managing the relevant entitlements vis-à-vis commercial users of protected contents. Such management consists in issuing licenses to users, monitoring uses, collecting fees from licensees and distributing royalties to right holders.[1] The economic literature concerning collective management of rights emphasizes the economies of scale and scope that can be realized through aggregation of the administrative functions with a single intermediary. In particular, an important advantage lies in the representativeness of collecting societies for a multitude of right holders and in their accessibility for commercial users. This emerges, for example, in the field of music exploitation and dissemination, where collecting societies' activities have developed and expanded to allow content to be disseminated through various technologies and to different audiences.[2]

This particular and universal nature of collecting societies' action is the

---

[1] Mihály Ficsor, 'Collective Management of Copyright and Related Rights' (2002) WIPO Publication No 855(E) 17; Ruth Towse, 'Copyright and Economic Incentives: an Application to Performers' Rights in the Music Industry' (1999) 52 Kyklos 382.

[2] This chapter focuses on music collecting societies (and performing rights organizations in particular) in reason of their history and the volume of transactions they facilitate. As discussed by Ficsor, 'performing rights societies still. . . represent the fullest system of joint. . . management of rights' (37). However, it must be noted that other collective organizations exist, for example for the

focus of this chapter. Starting from the justification of collective manage-ment offered by the economic literature, the analysis seeks to provide a critical outlook on the current initiatives of reform and on the impact that those initiatives could have on the public interests goals that col-lecting societies traditionally pursue. Specifically, Section 2 considers the justification offered by the economics literature to the emergence of music collecting societies and their subsequent evolution into monopoly insti-tutions acting within national boundaries, thus implementing copyright regimes on a territorial basis and without competition. Section 3 discusses two business practices normally adopted by collecting societies, namely blanket licenses and reciprocal representation agreements, to illustrate the possible impact of the societies' action acting as monopolists in their respective markets. Section 4 analyses the challenges to the initial justi-fication in light of jurisprudential and regulatory approaches offered by European authorities in their effort to encourage collecting societies to adopt modern solutions. In particular, it evaluates how competition law enforcement is attempting to attenuate the side-effects emerging in highly concentrated markets, and how more radical changes coming from a pos-sible regulatory reform could impact the representativeness of collecting societies' membership and the overall cultural significance of the collective action performed by them.

2. COLLECTIVE MANAGEMENT JUSTIFICATION AND NATIONAL MONOPOLIES

In order to understand the complexity of the current issues surrounding collective management, it is relevant to consider the emergence of collect-ing societies in relation to the fundamental function they play in aggregat-ing different entitlements. The form of aggregation realized by the societies gives rise to a large membership in quantitative and qualitative terms. Diverse rights holders appoint collecting societies to perform four main tasks: to license users, monitor them, collect license fees and, finally, dis-tribute remuneration to the right holder. In order to perform these tasks, collecting societies charge their members an administration fee, generally consisting of a deduction from royalties distributed to right holders and which can be considered each member's contribution to the functioning of the collective body.

---

administration of reprographic reproduction rights (Stanley M Besen et al., 'An Economic Analysis of Copyright Collectives' (1992) 78 Va LR 383, 386.

The economic literature emphasizes that efficiencies arise when the above four tasks are performed not individually by each right holder, but in an aggregate manner by an organization that groups the different interests. As Besen, Kirby and Salop (1992) have noted:

> [i]t is less expensive for a single agent to monitor establishments on behalf of a large number of songwriters than it is for multiple agents, each representing a single songwriter, to monitor the same establishments. By combining their efforts, a group of songwriters may find it feasible to identify unauthorised uses, and either prevent them or collect for them, when individual songwriters might not.[3]

Besen and Kirby earlier identified (1989) a condition under which collective administration ought to be the preferred solution. They consider that:

> [c]ollective administration of the copyrights of a group of publishers is efficient if its cost is lower than that of administering the copyrights of all possible subsets of the same group of publishers. . . This condition will be satisfied if the licensees of [the members of a society] are the same people and the costs of administration for a given licensee do not rise in proportion to the number of licenses he obtains. In such circumstances, a visit by one inspector to the premises of a given user will suffice to administer the licenses of several producers and will be less costly than separate visits by inspectors for each licensing producer.[4]

In practical terms, a broadcaster who seeks a license would generally be interested in many different parts of the repertoire and would find it useful to go to a collecting society where he could obtain a single authorization for the use he wants to make of the repertoire. When the number of works sought to be licensed is high, efficiencies in licensing and monitoring increase, as the costs incurred in performing each task are in fact split amongst the many right holders for whom the task is performed.

In situations where this relevant condition of efficient collective management is fulfilled, it makes economic sense for right holders to appoint such an intermediary. This allows access to content and enforces the exclusivity granted by copyright law to authors, other types of right holders and their successors in title. The delegation of powers from right holders

---

[3]   Besen et al. (n 2), 390.

[4]   See Stanley M. Besen and Sheila N. Kirby, *Compensating Creators of Intellectual Property: Collectives That Collect* (RAND Corporation, Santa Monica 1989) 4. Summary available at <https://www.rand.org/pubs/reports/R3751/> accessed 28 August 2009.

to the intermediary, however, necessarily generates the effect of the inter-mediary acquiring market power, by virtue of the aggregate volume of property rights that it administers.[5] This is factually confirmed by the current position of collecting societies within the markets they serve. In most countries, collecting societies act as monopolists entrusted with the interests of a broad spectrum of right holders of different size and from different areas of cultural industries.[6] Intuitively, right holders want to be members of strong collecting societies that, thanks to their bargaining power, are in the position to successfully negotiate with users, such as large commercial broadcasters and their representatives.[7]

The question of why monopolies arise more frequently in this context than oligopolies or less concentrated market solutions is also relevant to our analysis. In fact, while it has become clear that aggregation produces efficiencies, it is not clear which is the optimal form of aggregation that best serves the interests of collecting societies' members, considering that concentration generally produces welfare losses. With these caveats in mind, it is helpful to discuss the argument introduced by a segment of the economic literature that identifies in collecting societies the characteristics of natural monopolies.[8] Arguably, it is more efficient to have a single performing rights society per country to ensure that the costs of running such an organization are not duplicated. Further, such duplication nega-tively affects the amount of royalties that could be returned to the soci-ety's members. As suggested, most European countries (e.g. UK, France, Germany, and so on) have only one society, apart from whether national legislation actually imposes legal barriers or authorization procedures for

---

[5]   See Giovanni B Ramello's, 'Intellectual property, social justice and economic efficiency: insights from law and economics', Chapter 1 in this book.

[6]   The nature and form of the collective administration of any given set of rights will be similar in all countries. This is so for three basics reasons. First, reciproc-ity – whereby rights holders who reside in one country obtain payments through the copyright collective in the country in which the right is licensed – is promoted where collectives have similar forms. Second, newer collectives are likely to model themselves after successful collectives that administer the same set of rights in other countries. Finally, the similarity of rights themselves leads to similar forms of administration. Besen et al. (n 2), vi.

[7]   Case 127/73 *Belgische Radio en Televisie* v *SV SABAM and NV Fonior* [1974] ECR 313, § 9.

[8]   Ruth Towse and Christian Handke, *Economics of Collective Management of Copyright: Análisis Económico de las Sociedades de Gestión de Derechos de Autor* (Ediciones Autor, Madrid, 2007), 18, 19–20; KEA European Affairs, 'Study on collective management of rights in Europe: the quest for efficiency' (2006), European Parliament Study 17 <www.europarl.europa.eu/comparl/juri/study/rights_en.pdf> accessed 28 August 2009.

the establishment of collective management institutions. The USA, where more than one performing rights society exists for the same territory, is sometimes identified as an exception.[9] Yet even here there are only a few incumbents, which appears to suggest that a high level of concentration may be intrinsic to collective administration of copyright.

The question of whether lack of competition (or a reduced level of competition) is suitable in the market of music rights could be answered by verifying whether collecting societies are in fact natural monopolies. In the characterization of collecting societies as natural monopolies, it must be stressed that here the term 'natural monopoly' 'does not refer to the actual number of sellers in a market but to the relationship between the demand and the technology of supply'.[10] In other words, the costs associated with the management solutions provided by collecting societies make it economically preferable for one single entity to serve the entire market. In fact, collective management institutions can meet the wide and increasing demand for rights clearance only if equipped with the necessary tangible and intangible assets. These are, for example, the different local branches that performing rights society scatter across the territory they serve, the monitoring technology they use, the human capital they employ and train, or the databases on which they rely to administer the differ entitlements. These and other necessary investments allow collecting societies to properly perform, within the boundaries of their national markets, the four tasks for which they have been appointed.

3.   MANAGING PRACTICES

In the presence of a monopoly (or any other highly concentrated market), a number of regulatory countermeasures must be established in order to ensure that socially desirable outcomes are achieved. In particular, countermeasures should ensure that members of collecting societies are adequately and fairly represented, regardless of the nature of the repertoire they provide. Moreover, it is also important that collecting societies holding large market power allow rights clearance to all types of users,

---

    [9]   Besen et al. (n 2), 397.
    [10]   Ariel Katz, 'The Potential Demise of Another Natural Monopoly: Rethinking the Collective Administration of Performing Rights' (2005) 1(3) JCLE 552. The author continues his observation by specifying that 'the observed fact that in the United States there are three PROs [Performing Rights Organisations] is not necessarily inconsistent with the natural monopoly argument' (n 46).

at accessible conditions.[11] Only if these goals are ensured will collective management institutions have fulfilled their function in a manner preferable to any alternative method of administering the exclusive entitlements with which they are entrusted. Competition law enforcement is one of the several countermeasures that seek to maintain the equilibrium between the private, and often divergent views of the parties involved, and the institutional goals that societies should pursue.

EU competition law manifests its effects beyond the national boundaries of the Member States where collecting societies traditionally operate, to facilitate supervision and, to some extent, harmonization of the societies' working mechanisms. Competition law enforcement has been relevant in limiting the possible problematic effects of monopolistic or oligopolistic powers in many directions, namely on the relationship of collecting societies and their members (that is, authors and other right holders) and of the societies and users, as well as on the international collaboration historically present amongst collecting societies. While a full discussion of the relevant case law is beyond the scope of this chapter, a consideration of collecting societies' possible anti-competitive behaviours and remedies could provide an interpretative lens through which to view the pivotal role of collecting societies within their markets, and on the licensing practices they adopt.

The relationship between collecting societies and their members gives rise to numerous pratical implications that must be considered. Following the natural monopoly justification, the marginal benefits of an increase in membership naturally leads to a situation where collecting societies become the administrators and enforcers of a variety of rights, held by a spectrum of right holders with different characteristics. For example, collecting societies' membership is open to small creators as well as corporate entities. While corporate entities such as major music publishers generate the largest volume of income and receive the largest amount of royalties in return, the participation of smaller right holders, such as unknown individual composers or songwriters, is also safeguarded. This provides a contribution in terms of diversification of works, as well as breadth of repertoire available to users. This system is also an attractive management solution for most types of right holders, as it mutualises risk and decreases individual responsibility for the costs of tasks performed by the society.[12]

---

[11] Consultation (MARKT/E4/AA/ D (2004) 6036) on the European Commission Communication on the management of copyright and related rights in the Internal Market (COM(2004)261final) 16 April 2004, <http://ec.europa. eu/internal_market/copyright/management/management_en.htm> accessed 28 August 2009.

[12] KEA European Affairs (n 8) 31–2.

The solidarity created as a result is practically implemented in the system of licensing and royalty distribution that has characterized the operations of collecting societies. In particular, blanket licenses issued to users have been useful instruments that allow access to the totality of a society's repertoire.[13] Users obtaining blanket licenses are not only permitted to use any work, but they are entitled to do so as many times as they want.[14] With this system, every work is covered and every right holder is involved. Even if the method of calculating royalties would especially reward successful ones, niche repertoires also obtain a certain degree of remuneration that would not be obtained under a system where users can limit their choice of the protected content they want to access. The problematic question is whether right holders of different size are given remuneration according to a fair approximation of their contribution to the repertoire that users obtain. The widespread use of blanket licenses has been heavily criticized as an opportunity for collecting societies to 'exploit their power against their individual members by imposing burdensome conditions upon them or discriminating among some members'.[15] In the light of this risk, it can be argued that the issuing of blanket licenses offers certain advantages but remains an imperfect solution and could lead to inefficient outcomes when members are not in a favorable position to influence a society's decisions on how the relevant royalties should be distributed.[16] Critically, as suggested by Besen and Kirby (1989):

> . . .[a]lthough some right holders may be dissatisfied with the payments that they receive, and may attempt to have their payment increased, dropping out of the collective is not an attractive alternative so long as the payments they receive from the collective are larger than the payments that they can obtain on their own.[17]

While it is accepted that the costs of individual licensing are traditionally too high to encourage right holders to leave their collecting society and manage their rights on an individual basis, the 'opt-out' option cannot be fully disregarded when considering new means of exploitation discussed in the final part of this chapter.

Blanket licenses and their possible anti-competitive outcomes serve also

---

[13]   Towse (n 1) 382; Paula Shepens, 'Guide to the Collective Administration of Authors' Rights', (2000) UNESCO 25; Ficsor (n 1) 43.

[14]   Besen et al. (n 2), 388.

[15]   Katz (n 10) 544–5.

[16]   Ruth Towse and Christian Handke, 'Economics of Copyright Collecting Societies' (2007) 8(38) IIC 937–57.

[17]   Besen and Kirby (n 4) 11.

to characterize the relationship between collecting societies as monopolists and users. Katz's following criticism of blanket licensing addresses the imbalance that such instruments create:

> Because the PRO [performing rights organisation] sets the price of licenses, it can set the price at the optimal monopoly price rather than the level at which the individual copyright holders would have set it. Because the PRO usually grants only blanket licenses, this all-or-nothing bargain forces most users to buy more units than they wish at a price that is higher than they otherwise wish to pay and enables the PRO to extract the higher value of the license.[18]

This submission should be carefully considered.[19] Blanket licenses have been under the scrutiny of competition authorities, particularly in the United States where it was questioned whether such practices were in fact unlawful restraints of trade and fell foul of the rules established under the Sherman Act.[20] The Supreme Court did not accept that blanket licenses were unlawful in and of themselves, but considered that they had to be evaluated according to a rule of reason.[21] The US case law also forced collecting societies to grant per-program and per-segment licenses as

---

[18]   Katz (n 10) 551.

[19]   See Will Page, 'Lost in Translation? A Critique of Katz Papers' (2007) MCPS-PRS Economic Insight, Issue 4:

> In reality, blanket licenses are based around a formula which usually takes account of the licensee's level of music usage and either the licensee's revenue or audience figures. Also, the blanket licenses are often negotiable to take account of the unique circumstances of the end users. Blankets also encourage a wider use of the available repertoire at no incremental cost.

[20]   *Broadcast Music, Inc.* v *CBS, Inc.*, 441 US 1 (1979).

[21]   For a review of the US case law on this point, see Besen and Kirby (n 4) 27. Reference to the US approach was made by Advocate General Jacobs, in his opinion delivered in relation to the *Tournier* (Case T-395/87 *Ministère public* v *Tournier* [1989] ECR 2521) and *Lucazeau* (Cases C-110/88, C-241/88 and C-242/88, *Lucazeau and others* v *SACEM* [1989] ECR 2811) decisions, where he indicates that '[u]nder a rule of reason, a court is required to weigh up the pro-competitive effects of a practice against its anti-competitive effects. . .', and that, in the cases he was asked to consider, '[I]t is for the national courts . . . to weigh up the benefits and disadvantages of the [blanket] license' (ECR 1989, p 2521, §§ 48–49) The ECJ, in delivering its decision (*Tournier* § 45), also appears to adopt the 'rule of reason':

> Another problem raised was whether the fact that a blanket or flat-rate royalty was charged should be taken into account in deciding whether or not the amount of royalty was fair for the purposes of [ex] Article 86. . . The fact that a flat-rate royalty is charged can only be criticized by reference to the prohibition contained in Article 86 if other methods might be capable of attaining the same

alternatives to blanket licenses, and to offer a 'genuine choice' among the different solutions, opening up opportunities for practices that better adapt to the needs of users adopting different and ever-changing technologies. [22]

The overall impact of blanket licenses, however, needs to be considered in light of the relationships that exist among collecting societies, acting as monopolists in their respective countries and collaborating at the regional and international level. Blanket licenses are instruments that allow not only the use of the national repertoire, but also of foreign repertoires that national collecting societies may be authorized to license by virtue of 'reciprocal representation agreements' concluded with other collecting societies across the globe. According to the European Court of Justice (ECJ), a reciprocal representation agreement is:

> a contract between [e.g.] two national copyright-management societies concerned with musical works whereby the societies give each other the right to grant, within the territory for which they are responsible, the requisite authorizations for any public performance of copyrighted musical works of the other society and to subject those authorizations to certain conditions, in conformity with the laws applicable in the territory in question.[23]

The nexus of contracts that a national collecting society establishes with other equivalent societies in other countries provides users with the opportunity to access the world repertoire.[24] It also widens the demand for national repertoires and the potential remuneration returned to right holders.[25]

---

legitimate aim, namely the protection of the interests of authors, composers and publishers of music, without thereby increasing the costs of managing contracts and monitoring the use of protected musical works.

[22]   *United States* v *ASCAP* 2001–2 Trade Cas (CCH) P73, 474. For an overall summary of collective management and competition law enforcement in the US, see Fred Koenigsberg, 'Performing Rights in Music and Performing Rights Organizations, Revisited' (2003) 50 J Copr Socy 355–98.

[23]   *Lucazeau and others* v *SACEM* (n 21) §11; and *Ministère public* v *Tournier* (n 21) §3.

[24]   *Ministère public* v *Tournier* (n 21) §19: '[reciprocal representation agreements] are intended to make all protected . . . works, whatever their origin, subject to the same conditions for all users in the same Member State'. See also *Lucazeau* v *SACEM* (n 21), § 13.

[25]   While seemingly obvious, this is not always true, due to a tangential but complicated issue. There is a difference existing between type B and type A agreements between collecting societies. In the first case, society X retains the money collected for the exploitation of society's Y repertoire but society Y compensates the loss of income by retaining society's X. Under type A agreements, there is an

As observed by case-law, the economic advantage obtained in the establishment of reciprocal representation agreements consists in the fact that they:

> enable copyright-management societies to rely, for the protection of their repertoires in another State, on the organization established by the copyright-management society operating there, without being obliged to add to that organization their own network of contracts with users and their own local monitoring arrangements.[26]

However, beyond the efficiencies that can be realized under reciprocal representation agreements, there are problematic aspects that diminish the social desirability of these instruments. For example, it is suggested that reciprocal representation agreements have been the main cause for the perpetuation of national monopolies in the field of music rights administration. Those agreements have traditionally contained membership restrictions, whereby societies require right holders 'to transfer their rights only to their own national collecting society',[27] and territorial restrictions, whereby societies 'oblige commercial users to obtain a license only from the domestic collecting society and limited to the domestic territory'.[28] These limitations have been addressed by a long series of cases and continue to be under the scrutiny of competition authorities.[29] At this stage, it is important to underline that discrimination of members on the ground of nationality has been rejected explicitly since the *GEMA* case,[30] while, for certain uses, the geographical vicinity of the local collecting society could make economic sense. This was recognised, for example, in the *Lucazeau*

---

actual transfer of money. If a society is not a large exporter of its own repertoire, the result could be that the potential increase in remuneration gets eaten up by the administration fees that the two societies would charge anyway. This is quite controversial and beyond the scope of this chapter.

[26] *Ministère public* v *Tournier* (n 21) §19.

[27] European Commission: 'Antitrust: Commission market tests commitments from CISAC and 18 EEA collecting societies concerning reciprocal representation contracts,' IP/07/829, available at <http://ec.europa.eu/rapid/start/cgi/guesten.ksh?p_action.gettxt=gt&doc=IP/07/829|0|RAPID&lg=EN>, accessed 28 August 2009.

[28] Ibid.

[29] For a review of the relevant decisions, see Maria Mercedes Frabboni, 'Collective management of copyright and related rights: achievements and problems of institutional efforts towards harmonisation', in Estelle Derclaye (ed), *Research Handbook On The Future Of EU Copyright* (Edward Elgar, 2009) 373–400.

[30] Commission's Decision (EC) 71/224/CEE] OJ L134/15 of 20 June 1971.

and Tournier cases, [31] where it was submitted that the practice of denying access to foreign users is not restrictive of competition when it can be justified by reasons other than the existence of a concerted action.[32] As illustrated below, however, this reasoning does not appear to hold when applied to licenses for Internet uses.

Following the observations that emerge from the analysis of two main managing practices adopted by collecting societies, it can be argued that the consequences of a highly concentrated market should not be underestimated. In fact, the economies of scale and scope that can be realized by collecting societies and the public interest goals pursued in the context of collective administration could be negatively affected by harmful conducts that the societies could adopt in absence of countermeasures designed for the supervision of their activities. As suggested at the beginning of this section, EU competition law has actively performed this supervisory role. The final part of the chapter will illustrate how judicial intervention in the EU is influencing efforts to refashion collecting societies, and how regulatory measures are also contributing to the process of adapting licensing solutions to new opportunities created by advances in digital technology.

4.   A DIFFERENT DESTINY FOR BORDERLESS EXPLOITATION

Despite the numerous advantages of collecting societies serving as a single place for rights holders and users to ensure lower individual transaction costs for access, use and payment for the use of protected content, their

---

[31]

[R]eciprocal representation contracts have a twofold purpose: first, they are intended to make all protected musical works, whatever their origin, subject to the same conditions for all users in the same Member State, in accordance with the principle laid down in the international provisions; secondly, they enable copyright-management societies to rely, for the protection of their repertoires in another State, on the organization established by the copyright-management society operating there, without being obliged to add to that organization their own network of contracts with users and their own local monitoring arrangements.

Lucazeau v *SACEM* (n 21) § 1; and *Ministère public* v *Tournier* (n 21) § 19.

[32]

[S]uch reasons might be that the copyright management societies of other Member States would be obliged, in the event of direct access to their repertoires, to organise their own management and monitoring system in another country.

Lucazeau v *SACEM* (n 21) § 18; and *Ministère public* v *Tournier* (n 21) § 24.

potentially anti-competitive practices have drawn controversy. Collecting societies have historically exercised discretion towards right holders, and users have mounted challenges and proposed changes to the way they do business. This section of the chapter focuses on those challenges as addressed by current judicial and regulatory efforts, which touch upon the collaboration among collecting societies, the accessibility of content to users and, ultimately, the right holders' interests that the societies are asked to represent. In particular, the analysis will consider the controversy concerning the International Confederation of Societies of Authors and Composers (CISAC). In a recent judgement addressed to collecting societies members of CISAC, the European Commission has called for a redefinition of reciprocal representation agreements, and of the relationship between collecting societies and right holders and between collecting societies and users. Accordingly, from now on these relationships should depart from any form of territorial allocation, in order to adapt to the borderless nature of Internet, satellite and cable retransmission. The decision appears to be an expected outcome of the judicial control offered by the European Commission and the European authorities over previous years. An examination of the Commission's recent attempt at regulatory reform will address the question of whether new uses should encourage a change of perspective in the economic reasoning underlying the analysis of collective administration, and of the goals pursued by licensing institutions.

4.1 Reciprocal Representation Agreements, Revisited

Reciprocal representation agreements (as defined above) increase potential access to content and demand for licenses, and raise the income of right holders whose works are going to be used beyond the boundaries of a national market. Importantly, under the agreements, collecting societies make available their tangible and intangible assets not only to their own membership, but also to members belonging to societies with which such an agreement is entered. It is argued, however, that the relevance of tangible assets is not as marked for 'digital uses' as it is for analogous uses, due to the borderless nature of the Internet.[33] Katz (2006) observes that 'the Internet allows users to locate licensors, communicate with them and obtain licenses much more efficiently than was possible in the offline

---

[33]   For example, in relation to the Santiago Agreement notified in 2001, the Commission considered that 'the territorial exclusivity afforded . . . to each of the participating societies is not justified by technical reasons and is irreconcilable with the world-wide reach of the Internet' (IP/04/586).

world.' If this is so, the question arises whether reciprocal representation agreements are adequate instruments for online licensing. Or should they adapt to the different technical nature of the demand from commercial entities using content over the Internet? These questions were addressed in the *CISAC* decision, issued by the European Commission in July 2008.[34]

CISAC traditionally drafts a model contract for its members, which typically are national performing rights organisations. CISAC members use the model contract as inspiration for reciprocal representation contracts among themselves. Even if the model contract is not mandatory, it is widely adopted. In the controversy presented to the Commission, it became clear that reciprocal representation agreements, which also affected licensing practices for Internet uses, still contained membership and territorial restrictions.[35]

As to the first of these, according to the wording of the model contract, a society is generally prevented from accepting as a member any member of another society or any right holder having the nationality of one of the countries in which another society operates, unless the other society consents. In its investigation, the Commission found that, even though most of the EEA CISAC members indicated that they had modified or wanted to modify their reciprocal representation agreement in order to remove the membership restriction, this had not actually occured and the clause in question continued to influence the relationships and behaviors of the societies.[36] The Commission considered that the restrictions created an *'artificial dependence* between collecting societies because purely national repertoires, although an important part of the repertoire of any society, are rarely a commercially attractive product for commercial users'.[37]

Turning to territorial restrictions, the Commission highlighted that, under the 'exclusivity clause', societies granted each other exclusive rights to license public performances for exploitations occurring in their respective territories. For example, this effectively means that if the Italian society grants the French society such exclusivity, the Italian society would not only not grant any other society the same right in relation to the French territory, but the Italian society itself would also refrain from licensing its own repertoire in the French territory. Such exclusivity is reinforced by an additional clause, whereby societies mutually agree to

---

[34] Commission decision (EC) on *RTL Music/Choice complaints against CISAC* (Case COMP/C2/38.698-CISAC) (hereafter *CISAC* decision).

[35] *CISAC* decision, § 4.4.

[36] *CISAC* decision, § 4.4.1.

[37] Ibid., § 7.4 (emphasis added).

avoid any intervention within each other's territory of competence.[38] The Commission acknowledged that some of the EEA CISAC members had started to remove this second clause from their contract, and decided not to intervene. However, in relation to the first of the territorial restrictions, the Commission expressly insisted on the opportunities offered by technologies that allow remote monitoring,[39] and on the advantages that could be derived if more efficient collecting societies could act in more than one territory, and granted multi-territorial licenses.[40] Interestingly, however, the Commission also agreed that territorial delineation could be justified by reason of the individual capabilities of the parties to the bilateral representation agreements. Specifically, the Commission indicated territorial delineation would not be considered a concerted practice restrictive of competition if it was 'due to the fact that the other collecting society [with which an agreement is entered] may not be seen as having the technical capability to ensure proper monitoring and enforcement'.[41] However, the model contract led to a situation where territorial delineation was systematic and could not be justified.[42]

The *CISAC* decision imposed on the concerned parties (CISAC and its EEA members) the obligation to modify their reciprocal representation agreements and to put an end to the concerted practices. The question is whether this will actually require a change in the traditional cohesion of collecting societies, in the monopolistic configuration that the Commission appears partly to justify as far as offline exploitations are concerned, and ultimately in the ability to provide users with multi-repertoire licenses. The attempt to break the existing collaboration among collecting societies could in fact oblige them to adopt non-cooperative strategies, which could result in societies being pitted against each other, not only in commercial terms, but also in the pursuit of the more general goals of making copyright enforcement practicable for all types of right holders, and access to content feasible for a large spectrum of users. The following section illustrates how this problem has become impellent and needs to be explicitly addressed.

4.2   The Two-Sided Nature of the Market for Online Music Licenses

A discussion of music rights administration would not be complete without a discussion on the European Commission Recommendation of

---

[38]   Ibid., § 25.
[39]   Ibid., § 189.
[40]   Ibid., §§168 and 212.
[41]   *CISAC*, § 182.
[42]   Ibid., § 183.

18 May 2005 on collective cross-border management of copyright and related rights for legitimate online music services, 2005/737/EC.[43] With this instrument, the European Commission (DG Internal Market) called for a change, in terms similar to, but also more radical and explicit than those contained in the *CISAC* decision. It encouraged and endorsed the adoption of collective management practices whereby right holders:

> should have the right to entrust the management of any of the online rights necessary to operate legitimate online music services, on a territorial scope of their choice, to a collective rights manager of their choice, irrespective of the Member State of residence or the nationality of either the collective rights manager or the right-holder.[44]

The election of this policy by the European Commission is said to have led to a restructuring of the supply of online rights in the music market. Large right holders have decided to appoint only one of the European performing rights societies for their online rights, subsequently withdrawing their repertoires available under the nexus of reciprocal representation agreements.[45] Accordingly, no other society apart from the one appointed can provide online licenses for the repertoire belonging to that right holder. Importantly, this new business model has meant that, as far as online licensing of music rights is concerned, the market has shifted from the fragmented situation of 'natural' monopolies existing on a territorial basis to a multi-territorial oligopoly, with the simultaneous abandonment of the reciprocal representation model. This is not merely a matter of market definition and establishment of new market powers. It can be argued that the new licensing solutions comprise a quite different relationship between collecting societies and right holders, as discussed further below. As a result, therefore, eventually there may be a need to redefine

---

[43]   [2005] OJ L 276/54, corrected by [2005] OJ L 284/10. A Recommendation is an instrument of 'soft-law'. Article 249, of the EC Treaty provides that: '[r]ecommendations and opinions shall have no binding force.'

[44]   Commission Recommendation (EC) (2005/737/EC), 21 October 2003, 3.

[45]   EMI has appointed CELAS (alliance of the UK and the German performing rights societies) to license its Anglo-American repertoire in Europe; similarly, Warner has appointed PEDL (alliance among the UK, German, Swedish and French societies); Universal (who has not withdrawn its repertoire) has established a joint venture with SACEM, the French society. More of these types of agreements are currently being formulated. See European Commission, 'Monitoring of the 2005 Music Online Recommendation' (7 February 2008); and Maria Mercedes Frabboni, 'From copyright collectives to exclusive "clubs": the changing face of music rights administration in Europe' (2008) 19 Entertainment Law Review 5, 100–105.

the relationship between collecting societies and commercial users seeking the relevant licenses.

In thus characterizing the relationship between right holders and collective managers, it must be observed that the current scenario of administration of online rights is one where collecting societies compete for the most successful right holders.[46] Consequently, a system of exclusive appointments is developing, whereby a right holder allows only one institution to administer his rights within the EU, and that institution holds the sole responsibility towards that right holder for the administration of his rights. This situation did not exist in the analogue world. There collecting societies have two main sources of revenue: the remuneration derived from licensing rights belonging to their members and, importantly, the license fees derived from the administration of foreign repertoires belonging to societies with which a reciprocal representation agreement had been concluded. Arguably, in this way they could afford the expense of administering the smaller, niche composers and other rights holders. This system is not completely ruled out if collecting societies continue to operate in a traditional way for offline uses. However, this is far from certain in light of the possible developments ensuing from the *CISAC* decision.

Moreover, in defining the new relationship between collective managers and users, it is also important to underline that users who are interested in obtaining an online license are now required to approach the specific collecting society (or alliance) that has received the mandate to license the segment of the repertoire they wish to clear. Therefore, in order to evaluate the impact of the new solution, it will be crucial to determine whether the demand for multi-repertoire licenses remains prevalent.[47] If users find that the online music services they want to operate do not need blanket or multi-repertoire solutions, collecting societies will also need to compete for their users and adapt their strategies, in order to persuade as many of them as possible to buy their licenses. Again, this was not the case under the model based on territorial fragmentation, where they naturally approached their collecting society as a one-stop-shop for all type of music content. The mechanism of online licensing could have relevant

---

[46] Commission (EC) staff working document, 'Study on a Community Initiative on the Cross-Border Collective Management of Copyright' 7 July 2005 (36, 56).
[47] Ariel Katz, in 'The potential demise of another natural monopoly: new technologies and the administration of performing rights' (2006), 1 JCLE 2, 250, argues that 'it does not seem that an ability to offer the whole worldwide repertoire is considered imperative for those [new online music] services.'

implications in this sense, in terms of visibility of diversified content and its affordability.

The competitive dynamics introduced under the new model lead to two crucial observations. Firstly, right holders such as major music publishers can hardly be defined as members[48] of the entities they have exclusively appointed to issue online licenses because, in fact, they are the sole participants in terms of repertoire. Secondly, both right holders and commercial users can be considered as customers to the online licensing platforms. The reasons for and impact of this new role of right holders and users can be understood if the online licensing solutions are scrutinized according to the economic theory of two-sided markets, explained by one scholar as follows:

> Two-sided (or, more generally, multi-sided) markets are roughly defined as markets in which one or several platforms enable interactions between end-users and try to get the two (or multiple) sides 'on board' by appropriately charging each side. That is, platforms court each side while attempting to make, or at least not lose, money overall.[49]

In the field of online licensing, platforms have to court right holders, and in particular those holding strong international repertoires, for which there is a large demand. But the 'courting' activity is not limited to one side of the platform. In fact, a right holder is likely to be 'on board' only if the right manager is able to show the potential of also getting a large number of users 'on board' the same platform, and consequently the reassurance of future earnings for right holders in terms of licensing revenue. The two-sided nature of the platform consists on the influence that each side can exercise over the other, now that licenses have become multi-territorial but are limited to specific segments of the world repertoire.

One of the likely usage characteristics of the new platforms is that, in many circumstances, one side will engage in multi-homing, in the language of two-sided markets theory.[50] That is, a portion of commercial users will connect to several platforms in order to obtain clearance to use repertoires of more than one right holder. Even if multi-homing is an assured development, uncertainties concerning the quantitative and qualitative character of the demand make it difficult to identify the effects of pricing

---

[48] 'Member: n., a person, country or organization belonging to a group, society, or team.' *Oxford Concise English Dictionary* (1999).
[49] Jean-Charles Rochet and Jean Tirole, 'Two-sided markets: a progress report' (2006) 37 RAND Journal of Economics 3, 645.
[50] Jean-Charles Rochet and Jean Tirole, 'Platform competition in two-sided markets' (2003) 1 Journal of the European Economic Association 4, 991–2.

in the presence of multi-homing. In other words, it is hard to say which and how many commercial users will need to connect to more than one platform. This leads to the observation that the effects of two-sidedness remain a matter of degree. It is suggested that sometimes the two-sided nature of the business can be critical in the analysis, while other times it is helpful but not determinative of the desirability of licensing solutions such as those considered in this section.[51] Here, the illustration of the dynamics of two-sided licensing platforms points at a fundamental change in the definition of those relationships that characterise the role and activities of traditional collective managers. In fact, as far as pan-European online licenses are concerned, the relevant platforms are in fact more competitive and selective than the traditional societies in deciding who is going to be 'courted' and who is going to be 'on board'.

Thus, it can be concluded that online licensing solutions are a logical evolution of the activities performed by traditional and historically established collecting societies, which emerged out of market developments.[52] Such evolution, however, has produced, as a result, the establishment of new institutions that perform the usual four tasks of licensing, monitoring, collecting and distributing, but do not appear to offer a collective service to right holders or users. Such an outcome is not exempt from criticisms. In particular, a main concern raised by the European Parliament is that smaller right holders holding weaker bargaining power could find themselves not satisfactorily represented if they get excluded from successful licensing platforms.[53] According to the Parliament, the effects of the model endorsed by the Commission are not limited to online licensing but, arguably, are likely to 'lead to the rapid extinction of national CRMs [Collective Rights Managers] and undermine the position of minority repertoires and cultural diversity in Europe'.[54] This comment highlights how removed the traditional collecting societies, with their all-encompassing action, are perceived to be from their newly structured presence in the market for online music rights.

---

[51]   David S Evans and Richard Schmalensee, 'Industrial organization of markets with two-sided platforms' (2007) 3 Competition Policy International 1, 151.

[52]   The natural course of market developments has of course also been heavily directed by regulation and judicial control.

[53]   European Parliament resolution of 13 March 2007 on the Commission Recommendation (EC) of 18 October 2005 on collective cross-border management of copyright and related rights for legitimate online music services (2005/737/EC), 5.

[54]   Ibid.

5. CONCLUSION

The economic rationale behind collective administration of copyright and related rights has long provided a solid foundation for the concentrated market structure in which national collecting societies have traditionally operated. Accordingly, national collecting societies have managed a multitude of rights for a varied spectrum of members and also various foreign repertoires, via the instrument of reciprocal representation agreements. The economic literature is unanimous in identifying efficiencies in the aggregate model, but also questions the effectiveness of those instruments that helped in preventing possible abuses by collecting societies against right holder and users. Competition law, as one of those instruments, has not imposed actual competition amongst collecting societies. Rather, it has required a *rule of reason* to be applied to some of the practices adopted by the societies. From this perspective, over time, a discussion has emerged on the need to safeguard collecting societies' national monopolies. In facing the demand for Internet licenses and the characteristics of Internet uses, it was increasingly perceived that the territorial connotation of the collective action was no longer justifiable. Now, licensing solutions offer users the opportunity to obtain online multi-territorial licenses from a single licensing platform, but only for specific segments of the world repertoire. This shows a change in the nature of the licensing entities, which have partly abandoned their special collective role to allow for more competitive models to arise. It also indicates that especially large right holders may be inclined, in the future, to integrate the rights management function within their organization, bypassing existing intermediaries altogether. A much-needed review of the initial economic results achieved by the existing platforms could indicate to what extent the favor accorded to the new licensing mechanisms has actually fulfilled the needs and preferences of the market and its participants, but could also signify that further action is needed to ensure that stakeholders who are willing to participate are able to find an appropriate commercial solution to do so.

8. Social justice, innovation and antitrust law

Mariateresa Maggiolino

1. THE ROLE THAT THE SOCIAL JUSTICE PERSPECTIVE COULD HAVE PLAYED IN SHAPING THE RELATIONSHIP BETWEEN DOMINANT FIRMS' PROPRIETARY INNOVATIONS AND ANTITRUST LAW

Pursuing 'social justice' may mean supporting a non-discriminatory distribution of resources and opportunities among people to give them fair treatment, a just share of collective wealth, and the right to affect social and economic developments. Thus, endorsing a social justice approach towards proprietary innovations, such as patented inventions and copyrighted creations, may mean – as the previous chapters have shown – discussing whether the existing IPRs allow, on the one hand, inventors and authors to receive a fair and just consideration for their efforts;[1] and, on the other hand, the whole society to benefit from the innovation, as such, and from the spread of knowledge that each innovation entails and triggers.[2]

Yet, how can a social justice perspective have relevance to antitrust rules regarding dominant firms' conduct and, in particular, dominant firms' conduct involving proprietary innovations?

Though promulgated in different years,[3] in the United States and in the European Union, section 2 of the Sherman Act and Article 102 of the

---

[1] See Federico Morando, Copyright default rule: reconciling efficiency and fairness, Chapter 2 in this book.

[2] See Jerzy Koopman, Chapter 4 in this book.

[3] In the United States such a 'social justice' approach to antitrust law took place in the years before the advent of the Chicago School, leading up to the 1970s. Instead, in the European Community the same approach has survived at least through the late 1990s, until the Commission began the so-called 'modernization process'.

TFEU[4] have been enforced in order to: (1) protect democracy, freedom, and citizens' self-independence by sheltering economic pluralism;[5] (2) prevent big companies from engaging in unfair and exploitative behaviors detrimental to their rivals, customers and consumers; and (3) guarantee a just wealth redistribution towards consumers.[6] Hence, it could be argued that pursuing a social justice approach to antitrust rules that deal with dominant firms' conduct means, *inter alia*, preventing dominant firms from impairing their rivals and, in a specific case, prohibiting dominant firms from using their proprietary innovations to reduce their rivals' profit opportunities.

Nevertheless, this conception of antitrust law is outdated. Indeed, since the advent of the Chicago School 'U.S. antitrust law aims to protect free markets as efficient mechanisms of allocation and to spur innovation that is the principal source of economic growth'. Therefore mere harm to competitors is not a basis for antitrust liability. Analogously, the European Commission (recently) maintained that 'what really matters is to protect an effective competitive process and not simply protecting competitors. This may well mean that competitors who deliver less to consumers in terms of price, choice, quality and innovation will leave the market'.[7] In particular, the Commission has clarified that a dominant firm's conduct will be deemed allegedly abusive if it is likely to lead to anticompetitive foreclosure, given that the term 'anticompetitive foreclosure' addresses a situation where the practice hampers, or prevents, actual or potential

---

[4]   With the Lisbon Treaty, OJ 2007, C306/1, the Treaty on the functioning of European Union (TFEU), OJ 2002, C325/33, replaces the Treaty on European Community (TEC), OJ 2008, C115/1, with Article 82 renumbered to Article 102.

[5]   Whereas the 'US soul' of such a conception of competition law has roots in Jeffersonian ideals, it was the Freiburg school which inspired the analogous 'EU soul'.

[6]   For the analysis of the objectives of the present US and EU antitrust laws see Phillip E. Areeda and Herbert Hovenkamp, *Antitrust Law: An Analysis of Antitrust Principles and their Application* (3rd ed Aspen 2006) 100–113, and Richard Whish, *Competition Law* (6th ed OUP 2008) 19–23.

[7]   See European Commission, 'The Guidance Paper on the Commission's Enforcement Priorities in Applying Article 82 EC Treaty to Abusive Exclusionary Conduct by Dominant Undertakings' (2008) §6 OJ 2009, C45/7. True, the Commission's Guidance Paper represents an example of soft law aimed at rewriting the existing law, as the same Commission stated at the time that the paper 'is not intended to constitute a statement of the law and is without prejudice to the interpretation of Article 82 by the European Court of Justice or the Court of First Instance' (§ 3). Nonetheless, the new approach to Article 102 that the Guidance Paper supports has been already articulated in recent decisions (i.e. *Microsoft*) that the European Courts have upheld.

competitors to effectively access supplies or markets so that the dominant firm is likely to be in a position to profitably act in detriment of consumers, by increasing market prices, reducing market output, limiting innovation, and reducing consumer choice.[8]

Nowadays, therefore, the key antitrust jurisdictions finally concur in considering that antitrust law must no longer protect economic pluralism, fairness, and equity[9] but rather must concern behaviors that harm consumer welfare and innovation, that is to say allocative and dynamic efficiency.[10] Thus, the *condicio sine qua non* for having the current antitrust authorities to scrutinize a dominant firm's proprietary innovation can no longer be – and, actually, it has never really been[11] – that such innovation gives to the dominant firm a competitive advantage in detriment of its rivals. Rather, the antitrust assessment of dominant firms' innovation should follow a three-step analysis. *First*, given that good or true innovation (that

---

[8]   See id. at §§ 9, 11, 20. What really matters in the paraphrased statement is that the Commission finally acknowledges that a practice's exclusionary effect (i.e. the fact that a practice may hamper or prevent actual or potential competitors to effectively access supplies or markets) entails antitrust concerns *only if* it becomes the vehicle whereby the dominant firm is likely to be in a position to profitably act in detriment of consumers.

[9]   To be sure, what the European Commission has recently stated in connection to the aims of Article 102 does not imply that future EU policies regarding the common market will not pursue fairness, justice and wealth redistribution. On the contrary, as maintained in G. Ghidini and Valeria Falce, Antitrust and consumer protection: the new regime on unfair commercial practices, Chapter 9 in this book, EU institutions are really interested in protecting consumers, which may impact definitions of fairness across regulatory regimes. Indeed, reading Directive 2005/29 together with the Guidance Paper shows that the EU Commission has chosen to fulfill different objectives using different legal devices.

[10] Allocative efficiency is a static concept that is achieved when the system of market prices allows the existing stock of (final and intermediate) goods to be assigned to those purchasers who value them most in terms of willingness to pay or willingness to forego other consumption possibilities. When allocative efficiency is reached, market prices are equal to the marginal costs of producing and supplying those goods. The concept of *dynamic efficiency*, instead, addresses both the possibility of maximizing welfare over time by trading off consumption and production gains across different time periods, and how well a market delivers innovation and technological progress. In this regard, hence, it addresses whether appropriate incentives and ability exist to increase productivity and induce firms to engage in innovative activity over time. The Guidance Paper does refer to harm to allocative efficiency when it states that a dominant firm acts in detriment of consumers by increasing market prices or reducing market output; and does refer to harm to dynamic efficiency when it states that a dominant firm acts in detriment of consumers by limiting innovation.

[11] See Section 4 of this chapter, especially looking at the US experience.

is, innovation that does not consist in mere tinkering with products and processes) does represent a key driver of economic progress and, as such, a crucial source of wealth and consumer welfare, antitrust authorities should distinguish such a good innovation from sham innovation by evaluating the inherent quality of the regarded patented invention or copyrighted creations. *Second*, they should use economics to establish whether the conditions under which dominant firms can employ innovations to harm allocative and dynamic efficiency hold. *Third*, perhaps by using an effective burden of proof rule, US courts as well as EU antitrust institutions should confront situations in which dominant firms' innovations produce benefits versus those in which they cause competitive harm.[12]

Accordingly, whereas Section 3 of this chapter will look at the economic theory to briefly address each of these steps in turn, Section 4 will consider *if* and *how* US courts and EU antitrust authorities apply the above three-step analysis. Finally, Section 5 will ponder whether the current US and EU jurisdictions grant any further space for a social justice approach to dominant firms' proprietary innovations, using what the Commission and the Court of First Instance have stated in connection to the integration between Windows Operating System and Window Media Player as a hint for a possible answer. In order to better understand the structure of Section 3 a clarification is needed about innovation, addressed in Section 2.

2.   A USEFUL DISTINCTION ABOUT DOMINANT FIRMS' PROPRIETARY INNOVATIONS

As one of the seminal economic papers about 'predatory innovation' teaches,[13] dominant firms' innovations may be led to two different categories:

(1)   Innovations that regard only the already monopolized product and, hence, the already monopolized market (hereafter 'Isolated Innovations'); and,

(2)   In a scenario where the monopolized product generates value when pooled together with other products produced by the dominant firm

---

[12]   After all, hard cases arise under section 2, Sherman Antitrust Act and Article 102, TFEU when dominant firms' practices enhances allocative efficiency or boosts innovation but, at the same time, excludes competitors through means other than simply attracting consumers.

[13]   Janusz A. Ordover and Robert Willig, An Economic Definition of Predation: Pricing and Product Innovation (1981) 91 Yale L.J. 8.

as well as by other firms, innovations that jeopardize the technological compatibility that makes the products work together (hereafter 'System Innovations') and, hence, affect both the primary already monopolized market and the secondary market.[14]

Then, the US and EU case-law teaches that dominant firms' System Innovations have been questioned in three analogous scenarios, namely the cases of a dominant firm that introduces:[15]

(a) A 'new' version of the monopolized product *closing* its interface, thus preventing rivals from knowing what they need to make their 'old' products work with the 'new' one;[16]

---

[14] In this way, the chapters looks at some cases of 'horizontal foreclosure' – i.e. cases where a dominant firm is present in two final adjacent markets, one monopolized and one competitive, and forecloses its competitors in the adjacent competitive market by 'linking' its monopolized product to its competitive product. For a more detailed explanation of 'horizontal foreclosure', see Patrick Rey and Jean Tirole, *A Primer on Foreclosure* 49–79 (2006) <http://idei.fr/doc/by/tirole/primer.pdf>.

[15] Though every firm can manipulate compatibility, only a dominant firm can be interested in using incompatibility as an anticompetitive device. Indeed, if a firm without market power introduces a new product that is supposed to be combined with others but that cannot work with them, the firm will surely lose customers, as consumers will prefer the rival's product that lets them enjoy the benefits of the system. See, e.g., Richard J. Gilbert, 'Symposium of Compatibility: Incentives and Market Structure', 40 The Journal of Industrial Economics 1 (1992); Carmen Matutes and Pierre Regibeau, 'Mix and match: product compatibility without network externalities' (1988) 19(2) Rand Journal of Economics 221. Also see Nicholas Economides, 'Desirability of compatibility in the absence of network externalities' (1989) 79(5) American Economic Review 1165 (noticing that firms that are the same size and have similar characteristics prefer compatibility to incompatibility). After all, this is the reason why, using the tying jargon, for tech-tying to be profit maximizing it is necessary that the firm has market power in the tying market. Nevertheless, for an economic model where tying is anticompetitive though, the regarded firm does not have monopoly power, see Eugen Kovác, 'Tying and entry deterrence in vertically differentiated markets' (2005) CERGE-EI Working Papers <www.ssrn.com>.

[16] In order to close the interface, the monopolist can either acquire an IPR on that interface or exploit the fact that the interface is too complicated to be understood by its rivals without her help. For instance, that was the case when Microsoft introduced its new version of the operating system for networks without disclosing the information necessary to interoperability. Similarly, consider a durable good producer who refrains from communicating a technical specification to manufacturers of spare parts, preventing them from building their compatible components with the monopolized good.

(b)   An innovation consisting of the *physical integration* into a single good of the system's components that the monopolist previously sold separately. As there will be no space in the 'new' single product for rivals' 'old' products, they will lack technologically equal access[17] to the 'new' version of the monopolized product;[18] or

(c)   A 'new' version of the monopolized product that is technically incompatible with all rivals' auxiliary goods. This 'technological tying'[19] relies on incompatibility to condition the sale of its own compatible auxiliary products to the purchase of the 'new' monopolized product.

Therefore, in outlining the economic theory about dominant firms' innovations the following section will consider the impact that both Isolated and System Innovations have on welfare, evaluating as well how such an impact changes as System Innovations take one of the above three different forms.

3.   DOMINANT FIRMS' PROPRIETARY INNOVATIONS AND WELFARE

In order to face the first step of the above-mentioned three-step analysis consider that, broadly speaking, both Isolated and System innovations that do not amount to mere sham better satisfy consumer preferences by being either superior or less expensive than existing products and processes. Moreover, true Isolated and System innovations tend to engender further good innovations, auto-feeding economic progress. Thus, good

---

[17]   See, e.g., Jean Tirole, *The Analysis of Tying Cases: A Primer* 7 (2004), <http://www.intertic.org/Theory%20Papers/Tirole.pdf>.

[18]   As occurred when IBM integrated in new versions of its CPUs several functions previously sold separately.

[19]   As explained by Frank H. Easterbrook, 'An economical and legal analysis of physical tie-ins' (1980) 89 The Yale Law Journal 769, technological tying must be distinguished from contractual tying for several reasons. First, while the source of a technological tie is compatibility of the new products with each other and their incompatibility with competing products, an arrangement is the source of traditional contractual tie. Moreover, the time period of a tying arrangement is defined by the initial parties and is potentially permanent, while a tech-tying lasts only as long as it takes a competitor to develop a compatible product. Further, with only a technological tie, the disposal of the bundled good may be costly or even impractical, while with a contractual bundle, there is at least the possibility of getting rid of the unwanted part of the bundle.

Isolated and System innovations are generally welfare increasing tools, as they bring static and dynamic benefits not only to their inventors, but also to society as a whole. In particular, since any kind of true innovation produces more public than private benefits,[20] one could argue that it entails a positive impact on social welfare even when it results from firms' irrational[21] investment choices.[22] Hence, named *SW*(i) the impact that any innovation has on social welfare irrespective of competition concerns, Isolated and System innovations that do not consist in mere manipulations or tinkering with products and processes enhance social welfare, even when they result from non-optimal R&D expenditures, so that it is true that:

---

[20]   See, e.g., Edwin Mansfield, 'Microeconomics of technological innovation' in Bruce R. Guile and Harvey Brooks (eds), *Technology and Global Industry 311* (1987), and Timothy F. Bresnahan, 'The Mechanisms of Information Technology's Contribution to Economic Growth' in Jean-Phillipe Touffut (ed), *Institutions, Innovation and Growth: Selected Economic Papers* 135–37 (Edward Elgar, London 2003).

[21]   Affirming that a firm is making an irrational investment decision regarding innovation means addressing the case when a firm undertakes wasteful investments in R&D, i.e. addressing the case when a firm is not optimizing, by paying more for the innovation than what it is expecting to gain from it. Now, given the rationality of economic agents, the only way to justify such a behavior is assuming that the wasteful expenditures are a part of a strategy, i.e. that they are actually counter-balanced not by the innovation's benefits (as it should usually be), but by the collateral gain that comes from strengthening the dominant position. In formulas, given $B(i)$ the private benefits that come with the innovation (i), and $C(i)$ the costs in R&D sustained for developing (i), an innovation is produced when $B(i) > C(i)$. Therefore, an innovation results from an irrational but strategic choice when it entails an indirect benefit $X(i)$ that changes the innovation's pay-off so that, whereas $B(i) < C(i)$, $B(i) + X(i) > C(i)$. In the Ordover-Willig model, *supra* note 13, the indirect benefit that the innovation entails is the chance for the monopolist to keep on making over-competitive prices.

[22]   Since, broadly speaking, antitrust law assumes that the optimization of social welfare comes via firms' rational choices this assumption should lead to the conclusion that innovations resulting from wasteful R&D investments always produce a negative impact on social welfare. Indeed, that is the conclusion that Ordover and Willig reached when discussing the predatory nature of an Isolated Innovation, and they did recognize that innovations bring welfare increasing effects. Perhaps taking inspiration from the Areeda-Turner reasoning about predatory investments, [see Philip Areeda and Donald F. Turner, 'Predatory pricing and related practices under Section 2 of the Sherman Act' (1975) 88 Harvard Law Review 697, 720] Ordover and Willig supposed that with socially wasteful R&D investments the innovation's positive impact on social welfare was overturned by the social consequences of non-optimal R&D expenditures. However, as innovation's social returns are greater than their private returns, such a conclusion does not always hold.

$$SW(i) > 0$$

Further, System Innovations that entail and rely on incompatibility produce several *efficiency gains*,[23] typically via tech-ties and integrations.[24] For instance, they may allow: (1) controlling product quality and goodwill reputation;[25] (2) responding to customers' different valuations of the assembled products;[26] (3) lowering production costs, taking advantage of technological spillover, learning effects, economies of scale and joint sales that occur in the development of the system's components;[27] (4)

---

[23]   Efficiency effects are the effects that a firm's behavior produces absent any competitive response to it. On the contrary, the strategic effects that a practice produces are conditioned to the competitive response that a practice entails. In this regard see, e.g., Bruce H. Kobayashi, 'Does Economics Provide a Reliable Guide to Regulating Commodity Bundling by Firms? A Survey of the Economic Literature' (2005) 1(4) Journal of Competition Law & Economics <http://papers. ssrn.com/sol3/papers.cfm?abstract_id=836724>.

[24]   For a detailed discussion of the economics of tying see Jurian Langer, *Tying and Bundling as a Leveraging Concern Under EC Competition Law* (Aspen, New York 2008). Further, consider that economists develop these efficiency-enhancing rationales for incompatibility, tech-ties and integrations looking at the case of secondary markets that are highly competitive. See, e.g., David S. Evans and Michael Salinger, 'Why do firms bundle and tie? Evidence from competitive markets and implications for tying law' (2005) 22 Yale J. Reg. 37; and David S. Evans and A. Jorge Padilla, 'Designing antitrust rules for assessing unilateral practice: a neo Chicago approach' (2005) 72 U. Chi. L. Rev. 27. Nevertheless, those justifications can work as well for the case of secondary oligopolistic markets. See, e.g., Patrick Rey, Paul Seabright and Jean Tirole, 'The Activities of a Monopoly Firm in Adjacent Competitive Markets: Economic Consequences and Implications for Competition Policy' (2001) <http://www.idei.fr/doc/by/seabright/activities.pdf>.

[25]   Assuming that the monopolist cannot prevent its monopolized product from working with its rivals' components and that the system fails to satisfy consumers' needs. As consumers may be unable to understand why the system fails, it is possible that the monopolist will bear the risk to be found responsible for the failure, even when the failure results from the low quality of rivals' products. In such a situation, therefore, creating incompatibility (maybe via tech-tying and integration) can be a proper way to fight both the asymmetry of information that affects consumers and the risk that rivals' products will ruin the systems' performance.

[26]   For instance, integrating different kinds of software in a unique operating system satisfies various consumer needs: software to write, calculate, or listen to music. Nevertheless, this integration is possible not only because the costs are low, but also because the industry of microprocessors has developed products that are increasingly powerful. See, e.g., Yannis Bakos and Eric Brynjolfsson, 'Bundling information goods: prices, profits, and efficiency' (1999) 45 Mgmt. Sci. 1613.

[27]   For instance, it is cheaper and less time-consuming for a computer manufacturer to assemble its parts instead of asking each consumer – most of whom

internalizing pricing externalities;[28] (5) allocating risk;[29] and (6) setting a proper pricing strategy in two-sided markets.[30] Therefore, in studying the impact that System Innovations produce on social welfare, the above described efficiencies – say, $E(i)$ – must be encompassed, given that they are welfare-enhancing by definition, so that it is true that:

$$SW[E(i)] > 0$$

Also, System Innovations that take the form of tech-ties, where the tied product is consumed in variable proportions, can work as vehicles of price discrimination[31] or metering devices.[32] In such a scenario the effect of this practice on social welfare is ambiguous because total welfare can rise or fall, depending upon the specific combination of costs, consumers' reservation prices, and the correlation between them. Thus, naming such a social welfare impact $SW[TT(i)^D]$ when the regarded tech-ties work as discriminatory tools, it occurs that:

---

are without the necessary expertise – to search for and buy the different components and put them together. Also, without themselves having to write Internet-related code, consumers get Internet-related functionality with their operating system and applications programs that use this functionality in creative ways. For a detailed analysis of these effects see, e.g., Steven Davis, Jack MacCrisken and Kevin Murphy, 'Integrating New Features into the PC Operating System: Benefits, Timing, and Effects on Innovation' (1998) <http://faculty.chicagogsb.edu/steven.davis/research/Evolution_of_the_PC_Operating_System_(with_Jack_MacCrisken_and_Kevin_Murphy)_June1999.PDF>; Joseph G. Sidak, 'An antitrust rule for software integration' (2001) 18 Yale Journal on Regulation 1, 15–20; and Yannis Bakos and Eric Brynjolfsson, 'Bundling and competition on the Internet: aggregations strategies for information goods' (2000), 19 Marketing Sci. 63.

[28] In other words, the creation of incompatibility, in case via tech-tying and integration, consents to reach the well-known 'Cournot effect' that is proper of the pure bundling among complements.

[29] See, e.g., Joseph G. Sidak, 'Debunking predatory innovation', (1983) 83 Colum. L. Rev. 1121, 1135.

[30] See, e.g., Tirole, *supra* note 17, at 12.

[31] See, e.g., George J. Stigler, 'US v. Loew's Inc.: a note on block booking' (1963) 1963 Supreme Court Review 152; William J. Adams and Janet L. Yellen, 'Commodity bundling and the burden of monopoly' (1976) 90 Quarterly Journal of Economics 475; and Richard Schmalensee, 'Commodity bundling by single product monopolies' (1982) 25 J. L. & Econ. 67.

[32] See, e.g., Sreya Kolay and Greg Shaffer, 'Bundling and menus of two-part tariffs' (2003) 51 J. Ind. Econ. 383. Metering cannot work with complements that are used only in fixed proportions, such as Explorer and the Windows operating system.

$$SW[TT(\text{i})^{\text{D}}] \; \substack{> \\ <} \; 0$$

Now, turn to the second step of the above mentioned analysis and think about the competition strategic concerns that stem from monopolists' Isolated and System Innovations in turn. First, a dominant firm can use its Isolated Innovations to harm competition, as such, when these innovations can work inside an effective predatory scheme that, thanks to some market hurdles and a consistent pricing strategy,[33] allows the dominant firm practicing over-competitive prices after the exclusion of its rivals.[34] Analogously, only in particular scenarios can a dominant firm use its System Innovations that create and rely on incompatibility to harm competition, as such.[35] This may occur, for instance, when the two goods are complementary and the entry in to the imperfectly competitive market may facilitate entry into the monopolized market. Here the dominant firm may foreclose the adjacent market to pre-existing producers of compatible products, preventing them from entering the primary market and so displacing its original monopoly.[36] In this case, foreclosing the secondary market permits the firm dominating the primary market to defend this original dominant position and, thereby to continue its *supra* competitive prices in that market. Therefore, under specific conditions, dominant

---

[33]   See Ordover and Willig, *supra* note 13, at 9–12 and 22–27.

[34]   Indeed, firms compete both on prices and on product quality. Therefore, it should not be a surprise that predation may result from both pricing strategies and strategies about product changes.

[35]   To be sure, there is at least one other way to use tie-ins (and, especially, integrations and tech-ties) in a strategic way, i.e. as entry deterrence devices. Yet, as this strategic use of tie-ins requires the goods involved to be quite independent, it could be injurious to apply such a theory to explain the competitive harm underpinning the tying between complementary goods such as razors and blades, mobile telephones and accessories, new cars and spare parts, and computers and component upgrades. On this topic, see Michael D. Whinston, 'Tying, foreclosure, and exclusion' (1990) 80 American Economic Review 837; Barry Nalebuff, 'Bundling, Tying, and Portfolio Effects' (2003) DTI Economics Paper No. 1. <http://www.dti. gov.uk/economics/papers.html>; and Rey and Tirole, *supra* note 14, at 51.

[36]   See, e.g., Robin Cooper Feldman, 'Defensive leveraging in antitrust' (1999) 87 Geo. L.J. 2079, 2087; Jay Pil Choi and Christodoulos Stefanadis, 'Tying, investment, and the dynamic leverage theory' (2001) 32 Rand Journal of Economics 52; Dennis W. Carlton, and Michael Waldman, 'The strategic use of tying to preserve and create market power in evolving industries' (2002) 33 Rand Journal of Economics 194; and Rey and Tirole, *supra* note 14, at 57 for a formalized explanation of the last two models.

firms' Isolated and System Innovations allow monopolists to keep on charging over-competitive prices, say [P^M(i)], and hence producing all the usual allocative and dynamic inefficiencies that produce a negative impact on social welfare, say *SW*, so that it is true that:

$$SW[P^M(i)] < 0$$

Moreover, looking at the competition strategic concerns that stem from monopolists' System Innovations that create and rely on incompatibility, it must be noticed that this kind of innovation may reduce dominant firm's rivals' incentives to innovate. For instance, a tying may represent a commitment for the dominant firm to have an aggressive R&D policy in the tied market and, hence, may discourage rivals' R&D investments in that market. Yet the welfare implications of this conduct are ambiguous, since in the short-run tying reduces prices and in the longer run it increases one firm's R&D incentives to innovate but reduces those of its rivals.[37] Calling I_{t1}(i), the R&D incentives pattern that follows the introduction of the dominant firm's System Innovation, it is true that:

$$SW[I_{t1}(i)] \gtrless 0$$

Thus, moving to the third step of the analysis, a correct assessment of the total impact of monopolists' innovations on social welfare should require antitrust authorities to make a kind of 'algebraic sum' of the above different variables – that is, SW(i), $SW[E$(i)$]$, $SW[TT$(i)$^D]$, $SW[P^M$(i)$]$ and $SW[I_{t1}$(i)$]$.

Unfortunately, these variables are difficult to 'measure'. For instance, the magnitude of SW(i) rests with the nature of the single innovation and with a prognostic judgment about the market's technological development.[38] Moreover, as the above discussion has demonstrated, such

---

[37] See, e.g., Jay Pil Choi, Gwanghoon Lee and Christodoulos Stefanadis, 'The effects of integration on R&D incentives in systems markets' (2003) 5 *Netnomics* 21.

[38] It may be argued that major innovations produce noteworthy benefits to social welfare; yet sometimes it is difficult to distinguish between major product change improvements and mere product differentiation representing mere redesign of the pre-existing product without deliberating on the inherent technological nature of the innovation (an inquiry that many lawyers are not well-equipped to do). In this regard, it is notable that even the existence of a

variables may have a positive or negative value, according to existing market conditions; consider, for example, the ambivalent nature of $SW[TT(i)^D]$ and $SW[I_{t1}(i)]$. Further, antitrust courts and authorities are not always well-equipped to verify whether the facts support the peculiar hypothesis underpinning the economic model that depicts anticompetitive good innovations – that is, in order to verify that $SW[P^M(i)] < 0$ can occur. Therefore, though the economic thinking seems to suggest that antitrust authorities strike a balance between all the good that may come with innovations and the harm that dominant firms' innovations may sometimes cause, it is questionable that US courts and EU antitrust institutions will be able to do it. The following section tries to answer this question.

4. THE US AND EU LEGAL STANDARDS ABOUT DOMINANT FIRMS' PROPRIETARY INNOVATIONS

Having considered the variable impacts that dominant firms' Isolated and System Innovations can have on social welfare, this section examines whether and how well the authorities of the key antitrust jurisdictions, the US and the EU, have been able to apply such analysis in the cases involving such proprietary innovations.[39]

---

patent or copyright cannot be used as a proxy for the quality of the innovation, as patents are granted even to minor inventions and copyright follows from mere creation and, in case, the combination between creation and fixation. Moreover, it is mere speculation to anticipate both the extent to which an innovation generates further innovation and the benefits yielded by those subsequent innovations. To perform such a judgment, indeed, one should estimate both the innovations that might subsequently be developed and the innovations that would have been developed in the absence of this new innovation, so as to conclude whether the innovations that belong to the former kind are superior to the latter.

[39]   To be sure, as the following discussion will show, in the regarded cases IPRs did not play a significant role. Indeed, as noticed *supra* note 38, the existence of patents and copyrights does not help in appreciating the inherent value of the regarded invention/creation. Nor does it give any hint in connection to the likely harm that the proprietary innovation could cause to allocative efficiency. See, e.g., Harry First, 'Microsoft and the evolution of the intellectual property concept' (2006) Wisconsin Law Review 1369, 1383–1384 (stating, in discussing the US competitive analysis of the integration of Internet Explorer in Windows (see notes 43–47 and accompanying text), that: 'the court of appeals' balancing approach had little to do with the scope of the actual IPRs that Microsoft might have had. . . The question for the court was whether. . . Microsoft's conduct constituted an

An examination of US cases shows that US courts have faced several instances in which the regarded innovation represented either a major cost saving step or a brilliant and significant improvement – for example the launch of a new revolutionary camera, or the integration in one single computer of several features and functions previously supplied separately.[40] In other words, in these cases US courts scrutinized innovations whose value was outstanding – that is, innovations that, thanks to their inherent quality, produced a clearly positive impact on social welfare, say $SW(i) \gg 0$. Therefore, these courts stopped their examination at the first prong of the above-mentioned three-step analysis, as if the inherent quality of the regarded innovations was enough to outweigh any likely anticompetitive effects. Indeed, these courts quickly rejected any plea of anticompetitive innovation stating, for instance, that a monopolist has 'the right to redesign its products to make them more attractive to buyers . . . [and has] no duty to help [its competitors to] survive or expand . . . [or] to facilitate sales of rival products';[41] and that challenging the monopolist's innovation sometimes permits rivals to avoid new rounds of reverse engineering and to the detriment of the dominant firm's incentive to innovate.[42]

On the other hand, US courts have also faced cases where the challenged technological changes either had deliberately caused an evident worsening of the product, or did not represent anything more than manipulations

---

exclusionary practice under Section 2 of the Sherman Act. . . product quality of Windows was a sufficiently strong justification to make Microsoft's conduct, on this point, not unreasonable and, therefore, not a violation of the antitrust laws').

[40]   See, e.g., *California Computer Products, Inc. and Century Data System, Inc.*, v. *IBM*, 613 F.2d 727 (9th Cir. 1979) (although the plaintiff claimed IBM made design changes of no technological advantage on certain CPUs, disk drives and controllers to the sole purpose of frustrating competition from plug-compatible manufacturers, Court held that technological changes comprised significant innovations; *ILC Peripherals Leasing Corp.* v. *IBM*, 448 F.Supp. 228 (N.D.Cal. 1978) and *ILC Peripherals Leasing Corp.* v. *IBM*, 458 F.Supp. 423 (N.D.Cal. 1978) (holding that plaintiff failed to prove that certain interface changes were predatory) both *aff'd per curiam sub nom; Memorex Corp.* v. *IBM*, 636 F.2d 1188 (9th Cir. 1980); *Telex Corp* v. *IBM*, 367 F.Supp. 258, 347 (N.D.Okla. 1973), *rev'd on other grounds*, 510 F.2d 894 (10th Cir. 1975) (despite allegations that IBM undertook predatory behaviors by introducing 'technological obsolesce hence through mid-life kickers' and by tying peripheral products, including memories and control units, to its CPU's, trial court's conclusion that practices made available improved devices at the earliest practicable time and represented technological advancements upheld; IBM found not to be dominant).

[41]   613 F.2d 727, 744 (9th Cir. 1979).

[42]   458 F. Supp. 423, 443 (N.D.Cal. 1978).

aimed at creating incompatibility[43] – that is, cases in which the inherent quality of the innovation was so low that its impact on social welfare was negative or, at least, not positive, say $SW(i) \sim 0$. In these cases, therefore, the courts shifted their focus to what the innovation's anticompetitive rationale was – that is, to the second step of the above-mentioned three-step analysis, though they have not always paid a lot of attention to this aspect.

For instance, in *C.R. Bard* v. *M3 Systems* [44] the jury, after having considered evidence showing that the innovation was never *intended to be* an improvement,[45] found *without explanation* that Bard had launched its innovation to raise rivals' entry costs into the secondary market. Differently, in *United States* v. *Microsoft Corp.*[46] (hereinafter, '*Microsoft III*') the court carefully elaborated the anticompetitive aspect of Microsoft's innovation. In particular, the court maintained that Microsoft's technological changes – that is the integration of Internet Explorer in Windows,[47] and

---

[43]   See, e.g., *In re IBM peripheral EDP Devices Antitrust litigation*, 481 F.Supp. 965 (N.D.Cal. 1979), *aff'd Transamerica Computer Company, Inc.* v. *IBM*, 698 F.2d 1377 (9th Cir. 1983) where the plaintiffs, who were manufacturers of peripheral computer equipment such as keyboards and printers compatible with IBM PCs, brought suit for antitrust violations when IBM redesigned its central processing unit (CPU) and made it incompatible with any peripheral product not made by IBM. The courts found lawful all but two design changes – System 370, Models 115 and 125 – that unreasonably restricted competition as they allowed operating just short of the speed that would have enabled peripherals to attach (481 F.Supp. 965, 1006–1008 and 698 F.2d 1377, 1383). Notwithstanding such a negative judgment about these two innovations, IBM was not condemned because it lacked monopoly power and because the court established that the plaintiff did not suffer any damages.

[44]   157 F.3d 1340 (Fed. Cir. 1998), where the plaintiff alleged that Bard had modified its biopsy gun and needles not for improving the operation of the gun, but for the purpose of preventing use of its rivals' needles so that they did not fit the gun without an adapter. The plaintiff contended that Bard's design changes were anti-competitive, pointing to Bard documents showing internal discussions of anti-competitive aims.

[45]   In other words, the subjective element was crucial. Indeed, given the unpredictability of innovation, it is impossible to infer its anticompetitive nature from the fact that it is not a significant improvement.

[46]   253 F.3d 34 (D.C. Cir. 2001).

[47]   Microsoft's integration of IE and Windows 'prevented OEMs from preinstalling other browsers and deterred consumers from using them' (*Microsoft III*, 63–4). The integration consisted in: (a) excluding IE from the 'Add/Remove Programs' utility; (b) co-mingling in the same files the code related to browsing to other codes, so that any attempt to delete the files containing IE would, at the same time, cripple the operating system; (c) designing Windows so to override the user's choice of a default browser other than IE.

the development of Microsoft's version of Java, incompatible with the other on the market,[48] – produced a foreclosure effect to the detriment of Netscape and Sun Microsystems, as it prevented their developing a way to bypass Microsoft's operating system. In other words, the Court concluded that Microsoft used those innovations to defend its original monopoly in the operating system market by acquiring a significant market power in secondary markets. In its analysis of these technological changes, the Court used in a pivotal way the burden of proof rule, requiring Microsoft to rebut the alleged anticompetitive effects of the innovations concerned with some objective justifications regarding their superior quality. When Microsoft was unable to justify from a technical/commercial standpoint the different practices that resulted in the integration between Internet Explorer and the Windows PC operating system, the Court deemed those practices anticompetitive. Yet, when Microsoft could justify its choice to override the user's preference for a default browser with 'valid technical reasons'[49] and the introduction of its own Java underlining its superior speed,[50] the Court did not strike these innovations. Therefore, while rejecting some of Microsoft's rivals' claims the DC Circuit were quite deferential in addressing the positive side of the monopolist's innovations.

In conclusion, it should be acknowledged that US courts in scrutinizing dominant firms' proprietary innovations did apply a test similar to the above three-step analysis: they considered whether the innovation was *'unreasonably* restrictive of competition'[51] (the third step) by comparing its

---

[48]　　Java is another type of middleware posing a potential threat to Windows' position as the ubiquitous platform for software development. The District Court found that Microsoft took four steps to exclude Java from developing as a viable cross-platform threat: (i) designing a JVM (Java Virtual Machine) incompatible with the one developed by its rival Sun Microsystems; (ii) entering into contracts, the so-called 'First Wave Agreements', requiring major ISVs to promote Microsoft's JVM exclusively; (iii) deceiving Java developers about the Windows-specific nature of the tools it distributed to them; and (iv) coercing Intel to stop aiding Sun Microsystems in improving the Java technologies. The first of these behaviors is the one here addressed.

[49]　　Although all three acts mentioned above had anticompetitive effects, only the first two had no offsetting justification and, therefore, 'constitute[d] exclusionary conduct [. . .] in violation of § 2.' As for overriding the user's choice of an Internet browser, the court held the plaintiffs had neither rebutted Microsoft's proffered technical justification nor demonstrated that its justification was outweighed by the anticompetitive effect. The court therefore concluded Microsoft was not 'liable for this aspect of its product design.' See *Microsoft III*, 66–7.

[50]　　Id., 74–5.

[51]　　See, e.g., 613 F.2d 727, 735–736 (9th Cir. 1979); 698 F.2d 1377, 1382–1383 (9th Cir. 1983); 510 F.2d 894, 902 and 906 (10th Cir. 1975); and *Caldera, Inc. vs.*

inherent value (the first step) to the likelihood of its anticompetitive nature (the second step). At the same time, however, it cannot be overlooked that by employing such a *net plus standard*[52] the US courts give more weight to the inherent value of the innovations than their possible anticompetitive effects, proving deferential to innovations. Moreover, as *Microsoft III* shows, it is likely that the distribution of the burden of proof will make easier the above three-step analysis, asking who is in the best position to explain the practice to do it.

Turning to the EU case law, a first peculiarity arises. The Commission did claim for the application of the refusal to supply doctrine in two of the most important cases where it challenged the introduction of a new product under Article 102.[53] Namely, in relation to the launch of the new integrated version of the IBM mainframe System-370 and in connection with Microsoft's introduction of its new operating system for networks. The former case ended with the IBM *settlement*,[54] whereas the latter

---

Microsoft Corp., 72 F. Supp. 2d 1295, 1323 (D. Utah 1999). In this way, hence, US courts rejected the per se legality rule that legal scholars suggested without imposing plaintiffs to demonstrate that a design choice was entirely devoid of technological merit.

[52] See Maria Lillà Montagnani, 'Predatory and exclusionary innovation: which legal standard for software integration in the context of the competition v. intellectual property rights clash?' (2006) 37 IIC 304.

[53] It is noteworthy that the Commission has also followed the same approach in Article 81 cases. See, for instance, Commission Decision (EC) of 21 December 1988 relating to a proceeding under Articles 85 and 86 of the EEC Treaty (IV/30.979 and 31.394, Decca Navigator System) [1989] OJ L43/27, §§ 108–110. Here the dominant firm (Decca) developed a radio signal transmission system for which there were no substitutes. After patent coverage elapsed, Decca entered into licensing agreements and changed its signals in order to prevent competitor's unlicensed equipment from interoperating with the signalling system. The Commission initially concluded that Decca's practice of modifying the electronic signals without notice and without justification rendered competing equipment useless, so as to represent an anticompetitive agreement. The Commission subsequently archived the file when Decca voluntarily ended the agreements and the regarded practice.

[54] See Commission Case IV/29.479 [1984] *XIV Report on Competition Policy* 78, where the Commission focused upon not only IBM's choice of integrating the operating system in the central processing unit (CPU) for its most powerful range of computers, but also the IBM System/370, and IBM's practice of not disclosing interface information about the new product until it had actually marketed it. More specifically, the Commission observed that: (i) the incompatibility created by the new IBM System-370 with non-IBM peripheral equipment would have foreclosed such complementary markets to the detriment of independent manufacturers of peripheral equipments; (ii) the non-disclosure of the IBM System-370 source code would have prevented companies from designing and preparing

behavior comprised the first of the two abuses contested in *Microsoft IV*.[55] In both cases the Commission, rather than discussing whether the advantages that the innovations brought to society as a whole outweighed their anticompetitive effects (third-step), deemed the interface data needed for compatibility as an essential facility, despite Microsoft's alleged IPRs in that information. In other words, when faced with cases of straight-forward innovations, that is, innovations whose inherent quality was so outstanding to produce a clear positive impact upon social welfare, say $SW(i) >> 0$,[56] EU antitrust institutions, instead of stopping their action as the US courts did in their decisions,[57] applied the refusal to deal

---

software that could have worked in conjunction with IBM software; and that (iii) the non-disclosure of the interface information relating to IBM's system network architecture would have affected industry efforts to develop its own standard. As part of the settlement, IBM agreed to disclose, in a timely manner, sufficient inter-face information to enable competing companies to attach both their hardware and software products to the IBM System-370. Further, IBM agreed to disclose adequate and timely information to rivals to enable them to interconnect their systems or networks with IBM's System-370 using a set of network protocols – the Systems Network Architecture – which IBM had developed. On this case see, e.g., Frederic M. Scherer, 'Microsoft and IBM in Europe' (2003) 84 Antitrust & Trade Regulation Report 65.

[55]   Commission Decision (EC) of 24 March 2004 relating to a proceeding under Article 82 of the EC Treaty (Case COMP/C-3/37.792 Microsoft) <http://ec.europa.eu/competition/antitrust/cases/decisions/37792/en.pdf >.

After Microsoft moved from Windows NT 4.0 to the Windows 2000 generation of its operating systems for both client PCs and work group servers, Microsoft's competitors in the market for work group servers operating systems plead that Microsoft refused to supply them with the interoperability information necessary to make their own operating systems for work group servers dialogue with the Microsoft operating system for PCs. In other words, the first abuse consisted of Microsoft's refusal to disclose the technical specifications that could have allowed its competitors to develop compatible products.

[56]   Indeed, in both cases there were sufficient technological reasons to qualify the relevant changes so that claims of alleged anticompetitive nature would have been frivolous. For instance, though the quality of the regarded innova-tions seem to stem out as a matter of fact, it is worthwhile to consider that in *Microsoft IV* the Commission itself recognized that the Windows NT 4.0 replaced by Windows 2000 was an 'already outdated technology' (see decision infra note 61 at 583).

[57]   In the US, as courts traditionally dislike imposing duties to deal, and admit the obligation to disclose interface information only as a remedy to a different antitrust violation, plaintiffs prefer to claim the predatory nature of the innova-tion in question – a claim that regards the advantages and disadvantages that flow from the innovation and that, hence, does not really question the existence and enforcement of the IPRs that may protect the innovation.

doctrine,[58] irrespective of the fact that imposing such a duty to deal meant reshaping the scope of the existing IPRs.[59]

In contrast, in *Microsoft IV* and in *Microsoft V*[60] the European Commission and the Court of First Instance evaluated the integration between Windows Media Player (WMP) and the Windows PC operating system by endorsing the same *net plus standard* employed by the US courts and, to some extent, by employing the same burden of proof rules. Under the heading of objective justification, indeed, they observed first that Microsoft did not submit either 'substantiated evidence' that the integration would have led to a superior technical product performance,[61] or 'evidence that tying of WMP is indispensable for the alleged pro-competitive effects to come into effect'.[62] Then, they disproved all the efficiencies that the integration would have allegedly produced.[63] Third, they ascertained the anticompetitive effects that it was likely to cause,[64] affirming that, due

---

[58]   After all, when a monopolist's System Innovation forecloses competitors from the related market, the monopolist' rivals have two choices: they can challenge the anticompetitive nature of the innovation or try to obtain a license either for the innovation itself or for what is necessary to restore compatibility with the new product (i.e. interface information).

[59]   Indeed, the present EU approach towards monopolists who refuse to license their IPRs seems to track the following reasoning: as long as the enforcement of a monopolist's IPR impairs future innovation and, hence, long run consumer welfare, the EU antitrust institutions must intervene. More exactly, in *Magill TV*, *IMS Health*, *Microsoft IV*, and *Microsoft V* – see *Radio Telefís Eireann and others* v. *Commission* (Joined Cases C-241 and 242/91 P) (1995) ECR I-743, and *IMS Health GmbH & Co. OHG* v. *NDC Health GmbH & Co. KG* (Case C-418/2001) (2004) ECR I-5039 – the EU institutions developed different criteria to establish how a monopolist can restrain dynamic efficiency by leveraging its exclusive IP right: from the new product (*Magill TV*) and new market (IMS Health) criteria, to the innovation's incentives test (*Microsoft IV*), to the final limitation to technical development criterion (*Microsoft V*).

[60]   *Microsoft* v. *Commission* [2007] EUECJ T-201/04, available at http://curia. europa.eu/.

[61]   See *Microsoft IV*, § 962, where the Commission made reference to the US District Court judgment where, as stated earlier found that '. . . according to several standard programs used by Microsoft to measure system performance, the removal of Internet Explorer by the prototype program slightly improves the overall speed of Windows 98.' Afterwards, the CFI concurred observing that Microsoft's reply to the Commission' finding was 'unsupported' – see *Microsoft V*, § 1159.

[62]   See *Microsoft IV*, § 963 affirmed in *Microsoft V*, §§ 1097–8.

[63]   See *Microsoft IV*, §§ 956–61 and 962–69 affirmed in *Microsoft V*, §§ 1097–8.

[64]   See *Microsoft IV*, §§ 971–72, where the Commission wrote that 'it may be true that media players today are not substitutes for client PC operating systems

to Microsoft's dominant position and the network effects of the industry, Windows Media Player enjoyed an extraordinary distributive advantage so to force content providers to standardize their content on Windows Media Player. Such standardization,[65] in particular, would have led to a situation where content would have been available only for Windows Media Player, with spillover effects on competition in the market for client PC operating systems, thereby strengthening Microsoft's monopoly.[66] Finally, the Commission and the Court of First Instance concurred that the integration would have 'deter[ed] innovation in the whole market to which the integrated product belongs'.[67] In other words, the Commission and the Court of First instance did endorse the above-mentioned three-step analysis: they evaluated that the regarded innovation did not have a peculiar inherent value, say $SW(i) \sim 0$, and that it did not produce any significant efficiency, say $SW[E(i)] \sim 0$ (first step); they showed that the integration harmed allocative efficiency so that $SW[P^M(i)] < 0$, and impaired dynamic efficiency so that $SW[I_{t1}(i)] < 0$ (second step). Finally, they

---

insofar as no general purpose application programs can be written using a media player's APIs only. However, "limited purpose" application programs, in particular media applications, can be written using a media player's APIs. . . . The possibility cannot be ruled out that, if such a limited platform for applications became wide-spread, there would be incentives to expand the available APIs so as to allow the writing of applications which would no longer be for "limited purposes" only. Second, middleware such as Java *in combination with* a media player could in fact *be* a general purpose platform substitute today. As such, the media player can be deemed a necessary component of a "full-fledged" platform threat. In this sense, Microsoft has incentives to foreclose third party media players through tying.' The CFI concurred with the idea that 'by means of the bundling, Microsoft sends signals which deter innovation in any technologies in which it might conceivably take an interest and which it might tie with Windows in the future' – See *Microsoft V*, 1088. The Commission's choice to pay attention not to actual but potential foreclosure effects (and, so forth, to the way in which markets are likely to evolve) represents a peculiarity of the EU approach to foreclosure – a peculiarity that has been criticized. Then, it is necessary to acknowledge that with *Microsoft IV* the Commission took a step forward in examining the integration's effects, rather than merely considering – as is the norm in cases of tying – that the tying has, by its inherent nature, a foreclosure effect.

[65]   In the event that suppliers will standardize their technologies so to be compatible with the platforms when the degree of hardware differentiation is sufficiently small, see J. Church and N. Gandal, 'Networks effects, software provision and standardization (1992) 40 Journal of Industrial Economics 85.

[66]   See *Microsoft IV*, § 842.

[67]   More exactly the Commission wrote that whereas in a competitive scenario market forces attenuate the deterrent effect that tying a software with an operating system produces on innovation since competing platforms still exist, 'this is not the case where the platform market is virtually monopolized' – see *Microsoft IV*, § 961.

concluded that the regarded innovation produced a negative net social welfare effect (third step). In making this reasoning, the EU institutions did not assign any role to the existing IPRs.

It can therefore be concluded that, especially in the Microsoft cases, the EU antitrust authorities shared with US courts the standard adopted to judge the questioned innovations, the distribution of the burden of the proof, and the anticompetitive theory underpinning Microsoft's conduct (that is, that the innovations were intended to defend the monopoly in middle ware). Yet, the Commission and the Court of First Instance seem to have given, irrespective of the risk of false positives,[68] more emphasis to future and partially speculative anticompetitive effects than the DC Circuit did, which in turn assumed a short-run perspective. The EU antitrust institutions risked assessing the impact that Microsoft's conduct had on dynamic efficiency, as the Commission has recently done in *Microsoft VI*.[69] In this case concerning the integration between Internet Explorer and the Windows Operating System – a case which ended with a commitment decision pursuant to Article 9 of Reg. 1/2003[70] – the Commission justified the alleged harm to competition also looking at Microsoft's ability to impair future innovations. Indeed, in commenting on the case, and the subsequent separation between the Windows Operating System and Internet Explorer, Commissioner Neelie Kroes observed that it will 'act as an incentive for web browser companies to innovate and offer people better browsers in the future'.[71]

---

[68]   That is to say that the EU institutions made their decisions irrespective of the risk of prohibiting lawful conduct and, hence, of over-deterring dominant firms from undertaking conduct that generally serve to improve consumer welfare, such as product development.

[69]   Cfr. MEMO/09/15, 17 January 2009, available at <http://europa.eu/rapid/pressReleasesAction.do?reference=MEMO/09/352&format=HTML&aged=0&language=EN&guiLanguage=en>.

[70]   See IP/09/1941, 16 December 2009, available at <http://europa.eu/rapid/pressReleasesAction.do?reference=IP/09/1941&format=HTML&aged=0&language=EN&guiLanguage=en>. There, it explained that 'under the commitments approved by the Commission, Microsoft will make available, for five years, in the European Economic Area (through the Windows Update mechanism), a "Choice Screen" enabling users of Windows XP, Windows Vista, and Windows 7, to choose which web browser(s) they want to install in addition to, or instead of, Microsoft's browser Internet Explorer. The commitments also provide that computer manufacturers will be able to install competing web browsers, set those as default and turn Internet Explorer off'.

[71]   Cfr. IP/09/1941, 16 December 2009, available at <http://europa.eu/rapid/pressReleasesAction.do?reference=IP/09/1941&format=HTML&aged=0&language=EN&guiLanguage=en>.

5. THE IMPORTANCE OF DYNAMIC EFFICIENCY AND THE FUTURE ROLE THAT THE SOCIAL JUSTICE PERSPECTIVE COULD PLAY IN SHAPING THE RELATIONSHIP BETWEEN DOMINANT FIRMS' PROPRIETARY INNOVATIONS AND ANTITRUST LAW

The reference to innovation that the EU antitrust institutions made in the Microsoft saga encourages the following observation that, however, would deserve a further analysis in the light of future case-law.

As stated in Section 1 of this chapter, the importance currently given to efficiency and consumer welfare prevents competition authorities from pursuing a social justice perspective to antitrust law aimed at sheltering dominant firms' rivals from monopolists' aggressive practices such as product and process developments. Yet, given that in the Microsoft cases the EU institutions justified their ban stating, *inter alia*, that the integration between the Windows Operating System and other software deterred Microsoft's rivals' innovations, it could be argued that in the present EU jurisdiction there is still room for a social justice approach to antitrust law. Indeed, if pursuing social justice means, among others, promising to the whole society a fair and just spread of knowledge and innovation, focusing the enforcement upon the impact that dominant firms' innovations have on the incentive to innovate for the whole industry could resemble a social justice perspective.

After all, in *Magill TV* and *IMS Health*, and in the sections of *Microsoft IV* and *Microsoft V* dealing with the refusal to share interface information, the EU antitrust authorities did change the scope of national IPRs owned by dominant firms, in order to allow their rivals to develop follow-on innovations. Therefore, one could argue that in those duty to license cases the EU antitrust authorities endorsed a social justice perspective because they gave monopolists' rivals' the opportunity to be 'dwarfs standing on the shoulders of giants' – that is, the opportunity to overcome the existing IPRs to develop their (incremental) innovations.

Nevertheless, still now this last statement seems far from being certain: even in those decisions, as well as in the decision and judgment regarding the integration between some software and Windows, the EU antitrust authorities did ascertain that the regarded practices harmed allocative efficiency. More importantly, when they chose to protect follow-on innovations and the incentives to innovate for the whole industry, they appeared more concerned with dynamic efficiency and long run consumer welfare than with what could be deemed as 'the social dimension of innovation'.

In other words, it could be argued that if dynamic efficiency rationales have been enough to prevent the blockage of rivals' innovation, changing the antitrust law's aims to encompass a social justice perspective on an issue, such as the spread of innovation, could be a useless choice.

9. Antitrust and consumer protection: the new regime on unfair commercial practices

Gustavo Ghidini and Valeria Falce

1. INTRODUCTION

Competition law and consumer protection policies are complementary and mutually reinforcing. Competition in the market increases efficiency, encourages innovation, and also incentivizes product differentiation and the improved quality of goods and services provided. In this sense, competition enhances consumer welfare by providing consumers with a wider choice at competitive prices – that is, consumers make informed decisions in their preference for goods and services when they are well informed.[1] Still, the two disciplines cover autonomous and independent scope and ambit of application with the natural consequence that, at their various level of intersection, they reflect both synergies and tensions.

From such a starting point, this chapter aims to explore certain overlapping areas between aforesaid 'intricately'[2] connected disciplines that are reflected in the Directive 2005/29/EC of the European Parliament and of the Council of 11 May 2005 concerning unfair business-to-consumer commercial practices in the internal market (hereinafter, 'Unfair Commercial Practices Directive' or also 'Directive'). After a brief introduction on the Directive on Unfair Commercial Practices, we will identify its different functional guidelines as respectively centered on the value of consumer protection, competition law and fairness. Having examined from this

---

[1]   H Qaqaya and G Lipmile (eds), *The Effects of Anti-competitive Business Practices on Developing Countries and their Development Prospects* (United Nations, 2008) vi.

[2]   V Dhall, 'Competition Law And Consumer Protection: Insights Into Their Interrelationship' in H Qaqaya and G Lipmile (eds), *The Effects of Anti-competitive Business Practices on Developing Countries and their Development Prospects* (United Nations, 2008) 2.

perspective the complex legal background to the Directive, we will investigate the different level of intersection between its fundamental components, questioning whether – through the Directive – the Community Legislator is promoting the gradual convergence of competition policy and consumer protection with a view to defining a *statute of fairness* as the archetype of market relations.

2. THE UNFAIR COMMERCIAL PRACTICES DIRECTIVE

In tackling unfair business-to-consumer commercial practices in the internal market,[3] the Unfair Commercial Practices Directive stands at the crossroads of various interconnected community policies. On the one hand, as a harmonization step, it allows – pursuant to Article 95 of the EC Treaty – the establishment and safeguarding of the operation of the single market as a space without frontiers, where fundamental freedoms are effectively enforced in a harmonized competitive environment. On the other hand, and in relation to Article 153 of the EC Treaty, it safeguards the economic interests of consumers and raises the level of protection of 'civil rights inside the market'.[4] This shows, therefore, how the very legal foundations of the Directive encourage the convergence of different

---

[3]   For an in-depth analysis, G De Cristofaro (ed) *Le 'pratiche commerciali sleali' tra imprese e consumatori* (2007); E Minervini and L Rossi Carleo (eds), *Le pratiche commerciali sleali* (2007); AAVV, *Cinque voci sulla direttiva comunitaria 2005/29/ CE in tema di pratiche commerciali sleali* in *Contratto e Impresa Europa*, 2007, 1; Assonime Circular Letter no. 80 of December 17, 2007; J Stuyck, E Terryn and T Van Dyck, 'Confidence Through Fairness? The New Directive on Unfair Business-to-Consumer Commercial Practices in the Internal Market' (2006) Common Market Law Review 107–152; G G Howells and others, *European Fair Trading Law: The Unfair Commercial Practices Directive* (Ashgate 2006); G B Abbamonte, 'The Unfair Commercial Practices Directive: An Example Of The New European Consumer Protection Approach' (2006) CJEL 695; M Kenny, 'Constructing A European Civil Code: Quis Custodiet Ipsos Custodes?' (2006) CJEL 775.

[4]   G Ghidini and C Cerasani, 'Antitrust and Consumer Protection' in *Enciclopedia del diritto* (5th edn, Milan 2001) 264. For a different view, F A Schurr, 'The Relevance of the European Consumer Protection Law for the Development of the European Contract Law' (2007) Vict U Wellington LR 131 (according to the author: 'As far as consumer protection is concerned Article 153 of the ECT states that consumer protection requirements shall be taken into account in defining and implementing Community policies and activities. This treaty provision is therefore not suitable as a legal basis for the European legislature for the enactment of a new consumer law').

features of the community action – competition and consumer protection – and hence the integration of the corresponding set of rules with a view to an effectively integrated system.

Moreover, and as will soon be clarified, the Unfair Commercial Practices Directive suggests and points to the more ambitious idea of promoting fairness as a yardstick that dominates and informs the interpretation of the rules governing market relations for any reason whatsoever. This holds both when these apply between equals, or '*inter pares*' (in terms of power, whether bargaining or not), between businesses or traders according to the terminology of the Directive, as well as *pratiques commerciales déloyales* – those between businesses and consumers.[5]

3. THE DIFFERENT FUNCTIONAL GUIDELINES OF THE UNFAIR COMMERCIAL PRACTICES DIRECTIVE

To appreciate this emphasis on fairness, it may be helpful to explore the gradual path that the EC has taken in its approximation of competition policy and consumer protection. This will aid the attempt that follows to define a statute of fairness as the archetype of market relations.

3.1   The Value of Consumer Protection

'Consumer welfare' has long been a subject of Community law, dating back to a scheme adopted in the second half of the 1970s following a painstaking process. The European Economic Community was then working on implementing a so-called '*politique consommateurs*' based on specific programmatic guidelines aimed at protecting those 'five basic rights' – health, safety, economic interests, information, representation – to which John F Kennedy referred in his memorable 1962 speech to the US Congress. ('Consumers by definition include all of us').[6]

---

[5]   Back in 1993, A Trabucchi urged a 'moralization of contract law,' with an 'ethical' shift of contractual focus (Id., 'Il Codice Civile di fronte alla normativa comunitaria' (1993) Riv Dir Civ, 1993 I, 717 *et seq.*).

[6]   In fact it is well known that civil rights came to the fore in the USA during the Kennedy Administration, championed by so-called consumer advocates like Ralph Nader and his followers (Nader's Raiders). Back in the EU in contrast, until recently, consumers were still grappling with a 'regulatory vacuum' (R Ferrara, 'Voce Consumatore (protezione del) nel diritto amministrativo' in Dig. Disc. Pubbl., 3rd Vol., Utet, 1989, 515 *et seq.*).

Consider the numerous resolutions adopted by the Council in furtherance of this agenda:[7] those in connection with the proposed Directive of 1978 concerning misleading and unfair advertising,[8] and, more recently, those regarding the Commission's three-year plans for consumer protection policies (1990–92; 1993–95; 1996–98), the 2001 Green Paper on consumer protection in the European Union[9] and the Communication on European contract law[10] and, finally, the consumer policy strategy of 2002.[11] This increased attention to the interest of citizens as consumers evidences a process of profound evolution, for both the legal means and the legal justification.

With regard to the legal devices alongside the policy documents cited above, there were numerous broad and sector-specific measures adopted. In the early stage these measures were for the most part disjointed, poorly coordinated and not homogenous, both as to scope of application and to substance; however, over the last decade they have been fine-tuned – including those here concerned. These measures now boast a strong supranational and legal imprint of harmonization. This is illustrated, for example, by a series of broad measures, such as the Directive 84/450/EEC on the approximation of legislative, regulatory and administrative provisions of the Member States on misleading advertising;[12] Directive 98/6/EC on consumer protection in the indication of the prices of products offered to consumers;[13] Directive 93/13/EEC on unfair terms in consumer contracts;[14] or Directive 1999/44/EC on certain aspects of the sale of consumer goods and associated warranties;[15] or Directive 98/27/EC on injunctions for the protection of consumers' interests.[16]

Sector-specific measures include Directive 79/581/EEC on consumer

---

[7]   First resolution of April 14, 1975 ([1975] OJ C 92/1); the second resolution of May 19, 1981 ([1981] OJ C 133/1); the third resolution of 23 June 1986 ([1986] OJ C 167).

[8]   [1978] OJ C 70 of 21 March 1978, 4. For comments, reference is made to N Reich, 'Protection of Consumers' Economic Interests by the EC' (1992) Sydney LR 33.

[9]   Commision (EC), 'Green Paper on European Union Consumer Protection' COM (2001) 531 final.

[10]   Id., 'Communication from the Commission to the Council and the European Parliament' COM (2001) 398 final.

[11]   Id., 'Communication from the Commission to the European Parliament' COM (2002) 208 final.

[12]   See EC OJ L250, 19 September 1984, 22, as amended by Directive 97/55/EC on comparative advertising, in the EC OJ L290, 23 October 1997, 18.

[13]   See OJ L80, 18 March 1998, 27.

[14]   See OJ L95, 21 April 1993, 29.

[15]   See OJ L171, 7 July 1999, 12.

[16]   See OJ L166, 11 June 1998, 51.

protection in the indication of the prices of foodstuffs;[17] Directive 76/768/ EEC on the approximation of the laws of the Member States relating to cosmetic products[18] and the many other laws that followed.[19] In the 2001 Green Paper, the Commission considered the advisability of sticking to the so-called specific or vertical approach, rather than resorting to a framework directive, thereby protecting the possibility of regulating individual cases separately.

Turning now to the legal justification, the second aspect of which is strictly correlated to the first, a survey of EC measures adopted shows how consumer welfare was initially pursued only as a means to an end, subordinate to the supreme priority of Community integration as an economic entity, and in respect of which the other objectives played a subsidiary if not ancillary role. Against this backdrop, the creation of a single and effective market required a set of common rules that could guarantee smooth market operation, free movement of goods, services and competition, as well as fairness, transparency and fair contracts.[20]

---

[17]   See OJ L158, 26 June 1979, 19.

[18]   See OJ L262, 27 September 1976, 169.

[19]   The various measures include Directive 96/74/EC on textile names, EU OJ L32 of 3 February 1997, 38, as amended by Directive 97/37/EC, EU OJ L169 of 27 June 1997, 74; Directive 92/28/EEC on the advertising of medicinal products for human use, EU OJ L113 of 30 April 1992, 13; Directive 90/314/EEC on package travel, package holidays and package tours, EU OJ L158 of 23 June 1990, 59; Directive 85/577/EEC to protect the consumer in respect of contracts negotiated away from business premises, EU OJ L372 of 31 December 1985, 31; Directive 87/102/EEC on consumer credit, EU OJ L42 of 12 February 1987, 48, as amended by Directive 90/88/EEC, EU OJ L61 of 10 March 1990, 14 and by Directive 98/7/EEC, EU OJ L101 of 1 April 1998, 17; Directive 97/7/EC on the protection of consumers in respect of distance contracts, EU OJ L144 of 14 June 1997, 27; Directive 90/384/EC on non-automatic weighting instruments, EU OJ L189 of 20 July 1990, 1; Directive 94/47/EC on the protection of purchasers in respect of certain aspects of contracts relating to the purchase of a right to use immovable properties on a timeshare basis, EU OJ L280 of 29 October 1994, 83; Directive 2000/13/EC on the approximation of the laws of the Member States relating to the labelling, presentation and advertising of foodstuffs, as well as the related advertising, EU OJ L109 of 6 April 2000, 29; Directive 2001/83/EC of the European Parliament and of the Council on the Community code relating to medicinal products for human use, EU OJ L311 of 28 November 2001, 1, as amended by Directive 2004/24/EC, EU OJ L136 of 30 April 2004, 58; Directive 2002/65/EC concerning the distance marketing of consumer financial services and amending Directive 90/619/EEC of the Council and Directives 97/7/EC and 98/27/EC, EU OJ L271 of 9 October 2002, 16, and Directive 2000/31/ EC on certain legal aspects of information society services, in particular electronic commerce, in the internal market, EU OJ L178 of 17 July 2000, 1.

[20]   M Gambini, 'Il nuovo statuto del consumatore europeo: tecniche di tutela del contraente debole' (2004) Giur. Merito 12, 2605.

The Maastricht Treaty[21] and in particular the 1997 Amsterdam Treaty dealt a final blow to this legal order where market integration was the primary goal of community policy.[22] In fact, it was only with the adoption of Article 129A, amending the Treaty establishing the European Community (Article 153, EC Treaty), that the Community was even able to adopt minimum 'social' measures in their own right for 'protecting the health, safety and economic interests of consumers,' as well as for 'promoting their right to information, education and to organize themselves in order to safeguard their interests'. In such context, Article 153 marks a watershed in the Union's hierarchy of objectives and in defining European citizenship, expressing the Community's commitment to promote consumer interests and ensuring an adequate level of protection.[23] However, as no 'emancipation' followed in terms of legislative powers,[24] the laws protecting consumers typically rest upon the single market powers of Article 95 of the Treaty. They are thus adopted with a view to the accomplishment of the single market[25] and to its smooth working.[26] The sole exception is Directive 98/6/EC on indication of the prices of products offered to consumers,[27] whose legal foundations rest exclusively upon Article 153.

---

[21]   As to the evolution of protection at a community level, see also H W Micklitz and S Weatherill, 'Consumer policy in the European Community: Before and after Maastricht' (1993) Journal of Consumer Policy 285.

[22]   Although this was often blended with other policies.

[23]   In this sense, see G Alpa, 'Sei voci sul "Codice del Consumo" italiano' in *Contratto e Impresa/Europa* (2006), 19, 20.

[24]   HW Micklitz, Norbert Reich and S Weatherill, 'EU Treaty Revision and Consumer Protection' (2004) Journal of Consumer Policy 367.

[25]   GG Howells, 'The Rise of European Consumer Law – Whither National Consumer Law?' (2006) Sidney LR 63.

[26]   If this point is beyond question (operations are easier to conduct in a standard regulatory framework), on the other hand, other elements – environment and language for instance, or more simply taste or preference that may differ from nation to nation – play a role in a consumer's decision to turn to a global market to satisfy his/her needs. In this regard, one must bear in mind that, according to the principles of competition law, demand substitutability is correctly defined not only by institutional and regulatory barriers, but also by commercial barriers and, in a broader sense, by more subjective aspects such as taste, preference and habits of consumer demand which a certain product addresses to satisfy its needs.

[27]   Directive 98/6/EC of the European Parliament and of the Council of 16 February 1998, on consumer protection in the indication of the prices of products offered to consumers.

3.2   The Value of Competition Protection

Basically competition law also followed the above path. In fact, competition made its debut in the first articles of the Treaty of Rome as a fundamental principle built around a set of provisions (the reference is clearly to Articles [now] 81, 82 and 90 of the Treaty). However, these provisions, as observed by G. Amato, were conceived in a limited context. On the one hand, they were considered to be only ancillary to the main priority of market integration, also in light of the Treaty's neutrality with respect to the public and private property of businesses. On the other hand, the political climate of the Member States was such as to impose on competition policy the limits of industrial and agricultural policies in the belief of their importance. This was a deadlock that would have been hard to break had it not been for economic growth, steady integration of the internal market and the gradual liberalization of the international marketplace, all of which contributed per se to bringing competition protection into the limelight.

Moreover, the fact that competition was ancillary to market integration operated not only (as it happened with reference to the *politique consommateur*) as a limit to the reinforcement of competition protection. In fact, the Treaty of Rome had already clamped down against business conduct that segmented the European market along national frontiers, thus clashing with the ultimate goal of integration.[28]

At any rate, a historical and ideological survey of the nature and evolution of EC competition protection undoubtedly shows that despite its being a valued and fundamental principle, it was classified by the Treaty of Rome as a tool *functional to the achievement of market integration*, sacrificing it if such market objectives required freedom of competition to be put aside.[29]

Competition became, at long last, a fundamental principle of itself, in tune with consumer protection, under the Single European Act of 1986, and more so, under the Maastricht Treaty. This gave form to the very fundamental spirit of European antitrust, hinged, in particular, on the precedence of market competition defense over the acknowledged value of efficiency generation (including 'pro-consumer') produced by

---

[28]   In this regard, Pera observes that the Treaty aimed to solve the disparities of the European Economic Area and create a more integrated market where businesses could freely compete. The development of a competitive market, in fact, has always been one of the priorities set by the European Constitution. Id., *Concorrenza e Antitrust* (2nd ed, 2001), 47.

[29]   V Donativi, 'Introduzione storica' in *Diritto Antitrust Italiano* (1991, 79).

strongly 'monopolistic' transactions and practices – each case judged differently, applying various degrees of severity (more rigorously for cartels,
more benevolently for concentrations).[30] A substantial elimination of
competition is out of the question, even for short periods, and even if
anti-competitive transactions or practices produce the highest economic
efficiencies, including for consumers. The creation of efficiency justifies
(since Regulation 1/2003)[31] a judgment of substantial compatibility with
the rules of competition *only* if the conduct under scrutiny does not stifle
competition to the degree that prevents the maintenance of a 'workable'
level of competition in the market. Workable essentially means *actual*
competition that gives 'consumers' enough choices and not merely *potential* competition. This is despite that potential competition is presumed by
various economists (especially those from the Chicago school) as helping
to re-establish an effective competitive landscape.[32]

The second typically European fundamental feature of competition is
the concept of special 'behavioral' responsibility imposed on companies
that, either individually or jointly (and beyond specific cooperation or
integration links and relations) enjoy a dominant position, that is such
market power as to influence its competitors. This power justifies the
imposition of enhanced responsibility on dominant companies, whereas
those with a lower degree of market power are left to regulation by a
competitive market that offers a wide range of choices and is able to (self)
correct any attempt of abuse and discrimination.[33]

---

[30]   For a different position, see M Maggiolino, Chapter 8 of this book, where
although acknowledging that other values underpinned EU competition law
until recently, suggests that efficiency alone is and should be the sole premise of
modern competition law over social justice or welfare, at least in connection with
innovation.

[31]   Council Regulation (EC) No 1/2003 of 16 December 2002 on the implementation of the rules on competition laid down in Articles 81 and 82 of the
Treaty, in [2003] OJ L1/1.

[32]   For a critical review, see G Ghidini et al., *Diritto comunitario e legge antitrust italiana*, forthcoming (on file with authors); P Fattori and M Todino, *La
disciplina della concorrenza in Italia* (2004) *passim*.

[33]   For a more extensive analysis, G Ghidini et al., *supra* note 32 (noting that:
'as it is known, the responsibility of dominant companies addresses the various
ways to prevent them from "abusing" of such market power (as anyone with such
power would be tempted to do, *dixit* Montesquieu, but not about the economy
. . .and, more brutally, Napoleon Bonaparte with "what good is power, if you can't
abuse it?").' Specifically, such responsibility is designed to prevent two different,
but in actual fact, converging situations: 1) preventing a company from abusing
its market power to determine competition distortion (including the extension
of its 'dominance' on a certain market and/or the adjacent markets) which is not

3.3   The Value of Fairness

The uncoupling of competition and consumer policies from the foregoing market integration priorities failed, however, to help such policies
converge with respect to the protection of the interests of the market
and of its main players, that is, traders and consumers. An authoritative
2003 research paper coordinated by R. Schulze and H. Schulte-Nölke[34]
shows that only a few Member States laid down an organic set of rules
for consumer protection (for example, the Swedish Marketing Act, the
Belgian Act on Commercial Practices and Consumer Information, as well
as the other piece of legislation also mentioned in Schulze-Schulte-Nölke
adopted in Germany, Greece, Austria and Denmark) aimed at protecting both competition and market players. In these countries the national
legislatures' choice actually consisted in preparing a unitary *corpus* that,
without distinguishing the type of relation under examination, is indif-
ferently applied to the relations between traders or between traders and
businesses. In other countries, in contrast, the approach followed by the
legislature was not *reductio ad unum*. Take Finland, for instance. Despite
a general climate of fair practice, its system is neatly subdivided into rules
governing relations between competitors (Unfair Trade Practices Act) and
rules governing consumer protection (Consumer Protection Act). This is
then complemented by some sector-specific regulations aimed at adapting
the general principle of fairness for special sectors. A third grouping of
countries, including Italy and the Netherlands, follow their own approach.
There, for example, unfair competition is regulated by the Civil Code and
by the Burgerlijk Wetboek, respectively, where a general clause sanctions
the principle of fair practice to be applied to relations between competitors.

---

realised thanks to the objective superiority of services (the 'consumerist' concept
of competition on the merits – *Leistungswettbewerb* – common to both sides of the
Atlantic, but, as recalled, only Europe imposes special responsibility on dominant
companies); 2) preventing a dominant company from using its power to significantly alter *in peius* the bargaining position of its counterparts: *in peius* with respect
to the bargaining equilibrium one would expect in conditions of actual competition, hence, without the range of effective options which would have prevented
from succumbing. In both cases, special responsibility forces dominant companies
to act 'as if' (*als ob*) there were an effective – and thus effective 'disciplining' –
competition situation. In this regard, reference is also made to Fattori and Todino,
La disciplina della concorrenza in Italia (2004), *passim*.

[34]   R Schulze and H Schulte-Nolke, 'Analysis of National Fairness Laws
Aimed at Protecting Consumers in Relation to Commercial Practices' [2003]
<http://ec.europa.eu/consumers/cons_int/safe_shop/fair_bus_pract/green_pap_
comm/studies/unfair_practices_en.pdf> accessed 24 August 2009.

Likewise, in France the principle of *concurrence déloyale* is based on the *Code Civil* for that concerning relations between entrepreneurs and on the *Code de la Consommation* for that regarding direct consumer protection. Furthermore, the UK and Ireland have no rules on commercial practices, and lack rules that shield the system from unfair practices, as well as sector-specific regulations sanctioning a general principle of fairness.[35] The relevant legal framework is outlined by common law and then adapted by the law governing contract and torts.[36]

The analysis of R. Schulze and H. Schulte-Nölke reveals how Member States have always striven to pursue the dual functional objective of raising the threshold of consumer protection and creating the conditions for a competitive market without, however, always finding common legal techniques and legislative (and substantial) choices.

4. THE BACKGROUND TO THE UNFAIR COMMERCIAL PRACTICES DIRECTIVE

Such a fertile, composite and diversified background set the stage for the 'particularly accurate'[37] preparatory work for the Unfair Commercial

---

[35] Despite the conclusions reached by R Schulze and H Schulte-Nolke in their article, *supra* note 34, in the UK some piece of legislation codified a general principle of fairness. See, inter alia, the Consumer Protection Act 1987 that: 1) prohibits the supply of goods not in accordance with the general safety requirement or are unsafe; 2) provides for the safety and protection of consumers by enabling Regulations or orders to be made controlling consumer goods; 3) provides for approved safety standards to enable compliance with general safety requirements; 4) provides powers for seizing and forfeiture, and the powers to suspend the sale of suspected unsafe goods; 5) identifies provisions as to the requirement for persons to publish notices warning of unsafe goods previously supplied; 6) provides for liability for damage caused by defective products: 7) prohibits misleading price indications. See also the European Communities Act 1972 that a) implements community obligations and the approximation of the laws of Member States; b) prohibits supply of goods not of prescribed standard or composition; c) imposes safety restrictions on certain goods; d) protects consumer's interests as to holiday travel and in respect of distance selling contracts; e) provides for controls connected to the packaging of products and their suitability for recycling as well as to the activities of traders who persist in a course of illegal conduct in a way which is detrimental to the interests of consumers.

[36] National Consumer Council (UK), Unfair Commercial Practices: Response to DTI Consultation on the Draft EU Directive, 2003; European Consumer Law Group, The Proposed Directive on Unfair Commercial Practices, 2004.

[37] For this sense, see L G Vigoriti, 'Verso l'attuazione della direttiva sulle pratiche commerciali scorrette' in *Europa e diritto privato* (2007) 521.

Practices Directive, which resulted in the publication of the 2001 *Green Paper on Consumer Protection in the European Union*. As early as the publication date of this paper, the Commission takes as its point of departure that consumer protection is a value in itself.[38] It acknowledges the need to create a perfectly working internal market of consumers by urging national regulations to overcome the fragmentation, which obstructs the full accomplishment of consumerism[39] and promotes recourse by the legislator to the framework directive[40] as the preferred legal technique. This option was confirmed in the Communication of 11 June 2002 (relating to the observations of governments, businesses and consumers associations to the proposals in the Green Paper) and the proposed directive made public on 18 June 2003 and adopted in its final version on 11 May 2005.

In the final text, with a view to the correct operation of the internal market, the competition policy is connected to the consumer policy under the banner of a maximum harmonization principle.[41] The Directive's rationale is that once distortions typical of the disparities of national legislation on consumers have been corrected, it will be possible to boost trade and investments, thus promoting intra-community trade and hence the international one.

From this perspective, a system of common harmonized rules, which lays the foundations for effective promotion of consumer economic interests, is consistent with the concept of a single market based on fair competition.[42] Effective rules on consumer protection may indeed help to

---

[38] In this regard, G Alpa, *Il diritto dei consumatori* (2001) 10.

[39] J Stuyck et al., 'Confidence Through Fairness? The New Directive on Unfair Business – Consumer Commercial Practises in the Internal Market' [2006] CMLR, 107, where the authors identify the typical features of unequal treatment of commercial practices in the various Member States.

[40] A decision recently endorsed by the Green Paper on the Review of the Consumer Acquis (COM (2006) 744, Final, 8 February 2007), which indicates the next necessary step in consumer protection as being the creation of one instrument for all contracts, a goal pursued by adopting a common approach across the various directives and implementing a horizontal protection of full harmonisation.

[41] In this perspective, the Directive then 1) represents a major advancement toward the supreme goal of full harmonization of the individual European national legislation and of the creation of a uniform European consumer law; 2) is functional to the development of a world-wide commercial system and fair competition among market players in an increasingly unified and universal market. A Tizzano, 'Appunti sulla cooperazione internazionale in tema di concorrenza' in *Il Diritto dell'Unione Europea* (4, 1999) 695.

[42] Resulting from the Explanatory Report itself accompanying the proposal (submitted by the Commission on June 18, 2003 [p 2]), the Directive is key to

increase trust in the market and, therefore, help increase the overall sales volume, to the benefit of the economic system in general and ultimately to competition itself.[43]

4.1   Unfair Commercial Practices Directive Looking for a Unitary Pattern of Market Relations

The Directive undoubtedly identifies the need to develop an organic *corpus* of harmonized rules on unfair practices to promote the effective operation of the internal market. But one must equally acknowledge – also in light of the brief discussion above – the EU legislator's efforts, through the Directive itself, to complete the meticulous, if still unfinished, work of drawing up EU Regulations on unfair competition,[44] for which, in our view, the new regime intends to lay the core foundations.[45]

---

achieving two distinct, yet correlated objectives: on the one hand, the harmonization of European market prices for the same goods and services at the lowest possible costs, and, on the other, the extension and diversification of the offer of products and services accessible to consumers, which would allow them to also access goods and services that are qualitatively better or more innovative with respect to those offered in their countries of residence, thus stimulating actual competition. Extensively, G De Cristofaro, 'La difficile attuazione della direttiva 2005/29/CE concernente le pratiche commerciali sleali nei rapporti fra imprese e consumatori: proposte e prospettive' in *Contratto e Impresa/Europa* (2007) 1.

[43]   Bocchini, 'Nozione normativa di consumatore e modelli economici' in *Studi in onore di Schlesinger*, (Giuffrè, Milan 2004) 2347; Alpa, 'Nuove prospettive della protezione dei consumatori' (2005) Nuova Giur Civ Comm II, 103, according to which contract law, as conceived by the Commission and the Court of Justice, has become a segment of competition law; likewise, A Monti, 'Il consumatore, operatore e beneficiario della politica comunitaria di concorrenza' in *Rass Forense* (2004) 27.

[44]   Vigoriti recalls that the subject was considered by the Commission already in 1962 when it asked the Max Planck Institute in Munich for an opinion on the different national legislation on unfair competition (see 523, note 8).

[45]   Incidentally, G De Cristofaro, 'Premessa' in AAVV, *Le 'pratiche commerciali sleali' tra imprese e consumatori*, edited by G. De Cristofaro, 2007, as well as, *amplius*, C Wadlow, 'Unfair Competition In Community Law: Part 1: The Age Of The "Classical Model"' (2006) EIPR 28(8), 433–41, and 'The case for reclaiming European unfair competition law from Europe's consumer lawyers' in S Weatherill and U Bernitz (eds), *The Regulation of Unfair Commercial Practices under EC Directive 2005/29: New Rules and New Techniques* (Aspen Publishers, 2007). About community law on unfair competition, Beier, 'The Law of Unfair Competition in the European Community: Its Development and Present Status' (1985) EIPR 284; Schricker, 'The Efforts Toward Harmonization of the Law of Unfair Competition in the European Economic Community' (1973) IIC 201; Schricker, 'European Harmonisation of Unfair Competition Law – A Futile Venture?' (1991) IIC 788;

4.2   First Level of Intersection

As must be recalled, the Directive follows in the footsteps of a number of measures adopted for both competition and consumer protection to gradually rebalance the value of a market without frontiers and consumer welfare, in order that both co-exist on equal and fair terms in a harmonized legislative framework. This is the purpose, at least. This is (also) the meaning of the developments in the key legislative texts of the European Union referred to above (see discussion at Section 3.2), and of the different role assigned to 'consumer policy' in the Treaty of Rome with respect to that of Amsterdam. It is also evident how application of the rules protecting competition guarantees a primary role to the consumer as the holder of a direct, immediate and qualified right. Consider the indications from Article 81(3) in relation to the possible exemption of restricted agreements,[46] from Article 82 in relation to abuses of exploitation[47] and

---

Schricker, 'Twenty-Five Years of Protection against Unfair Competition' (1995) IIC 782; Wadlow, 'The case for reclaiming European unfair competition law from Europe's consumer lawyers' in S Weatherill and U Bernitz (eds), *The Regulation of Unfair Commercial Practices under EC Directive 2005/29: New Rules and New Techniques* (Hart Publishing, 2006). Finally, P Bartolomucci reports that some rules laid down in the Directive are strongly evocative of the national regulations on unfair competition (Id., 'La proposta di direttiva sulle pratiche commerciali sleali: note a prima lettura' (2005), Contratti, 956).

[46]   Any assessment under Article 81 consists of two parts. The first step is to assess under Article 81(1) whether an agreement has an anti-competitive object or actual (or potential) anti-competitive effects. The second step, which only becomes relevant when an agreement is found to be restrictive of competition under Article 81(1), is to determine the pro-competitive benefits produced by that agreement and to assess whether these pro-competitive effects outweigh, under Article 81(3), the anti-competitive effects. According to the first condition of Article 81(3), the restrictive agreement must contribute to improving the production or distribution of goods or to promoting technical or economic progress. According to the second condition of Article 81(3), consumers must receive a fair share of the efficiencies generated by the restrictive agreement. The concept of fair share implies that the pass-on of benefits must at least compensate consumers for any actual or likely negative impact. The third condition implies a two-fold test: 1) the restrictive agreement as such must be necessary in order to achieve the efficiencies; 2) the individual restrictions of competition that flow from the agreement must also be necessary for the attainment of the efficiencies. According to the fourth condition of Article 81(3), the agreement must not afford the undertakings concerned with the possibility of eliminating competition in respect of a substantial part of the products concerned.

[47]   Exploitative abuse is one of the three main categories of abuse of a dominant position, along with exclusionary abuse and discriminatory abuse, which may be prohibited under Article 82. In general terms, an exploitative abuse can be

from the rules in relation to concentrations.[48] Or finally also, consider the latest measures involving class actions for damages, which envisage the consumers' immediate – and no longer only indirect – interest in not being harmed by the conduct of businesses on the market.[49]

It will come as no surprise, therefore, if the distinctive feature of any EC action stemming from the Unfair Commercial Practices Directive sees the integration and combination of competition and consumer protection policies[50] in a context in which both regulate to promote consumer welfare and therefore each concurs in defining the other's scope and features. Hence, for instance, if comparative advertising does not aim to promote competition on merits, then it may be unlawful and, in any case, unfair. Similarly, the sharing of business information may be manifestly anticompetitive in the absence of information transparency necessary to make informed and reasonable choices.

In the Directive, this convergence of the above-mentioned different regulatory areas, that is, competition law, consumer protection and the unfair competition regime, merges from both the rationale and the wording of its provisions. In fact, the following combined provisions clearly show that the legal interest protected hinges on the *consumer's freedom of choice*, as a 'fundamental prerogative acknowledged to him/her by the primary community law, in particular within the context of the dynamic profile of the principle of an open market-oriented competitive economy':[51] Article 2, subparagraph

---

characterized as a use of a dominant position that is illegitimate because of a direct adverse effect on the interests of customers.

[48]   For instance, in the new horizontal merger guidelines, [2004] OJ (C 31) 5, adopted by the European Commission in February 2004, it is indicated at paragraphs 79–84 that to be compatible with competition law the efficiencies resulting from a horizontal merger must be 'passed-on' to consumers in the form of reduced prices, increased output/quality or enhanced innovation, so that consumers 'will not be worse off as a result of the merger'.

[49]   See Commission (EC), 'White Paper: Damages actions for breach of the EC antitrust rules,' SEC (2008) 404, SEC (2008) 405, SEC (2008) 406.

[50]   Recent comments on jurisprudence point to the notion that the rules governing consumer protection are very often seen as the vertex in the logical hierarchy of corporate businesses. Such an order, and the relevant regulations, is, in turn, considered the indirect, though fundamental guarantee for the true freedom of choice of consumers on the market. It appears that the two regulatory systems cannot be distinguished by discerning the protected interests, since both are too closely interdependent, determining their respective efficiency. R Di Raimo, 'Note minime sulle implicazioni sostanziali dell'art. 14 della direttiva 2005/29/CE: a margine di una proposta per il suo recepimento' [2007] *Contratto Impresa/Europa* 1.

[51]   L. Di Nella, 'Prime considerazioni sulla disciplina delle pratiche commerciali aggressive' [2007] i Contratto Impresa / Europa 39.

(k), identifying the decisions of a commercial nature made by the consumer; Article 5, paragraph 2, subparagraph (b), defining as unfair the conduct which is likely to significantly distort the economic behavior of the average consumer and; Article 6, paragraph 1, and Article 7, paragraphs 1 and 2, which explain how unfairness materializes when a consumer takes a decision he/she would not have otherwise taken, thus limiting the consumer's freedom of choice or conduct. In other words, the Directive points to the mechanism of competition as the assumption, the *condicio iuris* for consumers to freely express a conscious and informed decision, a basic legal right indeed, provided there is sufficient competition on the market.

In brief, the Directive represents a further step toward narrowing the gap between competition law (which today stands on a common and harmonized *acquis*, following a process of integration and modernization) and consumer protection. An objective which is much harder to achieve – owing to a confusing totality of disconnected measures and misapplications[52] – is creating a true European consumer legal framework hinged on all those typically consumer-type relations that drive and may affect the market.

4.3   Second Level of Intersection: Fairness as a Pattern of Market Relations

The Unfair Commercial Practices Directive, whose language and definitions 'strongly evoke' the regulations on unfair competition,[53] elevates the principle of fairness to the paradigm governing market relations. Against this backdrop, fair practice is the principle that moves across and connects the consumer and competition law systems, thus becoming the criterion to measure behavior. In this novel scenario, fair practice, in light of pro-competitive inspired principles, is both the regulatory theme and an interpretative instrument, connecting the different regulations governing consumer protection, competition protection, and the suppression of unfair competition.

First, the definition of fair practice at Article 2(h) of the Directive suggests a *continuum* between such notion and the *usages honnêtes en matière industrielle ou commerciale* (honest practices in industrial or commercial matters) under Article 10 *bis* of the Paris Convention for the Protection

---

[52]   In this sense, Commission (EC), Green Paper on consumer protection in the European Union, Brussels, 2.10.2001 COM(2001) 531, final.

[53]   Isdaci, 'Istituto per lo studio e la diffusione dell'arbitrato e del diritto commerciale internazionale, la proposta di direttiva sulle pratiche commerciali sleali: note a prima lettura', (2005) 10 Contratti 956.

of Industrial Property.[54] Any 'corporative burden,' thereunder, however, would appear not to also be ascribable to the framework of EC as measures adopted to raise the level of consumer protection.[55] Thus, while the evolution of unfair trade practice law between the Paris Convention and the Directive is worthy of a more extensive analysis,[56] to the extent that other than a consumer protection is seen as the Directive's primary foundation, such direct linkage may be denied.

Other examples of earlier legislation exist with theoretical underpinnings sounding in values other than purely the economics of the marketplace. If we consider, for example, the Italian context, it emerges that long before the adoption of the Unfair Commercial Practices Directive, Italy sought to equate fair practice with consistency and Constitutional values and not, as believed, with the interests of the entrepreneurial class involved in the game of competition.[57] In this perspective, both the principle of freedom of enterprise and that of social utility play a role in preparing the basic criteria to measure competitive behavior. As a matter of fact, it

---

[54] V Meli, 'Pubblicità ingannevole' Enciclopedia Giuridica, Aggiornamento XIV (2006) 7. Indeed, both instruments prohibit as unfair misleading the public as to the source, quality and characteristics of a product. See Article 10 *bis* (3) and Article 6 of the Directive, and the UK implementation of the Directive is included in at least one compendium of intellectual property laws, reinforcing that some may see the overlap as that comprising only the scope of traditional trade mark protections and/or purely market-based regulation of fairness. See M Dowie-Whybrow (ed.) *Core Statutes on Intellectual Property* (2d ed. Palgrave Macmillan 2009). But see Geraint G Howells, Hans-W Micklitz, Thomas Wilhelmsson, *European Unfair Trading Laws: The Unfair Commercial Practices Directive* at 98 et. seq. (Ashgate 2006) (suggesting that the two are not synonymous in their focus and use of similar language with the Convention possibly focused on honesty as professional diligence based on national notions of morality with tortious liability and the latter directed only to fair communication in the marketplace).

[55] See note 54. Though both concepts – honest commercial practices and fair practice – can be interpreted differently in principle, they are, in actual fact, basically considered to coincide. In the words of the Directive, if the professional has exercised the standard of special skill and care that can be reasonably expected, commensurate with honest market practice and the principle of good faith, then his behaviour may be considered fair. In contrast, practice is considered unfair when it harms the aware, prudent and informed consumer. See Article 2 (h) of the Directive.

[56] See, eg., Dowie-Whybrow et al. *supra* note 54; H Collins, 'The Forthcoming EC Directive on Unfair Commercial Practices: Contract, Consumer and Competition Law Implications', 66 Kluwer Law Int'l 2004.

[57] Ex multis, P Marchetti, 'Il paradigma della correttezza professionale nella giurisprudenza di un ventennio' in *Rivista di diritto industriale* (1966); G Schricker, 'Twenty-Five Years of Protection Against Unfair Competition' [1995] IIC 782 *et seq.*

is indeed the economic foundation – at whose apex stand the combined principles of the first two paragraphs of Article 41 of the Constitution[58] – that suggests that the 'market' is enhanced by the legal system as the *point of equilibrium* of composite and diversified interests, which are at times hard to synchronise: those of the entrepreneurs, those of the consumers, the 'public' interest to an effective arrangement, and so on. [59] Therefore, within this new perspective, social utility constitutes a limiting principle that marks a watershed, including the systematic organization of the rules on unfair competition.

The Unfair Commercial Practices Directive follows in these footsteps. With the Directive, the EU legislator can continue at community level the work on unfair competition – already in several Member States – in the wake of the novelty introduced under this European competition law and policy: consumers are now the lead actors – not merely spectators – of the market.[60] After reshaping the status and function of consumers in market relations – and introducing consumer *ethos* also in competition law – the principle of fairness can be rid, once and for all, of old protectionist and corporative barriers.[61] This would be true both in subjective terms and in terms of the interest protected.[62] 'Honest practices' can, at long last,

---

[58]   Article 41 of the Italian Constitution deals with the freedom of enterprise. Specifically, it provides that private economic enterprises are free; however such freedom cannot be carried out against the common good or in a way that may harm public security, liberty, or human dignity.

[59]   Extensively, in this regard, G Ghidini, 'Disciplina della concorrenza' in *Trattato di diritto commerciale e di diritto pubblico dell'economia* [1981] Cedam, 97.

[60]   Was it not the Supreme Court, in its well-known judgement no. 2207 of 4 February 2005, *Unipol* v *RM*, in (2005) 5 Giur It 967, which held antitrust law 'is not the law of entrepreneurs only, but also of market players, or of those who have a *locus standi* to see its competitive spirit upheld and consider it a crime to upset or diminish that spirit'?

[61]   Reference is made, as regards the national experience, to: 1) limitation to competing businesses of *locus standi* to sue for unfair competition for acts which also (or first) cause damage to consumers; 2) interpretation of typical unfair competition cases in terms of exclusive protection of entrepreneurial interests; 3) corporative interpretation of fair practice clauses.

[62]   For a critical analysis, M Libertini, 'I principi della correttezza professionale nella disciplina. della concorrenza sleale' (1999) Eu e Dir Priv 509; G Ghidini, 'Note sull'evoluzione della disciplina italiana della concorrenza sleale alla luce dei principi antitrust' (2002) I Riv Dir Ind 426; P Marchetti, 'Il paradigma della concorrenza sleale nella giurisprudenza di un ventennio' (1966) I Riv dir ind 180; PG Jaeger, 'Valutazione comparativa di interessi e concorrenza sleale' (1970) Id., 5; LC Ubertazzi, 'I principi della correttezza professionale: un tentativo di rilevazione empirica' (1975) Id., 105; G Ghidini, Slealtà della concorrenza e costituzione economica (Padova, 1978); P Auteri, 'La concorrenza sleale' in *Trattato Rescigno*,

represent a reference model in market relations *tout court,* and therefore in relations between entrepreneurs and between both 'traders' and consumers.[63]

Through the Directive's approach, the legislator proposes to solve the entrepreneur-consumer conflict for good (an ambitious plan it must be said) and instead of case by case, via a *corpus* of basic principles concerning the smooth working of the market.

Accordingly and in brief, the principle of fair practice tends to enhance a competitive market model that is 'socially compatible' through a harmonized yardstick used across the Union to measure competition. It logically follows – even though this is not the sole consequence – that unfair practices are solely those acts which, for no good reason, interfere with the interplay of competition to the detriment of consumers during the 'social contract' phase preliminary to the contract, at the pre-contractual and execution phase,[64] or during performance of the contract (and even subsequently throughout the entire period of use by consumers of the goods). These, in particular, take the form of methods of offering products that impair a free and informed consumer's choice.

Here, a caveat is required. As made clear by Recital 18, Directive 2005/29 refers to the 'average consumer' – the benchmark to be considered in order to verify whether an unfair practice occurs – as a person 'reasonably well informed and reasonably observant and circumspect.' Thus, it raises the bar of protection well above the traditional standard of the consumer of low attention and limited information. This approach

---

18, *Impresa e lavoro,* IV, (Turin, 1982); M Libertini, 'I principi della correttezza professionale nella disciplina della concorrenza sleale' in *Studi per Pavone La Rosa* (Milan, 1999) 575; G Ghidini, *Profili evolutivi del diritto industriale – Proprieta` intellettuale e concorrenza* (Milan, 2001).

[63] Assuming, as is obvious, that the consumer is 'one' and not the 'only' market player, the Directive sets, under the banner of a principle of maximum harmonization, the basic requirements to consider it an unfair or illicit business practice if professionals are providing a product or service, but concurrently harming, with their behaviour, the economic interests of the consumer (and not also the interests of competitors and professional clients: see Recital no 8 of the Directive). In this regard, the Commission deems it appropriate to accurately assess the need for a community action concerning unfair competition in addition to the objectives pursued by the Directive and, if required, to submit a legislative proposal contemplating these other classic aspects of unfair competition. In this sense, L Di Nella, 'Prime considerazioni sulla disciplina della pratiche commerciali aggressive' (2007) Contratto e Impresa / Europa 39, and in particular 40, note 3.

[64] On the limits of pre-contractual information see A Gentili, *'Informazione contrattuale e regole dello scambio'* (2004) Riv Dir Priv 555.

is apparently consistent with the contemporary context of diffuse market information. However, in our view, authorities and judges should not approve or rule out a practice based across-the-end on the notion of 'average well informed consumer', assumed as a general standard. Indeed there are facts that today's consumers know or can know only by paying reasonable attention, and facts that they simply cannot know. Consider, for example, with regard to the former the information conveyed by known trademarks, or by labels, and generally information 'carried on the surface' of products and presentation of services. In such a case, the criterion of 'well informed' average consumer remains fully satisfied. As to the latter, vice versa, consider information 'not revealed' by the products, such as methods of manufacturing (as in processed food), or effective levels of risk, such as in so-called structured financial instruments. In such cases, we suggest sticking to the traditional criterion of a 'lowly informed' average consumer. Otherwise, we fear, the new 'legal' definition of average consumer may not provide an effective – that is, adapted to the market context – consumer protection, in all aforementioned cases (not few, certainly) in which the relevant information cannot be accessed by an even reasonably informed and circumspect buyer.

Then, the Directive defines as acts that are unlawful in itself: unsolicited supply of services; commencing services regarding which consent has never been given; goods or services described as free if the consumer has to pay anything other than the unavoidable cost of responding to the commercial practice and collecting or paying for delivery of the item; market conditions other than effective conditions so as to alter the correct perception by the consumer; and so on. We hope these examples have given at least a rough idea of the meaning of convergence of different regulations (unfair competition, antitrust, consumer protection), toward common pro-competitive principles/values – that is, constitutional values.

5.   CONCLUSION

A convergence toward common principles/values does not necessarily imply a loss of autonomy in the rules governing unfair competition, consumer and competition protection. On the contrary, in the new framework, each regulatory framework keeps its distinctive function, since each has different although mutually coherent purposes.[65] Such mutual consistency

---

[65]   In this regard, it must be noted that the Directive neither harms nor interferes with the enforcement of competition rules (see Recital no 9), since each

enables each rule to be read through the same 'harmonised' lenses, including that of system relations, that is, relations between regulatory systems. Such relations are evolving. We are also advancing toward the growing use of administrative channels for legal protection. Both trends suggest evidence that because of the widespread importance of the protection of consumer interests[66] including issues of 'locus' and standing can no longer be dealt with in a private law context.[67]

---

regime adopts its own system in an incidental, but not necessarily coinciding way. For the purposes of constituting unfair conduct, impact on the market, or the ability to affect the normal competition game, both in terms of objective pursued, and in terms of effective consequences, is totally irrelevant. For the purposes of the rules on unfair practices, the only relevant form of interference is that affecting the economic behaviour of consumers, who are then induced to make a decision they would have otherwise not taken, which answers the different legal dimension of the rule-governed act: regulations on unfair practices deals with relations between professionals and consumers, while regulations protecting competition also interferes with the business activity as such.

[66] For a preliminary analysis of the 'administrative' proceeding introduced in Italy, see Falce, *Il commento* (2008) 1 Il Dir Ind.

[67] A dimension that started off with the Paris Convention, though suspended for a considerable period (for an in-depth analysis why the principle encroached into national law, see G Schricker, 'Twenty-five years of protection against unfair competition' (1995) IIC 782), and subsequently resurrected with the proceedings for the harmonization of rules on unfair competition in the European Union (in this regard, finally, see F Henning-Bodewig, 'International protection against unfair competition – Article 10 *bis* Paris Convention, TRIPs and WIPO model provisions', (199) *IIC* 166). For a clear summary, see also V Di Cataldo, '*Concorrenza sleale e interessi tutelati*' in *'Panorami'* (1998 pub 2001) 13.

Index